Behind Enemy Lines
with SOE

Behind Enemy Lines with SOE

Major Ernest Charles Roland Barker, BEM

Introduced and Annotated by
Michael Kelly

AN IMPRINT OF PEN & SWORD BOOKS LTD
YORKSHIRE – PHILADELPHIA

First published in Great Britain in 2021 by
FRONTLINE BOOKS
an imprint of Pen & Sword Books Ltd
Yorkshire – Philadelphia

Copyright © Ernest Barker, 2021

ISBN 978-1-52677-974-8

Typeset by Concept, Huddersfield, West Yorkshire, HD4 5JL.
Printed and bound by CPI Group (UK) Ltd, Croydon, CR0 4YY

Pen & Sword Books Ltd incorporates the Imprints of Aviation, Atlas, Family
History, Fiction, Maritime, Military, Discovery, Politics, History, Archaeology,
Select, Wharncliffe Local History, Wharncliffe True Crime, Military Classics,
Wharncliffe Transport, Leo Cooper, The Praetorian Press, Remember When,
White Owl, Seaforth Publishing and Frontline Books.

For a complete list of Pen & Sword titles please contact
PEN & SWORD BOOKS LTD
47 Church Street, Barnsley, South Yorkshire, S70 2AS, England
E-mail: enquiries@pen-and-sword.co.uk
Website: www.pen-and-sword.co.uk
or
PEN & SWORD BOOKS
1950 Lawrence Rd, Havertown, PA 19083, USA
E-mail: uspen-and-sword@casematepublishers.com
Website: www.penandswordbooks.com

Tommy

It's Tommy this an' Tommy that and Tommy 'ow's yer soul?
But it's 'Thin Red Line of 'eroes',
When the drums begin to roll.

Rudyard Kipling

Contents

List of Plates

1. The Castello Ceconi at Pielungo.
2. The Coroneo prison, Trieste.
3. Certificate awarded to Fr Cortese.
4. Fr Cortese.
5. Witness Record Fr Cortese, Posthumous Award.
6. Garibaldi and Osoppo commanders, 1944.
7. The members of the National Liberation Committee of the Province of Udine together with military commanders of Garibaldian and Osovan formations, Udine, 5 May 1945.
8. Squadron Leader Manfred Czernin, DSO, MC, DFC.
9. Captain Roderick Hall, OSS.
10. General Vlassov.
11. Major Barker with 'Barry'.
12. Mary Barker.
13. The Barkers' two children, Sarah and Charlie.
14. Captain Smallwood's father's letter to Mary Barker.
15. Fr Carra's letter to Charles, 20 August 1945.
16. Letter from Dr Bobleter, aka Dr Briefe, to Charles Barker.
17. Letter written in Stalag XVII A by Charles to his niece, Ann Lane.
18. The Helicopter Accident Report giving details of Charles Barker's death.
19. Grave of Major Barker, BEM.
20. Medals belonging to Major Barker, BEM.
21. Major Barker, BEM.
22. Map of Italy showing the Province of Friuli.
23. Map of Italy showing the Province of Belluno.
24. Map showing Smallwood and Barker's escape route from Forni Voltri.

Acknowledgements

I offer thanks to a number of people who have assisted me with this book. To Charlie and Margaret Barker for their willingness to share with me letters and personal items relating to his father. To Charlie's sister in Australia, Sara Tochterman, who has supplied family letters and photographs. Martin Mace and John Grehan for their valuable advice and assistance. Thanks go to the Battle of Britain London Monument for allowing me access to Squadron Leader Czernin's biography and Carlo Larosa of Genoa for his generosity in sharing details relating to the city of Trieste. To Marios Papaconstantinou for the Italian translations he initiated so expediently. Petra Vide Ogrin, Curator at the Slovenian Academy of Sciences and Arts, Library Novi trg 3, has been most helpful, allowing me to use information featured on his website relating to Fr Luigi Carra, the chaplain serving the Coroneo prison in Trieste during the Second World War. The unhesitating cooperation afforded by Stefano Perulli, Responsabile Archivio Storico dell'ANPI Provinciale di Udine. He supplied the photograph and biography of Candido Grassi aka 'Verdi', Commander of the OSOPPO. I must thank Michael and Kay Pope of Queensland, Australia without whom I would not have learned of the existence of the manuscript. I very much appreciate the book cover review by Nigel West. I am grateful to Martin Fielding, the son of Major George Fielding, and to Alan Ogden for allowing me access to SOE reports and to their invaluable paper 'The Clowder Mission In and Around Forni Avoltri'.

Introduction

'And now, set Europe ablaze.' The five words uttered by Winston Churchill in July 1940 to Hugh Dalton after the retreat from Dunkirk. These were dark days in Britain, the shadow of the Nazi Swastika threatened menacingly over the English Channel; the skies of England were teeming with German bombers and fighter aircraft, locked in mortal combat with the heavily outnumbered Royal Air Force. The future was decidedly uncertain, and England braced itself for the German invasion that would surely follow.

Dalton was a civilian, a Labour politician, he had opposed any manner of conciliation with the Nazis, and he was a firm supporter of rearmament in the 1930s, thus fortifying his relationship with Churchill. He had no military background but he soon attracted people with the relevant experience. Recruits from other intelligence sections were attracted to this new entity; to be called the Special Operations Executive, or SOE. It was responsible for both propaganda (SO1) and subversion (SO2).[1] The hierarchy were usually university educated but operatives were drawn from all walks of life – car mechanics, drivers, farmworkers. Their most important requisite was the possession of cool courage in tight situations where they would infiltrate behind enemy lines directing local inhabitants and Partisans, to commit acts of subversion and sabotage, proving to be a formidable driving force and a veritable pain in the side of the enemy.

Towards the end of 1940, SOE had established a headquarters in two family flats at 64 Baker Street, London. It was coincidental that Baker Street was the 'home' of Sherlock Holmes at 221b. Despite early setbacks, inter departmental arguments and jealousies, SOE flourished and by the end of the war the Department had a total of 160 officers and 2,000 men, not including those recruited in the field.[2]

Ernest Charles Roland Barker was born in Egham, Surrey on 6 January 1919. His father Ernest Barker was a serving soldier, joining in 1898, and initially attached to the 49th Battalion, Suffolk Regiment. He joined the Royal Flying Corps in 1915 transferring to the RAF on 1 April 1918 upon the reorganisation of the RFC. He met his wife Mary Lane in Ballincollig,

Cork, where she was working in a gunpowder factory. They married on 25 October 1906. Ernest served in the Colours for twenty-two years, being discharged in 1922 in the rank of flight sergeant. The family moved to Ascot in about 1919 and upon Ernest's discharge, they went to live in Gosport, Hampshire. Christened Ernest Charles Roland Barker, his diary refers to him as Charles. He went to school in Gosport and later secondary school at St John's College, Southsea. Charles' sister Emma lived all of her life in Gosport. He joined the army on 30 April 1934 at the age of 15 years and was attached to the Royal Corps of Signals. This was the beginning of a long and varied career. He turned 18 in 1938 and embarked for Egypt the same year. He saw service in the Western Desert Force in 1940 and, in April 1941, he was transferred to Greece. He spent most of the next three years in the Mediterranean Expeditionary Force, operating in Crete before returning to the UK in April 1944. It was then that he joined SOE. He was qualified in firearms and demolition and became a parachute instructor. His training as a signalman qualified him to be a radio operator in SOE and promotion to the rank of sergeant soon followed. In 1944, he and his officer, Captain Patrick Martin-Smith, parachuted into the Friuli area of the Northern Dolomites, Italy. Their task was to open routes from Italy into Austria and to infiltrate agents into Austria to encourage resistance amongst the Austrians.

I was extremely fortunate to have had the great pleasure of guiding Australians Michael, Kay and son Andrew Pope around the Great War battlefields in Belgium and France many years ago. It was through their recommendation that I contacted Charlie Barker, the son of Major Charles Barker, BEM. He told me he had a hefty manuscript written by his father after the Second World War, describing his actions as an SOE operative in northern Italy in 1944. For many years, he and his sister Sara had wanted it to be published but the opportunity had never presented itself.

When I examined the manuscript, I realised very quickly that this was not just an account of clandestine activities in extremely dangerous situations, but a work that most eloquently describes the beauty of the Northern Dolomites under Fascist occupation. This is a world where 'Beauty and the Beast' walk hand in hand. Using Charles' extraordinary descriptive powers, one can climb the challenging mountainous heights with him; we can walk through shadows in the deep valleys and marvel at the quaint little villages which nestle into the soaring ranges. We read of the everyday life of simple, honest people, many of whom harboured a fierce hatred of the Germans and the occupation of their homeland, but conversely there were some who would betray their presence to the Germans at the drop of a hat. We follow in Barker's footsteps to the villages where he stayed; the auberges, the hotels and mountain huts and always lurking in the background was the ever-present danger of discovery by the Nazis. Through his words, we can visualise the faces of the Partisans who assisted him, many of whom became his friends, many of whom put their lives on the line for the cause; some were captured and shot, others survived the war and became part of the new Italy. As for Charles, we cannot begin to imagine the physical and mental torture he endured at the hands of the Gestapo. He makes little mention of his treatment; almost as if capture and torture was something he accepted might happen and which walked hand in hand with the job. At the point of his capture, he selflessly elected to remain with his injured officer, fearful that the Germans might execute a wounded combatant. Sergeant Barker describes his journey in custody to Trieste; his interviews with the Gestapo; meetings with inmates, all with the constant threat of death by firing squad being foremost in his mind.

> Sergeant Barker was imprisoned about six weeks in the Gestapo Gaol in Trieste. He was subjected to about twenty interrogations, housed in very bad conditions with totally inadequate food and was subjected to solitary confinement and intense cold. He was severely beaten and several times threatened with death in an effort to extract information from him. In spite of this terrible ordeal he withstood all the tricks and resisted all the promises of the enemy of better treatment if he would talk.[3]

Sergeant Barker attached aliases to some Italians and Austrians he met, maybe in an effort to protect them. The Partisans already had nicknames which bore little resemblance to their true family name, making identification now virtually impossible. Despite best attempts, the identities of *most* of those brave Italians will remain firmly buried in the mists of time.

Barker's escape from Stalag XVII A to Budapest through territory being fought over by the Russians was a combination of luck and daring; he was successful and was eventually airlifted out of Hungary. After the war he chose to remain in the army. He was awarded the British Empire Medal (Military) in 1946. He was later accepted for officer training, serving in Palestine in 1948 and then the Far East. He was involved in the Malaya conflict and it was in that country in January 1953, that he was tragically killed in a helicopter accident. At this time, Major Barker was officer commanding 22 SAS in Malaya. This is his story.

Dramatis Personae

Squadron Leader Count Manfred Beckett Czernin, DSO, MC, DFC

Count Manfred Beckett Czernin was born in Germany in 1913. His father was an Austrian diplomat and his mother was the daughter of Baron Grimthorpe. The couple separated in 1914 and Czernin went with his mother to live in Rome.

In 1935 Czernin joined the RAF enlisting under the name Beckett.[1] He commenced flying training and was posted to 57 Squadron (Upper Heyford) and, latterly, 83 Squadron in 1936. He was placed on the Class A Reserve List in 1937.

Recalled upon the outbreak of the war, he was eventually posted to 504 Squadron at Debden in 1940, moving to RAF Wittering and, shortly afterwards, to 85 Squadron in France flying Hurricanes.

During his service he shot down over a dozen German aircraft and damaged several more. In October 1940, he was gazetted for the DFC.

Czernin was shot down by German ace Adolf Galland over Wattisham in Norfolk. This did not affect his appointment as 'A' Flight Commander in March 1941 and, later that year, Manfred was posted to 146 Squadron at Dinjan. He returned to England in 1943, being transferred to HQ 28 Group at Uxbridge. It was not long before he was officially transferred to an Air Ministry Unit but in fact a cover for SOE. He was the ideal candidate; he spoke fluent Italian and French and had a working knowledge of the German language.[2] The next eight months saw Czernin training for warfare behind enemy lines, and on 13 June 1944, he was parachuted into enemy-occupied northern Italy near the Austrian frontier. He operated in this area until late 1944 when he returned to the UK.

Awarded the MC in December 1944, in 1945 he went on a second mission and dropped south of the Swiss border, his work there culminating in the surrender of the German forces at Bergamo.

He was released from the RAF in October 1945, having been awarded the DSO and achieving the rank of squadron leader.

The citation for his DSO included the following:

On 28th April 1945 ... he, with the Partisan leader drove into Bergamo in a car draped with the Union Jack to demand the unconditional surrender of the German Forces. The Germans opened fire and Squadron Leader Czernin was forced to withdraw. He then ordered the Partisans to attack the city and arranged for the underground elements in Bergamo to rise simultaneously. At 7am on 28th April 1945, Squadron Leader Czernin obtained an unconditional surrender from the German General. Throughout his period in the field Squadron Leader Czernin displayed the highest qualities of leadership and by his courage and daring made a notable contribution to the Allied success in North Italy.

He was in a variety of jobs in Civilian occupation, his last being Sales Manager for Fiat in England. He died in his sleep on 6 October 1962 and his ashes were taken to the Villa Cimbrone, Ravello, Italy.[3]

Major William Francis Dayrell St Clair Smallwood, MC

Bill Smallwood was born on 6 June 1914 at Moulmein in Burma. His father was a group captain in the RAF. Bill attended Wellington College in Berkshire before joining the army in 1940. He was accepted into the Intelligence Corps and received his commission in April 1942. On 3 May 1944 he was a temporary major and by this time attached to SOE working in ME 66 CMF for operational work with the Clowder Mission.[4] In 1944 he was parachuted into northern Italy and linked up with 'Manfred' (Squadron Leader Count Manfred Czernin, RAF), Captain Martin-Smith, Sergeant Barker and Major Fielding. He was subsequently captured along with Sergeant Barker and taken into German custody. He survived the war.

Major George Fielding, DSO

George Fielding was born in July 1915, just a few weeks before his father was killed at Gallipoli. He studied German at Freiburg University and joined the 3rd King's Own Hussars as a commissioned officer. He was sent to Crete and when it fell, Fielding escaped with fellow wounded troops and was rescued by the Royal Navy. He re-joined his regiment in the desert, he was mentioned in dispatches and volunteered to join SOE. His mission was to infiltrate the Austrian provinces of East Tyrol and Carinthia, to encourage Partisans to commit acts of sabotage upon communication lines, disrupting contact between Germany and Italy.

With three colleagues, he parachuted into the Friuli district of Italy on 12/13 August 1944. He joined Captain Patrick Martin-Smith, Major Bill Smallwood, Squadron Leader Manfred Czernin and radio operator Sergeant Charles Barker. They were based at Forni Avoltri where they were entirely dependent upon their bodyguard, a group of twenty Partisans, for their security. In order to ensure their protection, Fielding promised to arm and supply the Partisans by airdrop. Fielding's code name was 'Rudolf' and the group was known initially as Force 133, later changed to Force 266 and again to Force 399.[5]

A combined American and British Balkan Air Force had been formed late in 1944 with the specific task of supplying SOE agents and Partisans. Although adequately qualified, the pilots had great difficulty locating the Drop Zones in mountainous regions which were subject to the speedy onset of bad weather. Fielding, as did many other SOE operatives in the field, became frustrated, he was trying to maintain his credibility with the Partisans at the same time suffering through lack of essential supplies, both to him and the promised arms to the Partisans.

Despite the problems, Fielding kept his party at Forni Avoltri for another six weeks, hoping that the Line of Supply would improve. In total frustration and in reply to radio messages that bad weather was responsible for the lack of air drops, he sent the message, 'More of the spirit of the Battle of Britain and less of the bottle of Bari.'[6] This cogent message was later to earn him a reprimand. He disguised himself as a peasant in an attempt to see what was happening in the Upper Gail valley, but he had no papers and if captured, he would have been executed as a spy. (SOE mostly wore uniform on operations.) On his return, German activity forced the group to disperse. Major Bill Smallwood and Sergeant Charles Barker were captured. There followed brave attempts by the Fielding group to escape the German net that was closing around them. Despite being betrayed and ambushed, Fielding, although wounded in the arm, was able to continue towards Slovenia, a 300-mile journey, and from there he and the survivors were flown to Southern Italy. It was estimated that over 6,000 German troops had been diverted in an attempt to catch him and he was awarded the DSO for his leadership, resourcefulness and courage.

Fielding survived the war. He farmed in the west of Ireland before returning to the Pays d'Enhaut in Switzerland, enjoying skiing and painting. He died on 23 January 2005 aged 89.[7]

Captain Patrick Martin-Smith, MC

Patrick Geoffrey Brian Martin-Smith was infiltrated by parachute to the Friuli district of northern Italy, then some 200 miles behind enemy lines, on 18 July 1944 to act as second in command to Squadron Leader Czernin, so Martin-Smith's personnel record tells us. The brief was to open up a route into Austria between the Plocken and Brenner Passes. He was accompanied by his radio operator, Sergeant Charles Barker. Martin-Smith himself was given the task of arranging safe houses and the actual crossings of the frontier by the various parties of agents. To do this, he established his base a few miles south of the Austrian frontier. Between the end of July and the end of November, Czernin's mission was exposed to repeated enemy attacks; Martin-Smith was most helpful, holding together the Partisan forces who had fallen into a low state of morale owing to the lack of supplies by aircraft. When the snow closed the passes, Captain Martin-Smith was ordered to close on Major Fielding who was in the same area and extract through Slovenia. This was a particularly hazardous journey of some 300 miles travelling through deep snow. (Fielding's account talks of German ambushes upon the party.) It was a successful journey and because of Martin-Smith's devotion to duty, his exemplary initiative during five months in German territory, he was recommended for the Military Cross.[8]

Captain Roderick 'Steve' Hall, OSS

In September 1943, 2nd Lieutenant Hall of the 270th Engineers, while stationed at Camp Adair, Oregon, wrote a letter to the Office of Strategic Services (OSS) outlining his various capabilities and applying to join OSS. He seemed to possess all the necessary qualifications for such work having been trained in demolition, mapping and reconnaissance, but most importantly for the task ahead, a knowledge of the Italian language and of the area of the Dolomites around Cortina D'Ampezzo, where he had skied before the war. It wasn't long before Hall was recruited, his team consisting of Captain Lloyd G. Smith, 'Smitty', in command (promoted to major shortly afterwards), 1st Lieutenant Joseph Lukitsch, radio operator Stanley Sbeig (navy specialist) and T-3 Victor Malaspino. In 1944 they were dropped by parachute to commence their subversive activities. Operational exigencies meant that Hall was separated from the rest of the group and he heard later that 'Smitty' had been caught between two attacking forces, 14,000 troops at Tolmezzo had overrun Carnia from the south and 3,000 Nazis brought in from Austria attacked from the south.

'Smitty' somehow evaded capture and escaped to Yugoslavia which had been an exit plan.

Hall started his own private war, blowing up bridges and power lines and generally making a nuisance of himself. Then, on the morning of 26 January 1945, he left his camp near Selva, to make his way to Cortina D'Ampezzo to blow up the railroad transformer station. He was advised not to go; his feet were still suffering from an earlier bout of frostbite and the weather was poor with heavy snowstorms. On 15 February, heavy snow forced Hall to rest at a house where an informer notified the Nazis of his presence. He was arrested.

Subsequent enquiries at the end of the war into Hall's disappearance led to the Gries Concentration Camp near Bolzano. In May 1945, Captain A.R. Materazzi found a grave marked by a small headstone bearing the number 17 in Row E. Cemetery records revealed it was the grave of Roderick Hall. Interviews with the Nazis who had been Hall's warders revealed that he had 'broken' under duress and told them he was a member of OSS and about the operations he had conducted in northern Italy. Hall was murdered on 19 February 1945. After being blindfolded, he was led to the machine room where a rope had been made into a noose and tied around a large valve wheel handle. The rope was placed over Hall's head and loosely on his shoulders so that he was unaware of its presence. At that, two of the Germans sprang on Hall, dragging down his shoulders and forcing the noose to tighten around his neck. After 10 minutes, they were sure that Hall was dead. Three of his murderers were subsequently captured and sentenced to death by hanging, carried out before 26 July 1946.[9]

Brigadier Edmund Frank Davies

In 1943, SOE appointed a new commander to the recently increased sized force operating in Albania. Brigadier Davies of the Royal Ulster Rifles was joined by his Chief of Staff Lieutenant Colonel Arthur Nicholls. Davies was a colourful character; he had been nicknamed 'Trotsky' at Sandhurst because of his 'disciplined bolshevism'. In January 1944, the SOE mission HQ was overrun by the Germans and Davies was captured. Nicholls died as a result of leading survivors to safety.

Davies was sent to Stalag XVII A. Placing his trust in Dr Carl Bobleter, he asked him to bury his personal diary.[10] The contents of the diary remain unknown.

Father Placido Cortese

Fr Placido's confessional was at the Basilica of St Anthony in Padua, Italy. The Basilica became a safe haven for many people who were in danger of being sent to Nazi death Camps, and Fr Cortese arranged escape routes for these people and for many British and Allied ex-prisoners of war and escapees, and it is thought that he saved the lives of hundreds of people. He was often heard to say, 'You cannot remain a spectator in war.' On 8 October 1944, he was betrayed by an informer, lured out of the sanctity of the Basilica by someone he knew, and arrested by the Gestapo. He was taken to Trieste and the Gestapo HQ where he was tortured remorselessly. It was here where Sergeant Barker saw him in a pretty sorry state. In November 1945, Barker deposited an attestation detailing what he saw:

> I myself saw many prisoners [in the bunker], Croats, Italians, and other nationalities who had been ill treated, had their limbs broken and had received so-called 'electrical treatment' which had often resulted in burns and other injuries to the body. There was in particular an Italian priest, the parish priest of San Antonio Church [*sic*], Padua, whose nails had been extracted by force, whose arms had been broken, whose hair had been burned off and who bore the marks of repeated floggings on his body. I was afterwards told that he was shot.

In another part of the affidavit Barker states, 'This man had helped British POWs ...'.[11]

In fact, Father Cortese suffered inhuman torture by the Gestapo. His eyes were gouged out, his tongue cut off and, eventually, he was buried alive. Exhumed later, his remains were cremated. Throughout, he refused to divulge the names of his collaborators, a truly brave and courageous man. On 29 January 2002 the beatification of Fr Placido was initiated in the Diocese of Trieste.

Father Luigi Carra

Fr Carra was the catechist and canon of the Cathedral Chapter of St Justa in Trieste. During the German occupation he served as a chaplain in the Coroneo prison between 1939 and 1 November 1946. He was held in a position of trust by the Germans, who allowed him free access to the prison. He prepared sixteen Slovenes/Partisans for their execution and supplied prisoners with items such as clothing. He wrote a letter to Charles Barker in August 1945 expressing the memories surrounding his stay in the Coroneo prison.

Dr Carl Bobleter aka Dr Briefe

On 22 July 1945, when he was living in Salzburg, Dr Carl Bobleter wrote a letter to Lieutenant Barker. Among many other things, while he had been the doctor at Stalag XVII A, he spoke of a diary belonging to Brigadier Davies, a previous occupant of the same living-quarters where Charles Barker was housed. He informed Barker that he had buried a diary at the request of that officer. In Barker's manuscript, he wrote of the same incident when talking to 'Dr Briefe', aka Bobleter.

No record of Bobleter can be located after the war; he appears as a 'Good Samaritan' to Barker and the British officers. In his letter he is most appreciative of what they did to assist *him* and he enquired after the welfare of a number of those incarcerated in the POW camp.

Candido Grassi aka 'Verdi'

At the time of the Italian armistice, the 34-year-old Grassi was in Udine and was one of the leading lights in organising anti-Fascist groups. His operational name was Verdi. He was instrumental in arranging a Partisan settlement in the upper part of Udine and the foundations of the Osoppo Brigade. Candido Grassi became the commander. They fought in the upper Friuli regions and between the Livenza and Isonzo alongside the Garibaldians organised by the Communist Party.

At the end of the war Grassi was commanding five Osoppo divisions comprising over eighteen brigades. He returned to teaching and painting. He was the Superintendent of the Udine Monuments Department and was elected Municipal and Provincial Councillor for the Partito Socialista Italiano. He died on 15 July 1969.[12]

Prologue

During the Second World War there were numerous adventures undertaken behind the enemy lines referred to as 'Special Operations'. In many respects these missions were similar. Some, nay many, experienced a full measure of success, others failure, but from their conception, the basic planning, the number of personnel involved, the spirit which carried the agents through differed little. Some went in search of information, accuracy demanding that they go to the very fountain from whence the rumour had sprung. For the majority, the original purpose and plan involved 'Sabotage', both active and passive. In all countries on the Continent of Europe before the close of the war British-trained para-militarists made their presence felt, if not destroying bridges or targets of equal importance, their representation on the ground in the midst of the enemy instilled morale sorely needed by people who favoured the Allied cause.

The story of one such mission is contained within the covers of this book.[1] I make no apology for its crude construction, the sequence is accurate, and to its very end that which could be truly rated success over the enemy is not sharply defined. It represents the passage of seven months spent in Nazi-controlled territory, some of the time in close liaison with the Italian Partisans, the remainder in the special care of the Gestapo. Both elements watched us closely. The Partisans asked questions about us, which was inconsiderate, the wings of verbosity cover a wide field. The Gestapo also chose to question us showing a keen interest, though the replies they received were of negative value. This operation was known as Arundel, a code-name which meant little to anyone other than those who were to carry it into effect.

'Sergeant Barker was dropped by parachute as W/T operator to a mission in northwest Italy which had the task of establishing a Base for the penetration of East Tyrol and Southwest Carinthia.'[2]

In the north-eastern area of Italy, the Dolomites, there are two Provinces called the Friuli and the Carnia. Our activities remained for the most part in the bounds of these localities until the time of our capture in

October 1944. The inhabitants of this neighbourhood did not experience the terrors of aerial bombardment. They did, however, feel the weight of the blockade, food was unfairly rationed, indeed most commodities were scarce, and even worse they felt the savagery of a nation maddened in defeat. The SS brigades had orders to deal effectively with Partisans and those that chose to assist them. The villagers of these mountainous Provinces made many sacrifices.

This then is the essence of this story, a tale of ordinary people committed to play a part, the results of which have yet to be defined. All suffered and continue to suffer for Liberty. Just how many strings liberty is tied with, for most people remains a problem. It was a problem during the period of this story, which appeared to be near solution. Unfortunately, the Osoppo and the Garibaldi Partisans who represented respectively the Christian-Democrats and the Communists tackled the problem in diverse ways, which remain untied.

My choice of subject has received much attention and study by authors of established prominence. They have recaptured thrilling incidents peculiar to special missions of the Late War, material which has given the layman a more comprehensive understanding of the meaning of 'Total War'. In so doing, they have performed a worthy task, for to understand the meaning of modern war, to feel the pain of a savage occupation, must enrol others prepared to defend the covenants of peace.

Chapter One

Friends

There were many appealing captions phrased to catch the eye of the potential young soldier. 'Join the Army and see the World' was one. This slogan has been the convincing factor influencing many would-be soldiers. In the late war many other countries were added to the lifelines of the Empire and were available for a 'tour'. Towards the end of 1943 Italy was added to that list. Security limited the number of advertisements inviting soldiers to make the best of their opportunities, in fact few with the exception of the troops stationed along the north-African coastline had any idea that a visit was to be paid in September, though many had an idea that it would be considered when Sicily fell. While the problem was being turned over in many minds the assault was made, and Italy became a battleground. Kesselring's Army moved northwards away from the heel and the toe, and in a few weeks Calabria, Puglia and the Province of the Basilicata were in the hands of the Allies.

Looking back over that particular period of the past there were several factors which together made the days of preparation for Operation Arundel wholesome and full of interest.[1] The Province of the Puglia for one freshly acquainted with foreign travel was a picture of bright colours which one might have seen in a geographic magazine, a brown countryside but with sufficient green, suggesting a hot but bearable climate, made additionally attractive by the brightly coloured houses distinct against the blue of the sky, which appeared to stretch all the way down to the horizon.

The main reason for our special interest in the calendar was surely the information received by radio from Manfred, who was then 300 miles behind the enemy lines. He sent short messages, between long intervals of silence, but they represented a wealth of adventure, and invitation was attached to every word. Progress reports were sent to Monopoli which was situated 3 miles to the north of the Country-Section house on the shores of the Adriatic.[2] Pat would return to the castle after a visit to Staff-Headquarters, looking very untidy in his ill-fitting khaki-drill shirt and shorts, sometimes with an expression of quiet boredom and always after the receipt of a message aggravated with a desire to be off, to take his place with our colleague, the originator of these short transmissions, which basically seemed to say 'hurry before you miss all the fun'.[3] We were certainly ready, having checked and re-checked our personal requirements and equipment.

There were other factors to be considered before we could follow Manfred.[4] The weather, which was so perfect in our Base area, was not always suitable in the neighbourhood of the DZ (Dropping Zone) which had been chosen. If the weather proved satisfactory, the situation on the ground at the receiving end was perhaps a little out of hand. These factors coupled with the availability of aircraft during the period of waiting, in our anxiety, seemed at times too complex to be surmountable. Then the day arrived. To be honest, though we had wanted so long, news of our departure was still in something of a surprise and now that there was limited time at our disposal there appeared to be too many things yet to arrange. Would I remember the cipher code for camouflage of future messages to Base? Now was the time to ask if I was not sure. A funny thing I had been sure right until this very moment. It was too late to make another test with the radio set; it was packed and ready for air-transportation. How long we had waited for this moment. Well, that is how it all was. Impatience one minute, anxiety the next, which helped strengthen the tense excitement, now well on the way to its climax. The Friuli, next stop but one, for we had yet to catch a plane at Brindisi.

Driving to the aerodrome from which we should take-off, my mind concentrated on the near future, full of conflicting alternatives possibly to confront us on the flight and later when we dropped over the DZ. The warmth of a typical Mediterranean summer day, with the waters of the Adriatic lapping the shore alongside the coast road over which we travelled, merely formed the stage and commencement of the first chapter of our own 'D-Day'. The car finally halted outside a small villa in the suburbs of Brindisi. Lunch was served when formal introduction to the caretaker had been completed. Contemplating a short rations era ahead, I ate a very filling meal which according to nature should have made me sleepy, but excitement over came the effect of the food and I remained very much awake, anxious to complete the remaining preliminaries prior to catching the plane. Take-off time had been arranged for 8pm. That afternoon we spent time at the packing sheds, personally supervising the arrangement of packages for air-transport. The caretaker took over from then on, assuming responsibility for on-loading.

Returning to the villa, we discussed the initial phase of the operation. In the bedroom Pat divided the currency. For once in my life I felt a very wealthy man in terms of lira. With care I fastened my operational wealth around my waist, for the money was carried in a cloth waist-belt. Taking a tip from Pat, I laid on the bed. If wine helps one sleep, I wish I had taken some with my lunch, for sleep was not easy. I was too full of excitement, my mind full of thoughts and conceptions of the next few hours and all that they might contain. Pat was deep in thought but appeared to have adjusted himself like an old campaigner. He always suggested complete control, a creditable quality of leadership and presence of mind, that I wished I could adopt. He had a habit of making conversation, which conveyed never more than security allowed you to know for your own good and well-being. He was uninformative but always interesting. I wondered whether he had previously undertaken an operation of this nature, a long time after I was still wondering, because he rarely spoke about his past, at least not to me.

I am always wondering about people, not necessarily with a touch of generosity, but because curiosity stimulates my imagination. Was Pat excited? That word 'obvious' tried to persuade me that he was, but as I have indicated, if looks convey anything, he certainly was not. I had utmost confidence in him, his calm approach to any situation was reassuring and at a later date in the field, many times this belief was confirmed. Forgetting Pat temporarily, I examined my own self, and disturbing though this was, I eventually succumbed to sleep. In the realm of dreams, for some reason, I am always more confident. The heat of the day helped quite a bit.

I slept for what seemed a noticeably short while and awakened to the clinking of china and the preparation of yet another meal. Tea was served. It was cooler in the room and looking at my watch, I calculated that we should be taking off in another hour. I describe my meals in the sequence they are served and not according to time. After a wash, I joined Pat at the table, feeling fresher but not hungry. The caretaker, a fat bustling little man, had returned from the aerodrome full of conversation and self-credit for work accomplished on our behalf. As an after-thought he mentioned that our Country-Section Staff Officer would meet us at the aerodrome before our departure to give us a final briefing. It would of course be Dickie, who had seen many of his charges off from Brindisi, giving them last-minute instruction based on up-to-the-minute intelligence reports or a recent transmission from the field.[5]

Draining a last glass of Chianti accepted in keeping with the spirit of the operation, rather than because we really wanted it, we gathered up our personal kit and drove off to the aerodrome. Taking the road north-east, we left the area of the port, the dust disturbed by our vehicle setting up a temporary screen obscuring our view to the rear as though we were finally divided from all that had been comfort and forcing our attention and interest to the front and the future. Indeed, at this moment time was not waiting for us and the hours ahead were full, leaving little time for meditation. As we passed through the Main Gate and Guard Room manned by our late enemies and more recent Allies, the Bersaglieri sentry saluted, drawing his weapon of ancient vintage close towards his chest.[6] We drove straight through towards the location of our aircraft. The crew was busy making a final pre-take-off check, the despatchers arranging our packages amidships, where they would remain until such time as we were airborne, when they would once again transfer them to a position closer to the aperture, for speedy dropping into space. We were watching this preparation when Dickie arrived.

Pep talks are always interesting or perhaps I am naturally gullible. I thought that Dickie's words were full of wisdom, for they sounded very comforting and oozed of a contemporary catch phrase, 'It's in the bag'. Briefly his conversation centred on a late message from Manfred, who had signalled that he would be waiting on the DZ for us and had added with cheerful emphasis that we should not forget to bring his whisky ration, required naturally enough for medicinal purposes. His overall report suggested that he had lost no time in organising safe bases which promised an uneventful landing. 'Time will tell' should always accompany wishful thinking. The next few hours were to provide us with a situation underlining reality and would, needless to say, quickly readjust our wide contemplation in the present.

Dickie had met the crew of the aircraft previously. When they had completed their preparation, he introduced us mentioning needlessly that we were now in their care for the period of the flight. They looked at us though we were labelled 'With Care'. They looked incredibly young to have so much responsibility, but the navigator brought me down to earth when he replied to a question, stating, 'Oh, it's quite alright we know this journey fairly well, we've been on this run several times before.' That was very reassuring, and fingering my parachute harness, I would like to have asked whether it was a quiet journey, but checked myself, thinking that it would probably be in bad taste. It occurred to me after a pause in the conversation that they would not relish any thrill they had not ordered. With a final 'Cheerio' we climbed aboard. The pilot was a Canadian and the navigator an Australian. The engines burst into life at the pilot's touch as he warmed up for take-off. The slipstream sent a cloud of dust scattering behind the plane, forcing Dickie to take cover further starboard and behind his car. We taxied down the runway coming to a halt at the coast end down wind.

There was a flux of conversation over the intercom. The engines revved to a roaring crescendo. Finally, the plane lurched forward gathering speed each second, wheels off ground and we were airborne. The ground raced past as we circled the drome before setting course over the Adriatic northwards. Still standing by his car, Dickie in miniature waved us a final 'Goodbye'. No sooner were we on course, than the despatcher lost no time moving the packages aft near to the aperture. When he had finished, he came amidships to where we lay on bunks arranged each side of the plane. Cupping his hands to his mouth he yelled, 'What order do you wish to jump?' and 'Do you wish to jump before or after the packages have been despatched?' Pat screamed back, 'I will jump first and Charles will follow me.' He further explained that once we were on the ground, on the second run over the target we would signal the plane to drop stores. The despatcher nodded his approval and added, 'Try and get some shut-eye.' With that he returned aft seating himself in the rear gun turret.

I was amused by his matter of fact manner and suggestion. What with the roar of the engines and the excitement, who the hell could contemplate sleep? I could not, but evidently Pat thought it was a sound proposal for cupping his hands behind his head, he settled himself to sleep. Turning his head towards me, he nodded wisely, confirming that he accepted the despatcher's advice, and thought I should follow suit. The man was not normal. I was hot and freely perspiring when we had climbed aboard but, having climbed to 10,000ft I was thankful for the flying suit. The despatcher noticed that I was unable to sleep and came forward again. 'We shall fly over the sea until we are adjacent Venice, after which we will fly to the north of that city changing course slightly east, heading for the Austrian border.' Having vouched this information, he returned to his turret. Sleep surprisingly overtakes one. The despatcher roused the pair of us. When we had fully recovered, he said, 'Adjust your parachutes, ready for checking.' This we did with the aid of the despatcher, who gave a final knock on the safety box and a confident 'thumbs up', grinning that all was in order. The times I had seen the parachute instructors do just that, I had often wondered whether they should adopt a more serious outlook. Weighing our reactions in turn he said, 'Relax' and as an after-thought, 'You have several minutes yet.' The radio operator made his presence felt. Apparently, we had been flying over the area for some minutes, the pilot had located three sets of fires, all close to the DZ. Only one set represented the right spot. Time marched on. We were ordered to take up positions either side of the aperture. This was it.

Flying conditions had changed for the worse, for the plane alternated at different levels in sudden lurches and we experienced a series of bumps, which the despatcher, who was seasoned to this unpleasantness, mentioned was due to the fact that we were now over the mountains. Looking forward towards the pilot, he waved his hand in recognition of a message understood, and passed on in turn, a warning that we should jump in 5 minutes. Assisted by the radio operator, the despatcher lifted the aperture housing, leaving an ominous hole all too plainly visible. A cold rush of air penetrated the 'craft. We could now vaguely distinguish the mountainous terrain below, towards which we should shortly plunge via the narrow aperture. I hadn't seriously considered dropping into space over this type of ground, but there was no time to reflect, for the despatcher pointed to the light about us which glowed an eerie red, meaning caution and action stations, and with a second's pause changed to green, meaning 'Jump'. Pat eased himself forward, hung for a brief moment over the hole and quickly disappeared through it. It was now up to me, and mind took an awful long time to persuade matter, my strength disappeared as quickly as Pat had passed through the hole. The despatcher patted me on the shoulder, I looked up at him as I passed from the plane into space.

How quiet and refreshing. An open parachute establishes supreme confidence in one's self immediately and, come what may, nothing for several seconds matters a damn. The wind whistled through my rigging lines and this was a tonic for the nerves. Gently I drifted earthwards, I could see Pat, not more than a couple of hundred feet away, I had not really taken long following him out. For some moments, the moon outlined the length and breadth of the valley into which we were drifting, then the nearby mountain peak shut off the light. Suspended in the darkness, swinging slightly forwards and backwards, my descent seemed interminable. Three small fires burned in a meadow. My reactions changed. Had the pilot dropped us on the right DZ? There were trees, hundreds of them, covering the slope of the mountains. It was not possible to see the narrow road showing up white as it curved through the trees. A gentle tap on the leg, and I drew my knees towards my face for protection, as I crashed through the upper foliage of a fir and into the branches of yet another. A jerk, and I was left suspended. Time had caught up with me, and I was down to earth or at least not too far from it. Releasing myself from the harness I fell several feet into a rocky bedded stream. The engine of the aircraft hummed pleasantly as it returned making its second run over the target area. Now I had to signal the OK for stores.

The woods were extensive, the darkness all the more complete. Climbing the bank of the stream I discovered that I was quite close to the roadway. There were cheerful voices, which gay as they sounded were not reassuring, I still doubted the efficiency of the pilot. Two strangely garbed men made their way towards me, excited and shouting, 'Bravo Amico, Bravo Amico il vostro cammerato e giu'.[7] 'Come, we go, here along this path.' On the pathway leading towards the road which they indicated I should take, I stopped to signal to the plane, hoping that the occupants would see the flashlight. Watching expectantly the plane passing quickly overhead, we saw twelve or fourteen parachutes mushroomed in the light of the moon. My recent acquaintances regarded this sight as a signal for further outbursts of cheering. The Partisans moved quickly down the road leading me to a small house where I found Pat surrounded by twenty or more Partisans. The house was opposite the meadow in which the fires had been burning, but which were now completely extinguished. Pushed through the gathering, we were led into a room where the ladies of the house offered us hot, sweet milk, which we gratefully accepted.

Chapter Two

Pielungo

The room was full of warmth, and every smiling face reflected a state of good cheer. Our arrival from the skies cast us in the role of 'Martian Men', certainly we could not have aroused more minute attention. The one-piece flying suits, with zip-fastener pockets, the jumping helmet and finally our sturdy footwear drew speculative comment followed by criticism condemning the Fascisti, and possibly for our benefit, praising British diplomacy and the men who were responsible for carrying it into effect. Conversational ebb and flow maintained for the most part a cheerful theme, had not 'The Inglesi come to help them?' This indeed was a joyful occasion, a shortage we did not regret, for we had yet another 20km to travel on foot. Having no further use for the flying suits, it was our pleasure to proudly present them to the ladies of the house, thus reciprocating their kindness and adding to the general flow of goodwill.

We returned to the area of the Dropping Zone to find that our packages had been gathered together and placed near the roadside. The woods had been alive with laughter and the merry chatter of the search party, while they crashed through the undergrowth looking for the stores.

Some parachutes were found suspended among the fir trees, while others including the package containing our ill-fated radio had crashed onto the road. Radio was a vital requirement for the execution of our work. It was the medium through which we had immediate contact with Base who in turn would require our information, yet another piece of jigsaw fitting the information pattern, a study of which defined the weaknesses of the enemy armour. Time was another factor to be considered, the value of the up-to-the-minute reports concerning the enemy receiving a priority of consideration and possible action. It was comforting to think that shortly we should link up with Manfred, through whom we could obtain a replacement radio.

Marco, the local commander, cried for silence! The sound of a vehicle approaching explained the order. Hurriedly issuing instructions which were obeyed with noisy alacrity, the ambush parties selected positions close to the road along which the vehicle would be forced to pass. Many, including Pat and myself, dispersed into the safer distance and cover of the woods. The searching lights of the lorry swept the valley, filtering through the foliage behind which we waited in silence. With obvious difficulty the straining engine pulled the lorry up the gradient and into view. It came to an abrupt halt when the ambush party rushed from cover, weapons levelled warning the driver that they meant business. With equal abruptness the tense atmosphere eased when the storekeeper from Pielungo made his identity known. This discovery boosted our morale no end, for a third-class ride remains to this day a better proposition than a first-class walk, especially at 1 o'clock in the morning.

Adding our personal kit to the already loaded vehicle, we bade hasty farewells to Marco and his friendly compatriots, delivering ourselves into the hands of the storekeeper whose cheerful demeanour was not in the least affected by the recent unforeseen halt and was only matched in magnitude by his rotund waistline which even the darkness failed to conceal. 'Ei tanta bella cosa.'[1] It was certainly his pleasure to aid friends of the Signor Majore Manfredo, to whom he would take us without further delay.[2] The drive proved uneventful apart from the abuse paid by the driver to turns of the road, some curves leading into the unknown. With the departure of the moon, the countryside was covered in a shroud of darkness, thus with no indication of the route the navigation appeared to be without caution.

On two occasions Partisan patrols held up the lorry for inspection. From time to time it was the habit of SS units to make unannounced patrols through the area, with the object of encircling villages harbouring Partisans. Informers still prevailed, supplying reports in exchange for money or favour. With the growth of the Partisan movement, both SS and informers were forced to relax their vigilance in the mountain localities. Their actions when planned demanded complete surprise if they hoped for any measure of success.

The Partisans prepared for all possible emergencies maintaining a watch day and night, so that friendly villagers as well as themselves knew of an impending attack. The journey lasted little more than an hour, it was 2.15am, the Pielungo church bell clanging in conjunction with our arrival. The village was fast with sleep, not a light showing. Guiseppi pulled up in front of the albergo, whereupon two figures moved from the cover of the entrance.[3] Familiarly Guiseppi greeted them making our presence known. In return the stranger beckoned us to join them, passing into the hotel. They explained that Manfred had gone over to the Tramonte dropping ground, where it was expected we should land. He would arrive soon. Almost as we received this message, an automobile drew up outside, the door opened and Manfred strode into the room, his face wreathed with a smile of welcome, as he extended his hands in congratulation. Shouting for Vermouth, a toast was called in celebration of our link-up, after we had been introduced to Verdi, Orellio [often spelt Aurelio] and Peppino, Manfred's young Italian wireless-operator, who had returned with him from the Body-Ground.[4]

Pat spoke of the days of preparation and waiting and our reaction to the messages which Manfred had originated. Manfred listened absorbed, punctuating the account with few questions until Pat had exhausted his news. Yet another bottle of Vermouth was produced, Verdi and Orellio, though rarely adding to the conversation, ensured that we should not lack inspiration in the form of local vintage. It would be convenient to add that, much as the stimulant was enjoyed, Pat and Manfred had little need of it, for the conversation contained much that was business, alleviated by the odd sparkle of humour. During a pause, the village bell invaded the silence, sounding 3 hours, a signal that we should retire. Preparation for bed was accepted unanimously. Leaving the warmth of the hotel room, we made for the castle [Castello Ceconi], which had been forcibly requisitioned by the local Partisans and was at present Manfred's temporary headquarters.[5] In a little more than 10 minutes Pat and I were installed in a room, with beds, and making full use of them. Luxuries of this form were not to be wasted, and sleep was not difficult. A tiny voice in the distance, but sufficiently loud to penetrate the inner consciousness of one expecting the alert, awakened me. 'Hurry up, we've got to get out of here, and QUICK!' Leaning up on one elbow, the impact of the sentence took time to catch up with me. Looking towards the door, around which Manfred had poked his head, I said, 'What's the matter?' He replied with emphasis, 'Come on you two, everybody else has gone.' Pat was now fully awake. Manfred continued, 'The Boche are approaching the village in strength, supported by armoured cars, there is no time to be lost, for God's sake hurry up.' That was enough. 'OK, coming.' I said. This was most unsatisfactory before breakfast, not that breakfast occurred to me. I was dressed, waiting for Pat, who had just left his bed. Anxious to be gone, I waited with feet that wanted to leave Pat behind, my valour certainly would not wait for him and I ran from the castle.

Once outside, I ran fast to the left along a track which led to the village, the route we had used after leaving the hotel. Then I remembered, doubling back on my tracks there was a small hedge through which I made for the cover of the woods. On a well-trodden path, I hoped that I would catch up the others, there were some in fire positions covering the track. It was at this moment that valour caught up with me or it may have been that I was temporarily out of breath, in any case, I slowed down to a trot, eventually joining a party of four, all going my way. We kept together, an Alpini officer, two now militant civilians in retreat and a tall blond-haired young man wearing battledress which was somewhat worse for wear. Pondering over my limited Italian vocabulary, I addressed the latter. 'Dove Andiamo adesso?'[6] He looked at me as though I was annoying him. He was obviously being difficult for I was certain that the sentence was grammatically sound in the colloquial sense. I tried again. 'Conoscete la vie?'[7] He chose not to reply for some moments, then surprised me saying 'I'm from Lonnon, an escaped prisoner, what d'ya want t'know?' I wondered where we were making for, we had started to climb. 'I reckon this Alpini chap is taking us up the Monte Rossa, it's a pretty tough climb from here.' It certainly was, we had just commenced the ascent and I had a feeling that my legs were not long enough or short enough, whichever were more adaptable to climbing.

Moving just within the shelter of the fir covered slopes, it was possible to trace the outline of the valley and the area of Pielungo, without actually seeing the village itself. The valley echoed with the rattle of machine-gun fire which was too close to be comfortable. A series of heavy crumps made it noticeably clear that we should continue with haste. Mortars would disturb the Partisans and the enemy would gain the initiative, enabling them to follow along the track. I knew from my short acquaintance with the Partisans that they held no effective weapon to oppose them. We carried on.

To complicate the proceedings, aircraft put in an appearance. The Alpini officer said that we should remain still, until they had passed over-head. It was not clear why we should, but as he had assumed command, we obeyed. The roar of the engines increased. The sky was a bright blue and the American Fortress bombers were like an orderly array of silver filings glinting in the sun's light. It was great to feel that they were on your side, until a series of whistles indicated they were jettisoning their remaining bombs, which had no doubt stuck in the bomb bays over the arranged target. The legend of the whistling shell was anything but comforting, for our frame of mind contained but a single thought as we dived flat among the dewy grass. The bombs landed near the village, the blast shaking the earth, the thunderous explosions ricocheting throughout the valley in rapid succession, the tempo matching our rapidly beating pulse. Later we learned that the SS unaccountably decided to retire, but this was still news as far as we were concerned. With the returning tranquillity our guide led us on towards the peak. At 3,000ft above Pielungo, probably more above sea-level, the air was crisp, invigorating and our attention was attracted to the natural beauty of the surrounding panorama demanding an easier pace than we had thus maintained. Jacko, the Alpini, became sentimental explaining the local folklore. 'It is the custom for a lover to search for Edelweiss,' he pointed to a little white starred flower. 'When he has found one, he returns to his sweetheart, presenting the flower to her, to confirm his love.' His face was pensive in keeping with tender moments of the past. This was interesting, I almost plucked the Edelweiss for future reference, but my sense of fair play rescued the flower just in time. We sighted the malga, and I hoped that we should rest there.[8] There were other bodies in various states of ease, sitting near the malga. When we were nearer, one walked to meet us. Apparently, they too were Partisans, though they carried no arms. When the first warning of the approaching enemy was given at Pielungo, they had escaped to Monte Rossa. One of them offered me a bowl of goat's milk, describing it as particularly good stuff, with active confirmation, raising his index finger against his blown-out cheek. I found that the milk was curdled; but showed my gratitude nonetheless by smiling and taking another sip. It was cold, even refreshing but I thought of other drinks that would have been preferable. Meanwhile Jacko was participating in a heated discussion conducted with much waving of hands, in conclusion of which it was decided we should mover further up the slope to another malga.

The next halt overlooked the Tramonte valley. With the setting sun taking its light to the west, the view was a tonic for those of the party who were tired. The three villages of Tramonte were plainly visible, together with the road connecting them. Stretching southwards from Tramonte di Mezzo, the road ran through the Meduna valley over the Tagliamento River and so to the plains. Absorbed in the view below me, I had not noticed that Pat had arrived with another party. He informed us that we should remain here for the night.

Feeling obliged to assume a cheerful disposition, which in my tired state I was loath to adopt, I asked Pat what had kept him. Meditating several seconds before he replied, Pat's tone conveyed a more serious turn of thought. 'I must have taken a longer route, I'm sure that we saw your party, moving in a more westerly direction.' With that he leaned against bank, surveying the darkening blue above.

Feeling a trifle guilty, but anxious to hear what had happened to him on the way, I explained my hasty withdrawal, mentioning the fact that we had another Englishman with us. 'On the way I met an English ex-POW. He is over by the hut at the moment.' There were several people standing near the hut, watching the preparation of a meal, but the soldier was not among them. 'I think he must be inside.' Turning the events of the morning over in my mind, I wondered what had become of the others. 'Do you know what has happened to Manfred, Sir?' I ventured to ask. 'I should think that he has returned to the village. The SS serve no purpose remaining in Pielungo. If they have left any buildings standing, Manfred will be there.' Feeling that he should clarify this assertion, he added, 'I saw him shortly after leaving the castle. He was with Verdi, helping to organise the withdrawal, placing Partisans in sniping positions. Manfred is averse to sustained exercise. It's my guess that he chose to remain in the vicinity of the village.' I had gathered that Manfred was not in the best of condition. There were many reasons supporting Pat's belief and the conclusion he had reached. The SS rarely moved far from the road, the woods offering cover for snipers, who, placed in a good firing position, could cause havoc. If Manfred had chosen to remain near the village, he must have been fairly close to the fallen bombs. This supposition prompted another question. 'Did you notice where the bombs fell?'

'Yes,' Pat answered, 'I was with Manfred a few moments afterwards. He had stopped to drink from a stream. Shortly he joined me further along the path. One bomb landed in this stream, close to the spot where he had quenched his thirst.' Smiling, Pat reflected for a moment. Verdi congratulated him, it certainly was a near miss. Shortly after this he suggested that we separate, telling me to make for Monte Rossa. We have had a very enthusiastic welcome taking things all round.

The remainder of his account referred to the route he had taken to reach the peak. After a meal of polenta and cheese, purchased from the shepherd who owned the malga, we went into the hut, our dormitory for the night.

Chapter Three

Manfred Recalls the Recent Past

The hut was damp, pungent with the odour of goats and sheep. Small branches stripped from the nearby trees were scattered over the earthy floor on which we slept, a limited protection against the cold. The murmur of voices gradually subsided into heavy breathing and a varied chorus of snoring. Throughout the night there were additional disturbances, caused by the sentries, who stamped their feet trying to warm themselves. On the hour, the church bells rang out in unison, the waves of sound reaching up the slopes carried on the cold, crisp air. Amidst these distractions we slept.

Came the dawn. 'Good morning, Sir, did you sleep well?' With uncanny consistency I have found it easier to say the wrong thing. Having bid Pat good morning, I realised what a silly question it was. Pat was not disgruntled, he replied casually, 'I regret to say that I slept badly, I'm pleased it's past.' Sitting up, he rubbed his eyes, speaking at the same time. 'Did you notice the hours when the church bells rang. They struck the hour a second time. I heard 4 and 5 strike.' Standing up, he rubbed his legs. 'Let's see what's happening outside.'

There was little activity with the exception of one man who was preparing another polenta meal. Polenta is fed to chickens in normal times. If you enjoy it, you are abnormal. I had my doubts about one or two of the Partisans for they appeared to enjoy it. I smoked a cigarette in lieu of breakfast.

Jacko returned with us to Pielungo, taking another route along a mule-track which he stated had been built by the Austrians during the Great War. It was much easier going, in addition to which we were proceeding down the slope. Towards midday we reached the village. Entering the main street, we saw Manfred in the company of Verdi and Orellio, sitting outside the albergo, drinking wine. Seeing us, he stood up, glass in hand, calling, 'You have arrived at the right moment, it is opening time.' Verdi and Orellio offered their chairs after which they excused themselves and walked off towards the church, situated at the end of the street. Manfred explained that they were going to see the local priest concerning the funeral of the one fatal casualty suffered in the recent clash with the SS.

Manfred was on good form and cheerfully outlined the skirmish. 'I'm sorry that you should have had such a hectic welcome, but fortunately this episode had a happy ending.'

He had obviously enjoyed himself, for he continued with some fervour. 'The Boche took over the village all right and set fire to our headquarters.' He pointed to the smouldering shell of what was once the castle. 'They decided against following us along the track and were content to fire their mortars in the general direction of our withdrawal. That gave us time to plan a counterattack. Assuming that they would return to Spilimbergo via the Clausetto route, we dispatched two ambush parties, who took up a position either end of a tunnel, through which the Boche made their way. As they entered the tunnel, one ambush party fired for all they were worth. The Boche lorries accelerated for the cover of the tunnel. Once they were inside, the tunnel ends were blown in and sealed. They made their way out at the other end after much digging, unfortunately the ambush parties had little ammunition left and so were forced to break off the engagement.'

There ended the tale of the skirmish, but Manfred had not run out of news, for he produced a newspaper, which he laid on the table translating the substance of the leading article, an account of the previous day's action. 'This is the local paper called *Il Picollo*, according to this the SS had a successful day out, they caused the bandits seventy-nine fatal casualties and numerous wounded in a battle lasting 4 hours. Ignoring the minor casualties, this magnificent piece of propaganda was just seventy-eight out.' Manfred concluded the translation, the essence of which inferred that the German troops had retired without loss to themselves. Pat produced his map, having heard the account of the skirmish, and asked several questions concerning the topography of the local countryside. 'Where is Spilimbergo?' Manfred had made a thorough reconnaissance of the Province, for he answered confidently with accuracy, 'Spilimbergo is about 20 miles to the south. It lies on the south bank of the Tagliamento River on the plain, just below the lower foothills.' He waited for Pat to put another question.

'Presumably, that is the nearest garrison town?' I listened carefully to the answer, for we had as yet discovered little with regard to enemy dispositions.

'No, not really. The Boche maintain a road barrier there, for it is the nearest town to the foothills. There is another town further to the east called Tolmezzo where they keep a larger number of troops. There is a road passing through Spilimbergo running on north into the mountains, but the bulk of the traffic is carried on the first-class road leading from

Udine through Tolmezzo, Paluzza and eventually to the frontier town of Timau. There is another excellent route which leads through Pontebba and then to Tarvisio, a town near the frontier.'

Manfred paused briefly, allowing us to absorb this information. 'Udine is roughly half-way between our present location and Trieste. It is both a reinforcement centre and rear rest position. Most troop movements from Austria to the Adriatic side of the front, pass through or make a halt at Udine. To date the Partisans, through shortage of arms and ammunition have remained quiet. Yesterday's visit was quite unexpected. I cannot account for it. One thing is clear, we must leave this neighbourhood without further delay. I propose to settle in the Tramonte valley, Verdi knows of a secure house there, just above Tramonte di Mezzo, called Rutizza.'

'Apart from the DZ we landed on, have you located any other suitable places?' Pat asked.

'Yes, in the Tramonte valley there is an ideal spot. It is about 2km square. You should have landed there. Do you know why the pilot chose to put you down on the stores ground?' Pat remembered equally well, the difficulty the pilot had making up which DZ to use, 'There were three sets of signal fires. He taxied over the area more than 10 minutes before he cautioned us to jump.' Manfred frowned showing his disapproval, fully aware of what had occurred. 'The locals are desperately keen to obtain weapons. They heard the plane circling the area and of course lit more fires in the hope that they would receive the drop. We must be incredibly careful in the future not to indicate when we will expect stores. Verdi and Orellio are absolutely trustworthy, but the remainder have no respect for security.'

Before he continued, Manfred called for more wine. 'Cameriere, possiamo avere un'altra bottiglia, per favore?'[1] The waiter brought the fresh bottle, filling the glasses before he withdrew, Manfred drank a little wine, then spoke about his own reception.

'I landed among the sugar beet which covers the Tramonte ground. Verdi arranged the reception, and I give him his due, he made his arrangements well. We were clear of the DZ and after 5 minutes drove off by car to Pielungo. We still have two cars, but naturally their use is confined to the local area and of course petrol is difficult to obtain. The Bergoli brothers steal it from German dumps near Udine.'

Many villagers were making their way to the church. 'I think it would be only right for us to attend the Requiem Mass and the funeral. The poor devil was a stranger, joining the local Partisan movement three weeks ago.

He got a stray bullet in the head, so he didn't know very much about it,' Manfred said.

'What time does the ceremony commence?' Pat asked. 'At 2 o'clock, the bell will give us warning. These people are a little premature. To continue with what I was saying. Bearing in mind that we have dual commitments, I have concentrated on the Friuli, leaving the Carnia and the frontier area to you. So that you will establish yourself up there with a minimum of delay, I have made the acquaintance of one called "Primus", who is the local Garibaldi commissar of Timau. I shall refer to him in a minute. It is essential that we observe fundamental radio security, keeping our two sets at least a Province apart. Secondly it would inadvisable to keep two such vital eggs in one basket. The sooner that you establish yourself in the Carnia therefore, the better.'

Checking the time at his disposal, before the commencement of the funeral service, Manfred continued, 'I should like you to be entirely responsible for the Operation Royal requirements. I have wired Base that they should not arrive before the end of August, which will leave you roughly six weeks to lay things on. Primus will be able to put you in touch with a smuggler named "Remus" who is bilingual, speaking Italian and Austrian. He is quite a character, for the police of Italy and Austria would like to get their hands on him, but he is too slippery for them, which is a form of recommendation. He is familiar with all the unfrequented routes over the frontier and therefore your man. To conceal the identity of your object, tell Primus that you are interested in meeting the local Partisans. Knowing that you are in a position to produce arms and ammunition he will be only too pleased to be of service. When you think fit, try to establish a meeting with Remus through Primus, they are particularly good friends, but Remus will play our game if we pay him well. You may find suitable dropping localities. Certainly, the local Garibaldi will know of some. Personally, it would be to our mutual advantage and the success of the operation if we ignored whatever DZs there are up there. To use them would attract unnecessary attention which of course would be prejudicial. For the time being we have enough grounds in the Friuli.'

Pat looked at his map again, and then asked, 'Is the frontier heavily guarded?' Before Manfred could reply, he put a second query forward, 'Presumably, the Boche maintain infantry patrols along the frontier?' 'No, it is not heavily guarded. There is a Company post above Timau. At irregular intervals, the Timau post send an armoured car carrying the mail to Tolmezzo, and in addition the Tolmezzo Garrison send an infantry company on foot up to Timau. On the Austrian side of the frontier, there is a form of Custom Gendarmerie, who patrol in pairs.'

Pausing, Manfred waited for Pat to ask another question. Pat preferred to listen, so Manfred continued. 'I prefer to remain in the Friuli, there will be plenty of scope here too. One of the main roads between Austria and Italy passes through the Friuli and the Carnia in addition to the Udine–Tolmezzo–Timau route. If Base will supply the necessary drops so that we can arm about 2,000 Partisans, we should be able to keep the Boche very busy from August onwards, distracting their attention from the frontier, thus enabling you to go ahead unhampered with your plans.'

I watched Manfred closely while he brought us up to date. At first glance he did not impress me. Certainly, he was tall and strongly built, he had an easy flow of conversation, which was witty, coupled with a charming disposition. Before he commenced the operation, he was erratic, full of energy and interest one day, complacent the next. I gained the impression that he was selfish, perhaps even wild. A man with a hit or miss nature. Listening to him now and all that he had achieved in the short time that he had been on the job, I thought differently. He planned well, leaving nothing to chance.

Manfred had one obvious failing he would have done well to counteract. He smoked almost continually, sometimes lighting a fresh cigarette from the unfinished one. Looking at his face and unlined forehead, it was difficult to believe that he was 40 years of age, yet seeing him attempting to run, you would be excused if you were to add 10 years to his 40.

The church bell rang, a doleful invitation to all within hearing. We stood up, waiting for Verdi who was walking towards us. Together we went to the church wherein the whole congregation was assembled. At the head of the aisle and in front of the main altar lay a coffin draped in black, three Partisans standing each side of it. The Mass was sung, the gathering loudly replying to the priest's lead. Without organ accompaniment, the voices were truly a mournful chant, a fitting incidental to a sorrowful occasion. Strong beams of light played onto the coffin, along whose rays a million particles of dust surged towards the windows. Standing to the rear of the church, near the open entrance, I was tempted to look outside, for the sunny countryside was a picture of living beauty, in contrast with the scene inside the church. It was a short service, after which the priest led the way to the graveyard behind the church, followed by the pallbearers. No relatives were present, but many in attendance wept, as though he were one of their own. The coffin was laid in the grave, the last rites performed, and silence returned once more to the graveyard.

Returning to the hotel, where a meal awaited us, few words were spoken, each aware of the fact that the dead man might easily have been one of us. A breeze carried a piece of paper along in front of us. Life during these tumultuous times seemed to be borne away just as easily. This theme of contemplation checked the flow of conversation, and since our thoughts were in harmony, there was no need for words.

Breaking into the melancholy of the moment, Manfred interrupted our thoughts, saying, 'I like this part of Italy, the landscape is beautiful, and the villages are medieval. You will love it up here after a while. The air is always so wonderfully fresh, I always feel very much more alert here. Don't you find it refreshing?'

Pat agreed with him, saying, 'Yes, even after our exacting climb, I don't feel a bit tired. Just a little stiff, that's all.'

The lunch table was set in a small room in the albergo. Verdi and Orellio joined us at the table. They wished us 'Bon appetito', a customary greeting before a meal. For their benefit, during lunch, the conversation was in Italian, my understanding of which was limited and therefore gave me the opportunity of studying our new friends. Verdi was the more arresting of the pair. He was of slight build, dark-haired, swarthy chin and had a pair of penetrating black eyes. He reminded me of the King of Abyssinia, there was a striking likeness. Unlike many other Italians, he had no mannerisms when he conversed, confining his sentences to a minimum, yet adequately conveying his point of view. When talking, he commanded attention for his choice of subjects covered a wide field, his deliberations based upon a comprehensive study and search, giving him an air of authority. He was a patient listener and therefore pleasant to talk to. At the same time, one gathered he did not appreciate idle chatter.

Orellio was Verdi's second in command, counsel and closest friend. He had been responsible for recruiting many of the Partisans. In ordinary life he was a priest but had left his parish to take a more active part in the fight for liberty, bringing with him into the mountains several young men of his parish. He was taller than Verdi and of stronger physique. He spoke with bewildering rapidity revealing a highly nervous temperament, over which in times of stress he exercised admirable control. He was short-sighted and wore horn-rimmed glasses, which gave him a learned air. His responsibilities included the financial and spiritual well-being of the movement, a position he was well equipped to fulfil, pursuing his self-adopted appointment with a will appreciated by all the Partisans, who in return showed him much respect. He was as loyal to Verdi as he was to his own conscience.

Their clothing was well worn but serviceable. Verdi wore boots, stockings, breeches and a bottle-green Italian Army jacket. He never used a hat. Orellio proudly wore the uniform of an Alpini soldier, a dark-green jacket and ski-trousers, which were tight at the ankle. To complete his dress, he wore an Alpini hat attached to which was a feather, denoting senior rank. In former times Verdi had been a half-colonel of Bersaglieri serving with the Regiment at Caporetto during the Great War, where he among the few distinguished himself when in close contact with the enemy. Orellio, Verdi's confidant, while recalling incidents of the Great War, mentioned Verdi's personal history, and referred to his present activities. Apparently as soon as Bagdoglio accepted the terms of surrender and it was clear that the German Army serving in Italy would continue the fight on Italian soil, Verdi made straight to the mountains to organise resistance.[2]

Coffee was served and with it Orellio developed the discussion along political lines, taking care not to allow Manfred to alter the course which he had carefully chosen. He spoke for some time in general terms of a much-propounded creation of Dr Goebbels' propaganda, who preached that it was inevitable that the Allies would break up into two camps, Russia leading the Eastern states and the US and Britain the countries of the West.

If Germany were beaten, the war would continue between these two camps. Avoiding personalities, Orellio narrowed the field to his own Friuli and the neighbouring Province of the Carnia. Before explaining the local position, Orellio paused to wipe his spectacles. 'There are a million cores of dissension floating on the tide of this war, which we are powerless to cast aside. Though the Nazis have overrun many countries in the course of this war, the people of those countries are dis-united in purpose. Certainly, they consider Germany the major enemy, who must be destroyed. What then is the reason for their inability to unite and thus strengthen the foundation of their nations?' Orellio chose his words with care. 'I will tell you we fear another war will develop. Even here we cannot ignore this possibility, and therefore we have friction and the formation of two Partisan elements opposed in their basic conception of liberty and the rights of the individual.' Orellio had spoken with undisguised conviction, flavoured by an undercurrent of frustration, hopeful that there might be a solution possibly that Manfred or Pat could offer. He waited earnestly for a reply.

Pat looked at Manfred who took another cigarette from a packet of Chesterfield, gaining a few seconds in which he formulated his answer, 'I'm afraid, Orellio, your convictions are dangerous though I must admit the signs that have guided you are real enough. Unfortunately, your sources of information have been restricted and therefore have fostered your opinions.'

Orellio made to answer but Manfred forestalled him for he continued, 'I know that you have listened to radio broadcasts from the United Kingdom, you have heard the "Voice of America", but these broadcasts have not taken up Dr Goebbels' challenge. As far as you are concerned, we represent the outside world. The Allies are bound together with a firm determination to rid the world of Nazism. Dr Goebbels' comments are received with unreserved contempt. I am firmly convinced that when this war is over, all differences will be discussed over the peace table. They will draw up a charter for the maintenance of peace guaranteeing the liberty of the individual and what is more they are powerful enough to carry this charter into effect, peaceably and with patience.'

I am sure that Manfred was right. Why, only defeatists listened to the propaganda of the enemy, but then Orellio had nothing to counter Dr Goebbels' arguments. His country had been fighting alongside the Germans, it was natural that he should think differently. But Orellio was not to be convinced easily. He did not reply, but there was no mistaking his attitude.

Verdi felt there was nothing to be gained by pursuing this conversation and inferring that there were things to be done excused himself and left the hotel accompanied by Orellio. When they left, Manfred smiled, but I could see that he was disturbed by the recent discussion. We were not concerned with political issues, though they might develop with the progress of the war, we were here for purely military reasons. Manfred voiced his concern. 'Possibly you would have answered far more ably Pat, but I felt he expected me to reply. It was rather a difficult one to answer. These fellows will not concern themselves with the military aspect and that alone. It is difficult to gain their confidence, essential if we are to be successful, yet remain aloof from their political intrigues. I will not suggest for one moment that I understand their problems but if you choose to refrain from political discussion, they may think you are not interested or that you are complacent. If you sympathise with them, you will become more deeply involved. The word will go around and later you will be accused of taking sides. We owe it to the Garibaldi and the Osoppo that we should remain strictly impartial. You will have learned from this that we must always emphasise our military commitments and refuse to become involved with their political harangue. It will be difficult, for it is their chief pastime.'

Changing the subject, Pat spoke of the future. 'Shall we go to Rutizza this evening?' Manfred said 'No, we will drive over there early tomorrow morning, it isn't far. When we use the cars, we make sure that the way is clear first. I have driven as far as the Ampezzo valley, having assured myself that there were no enemy patrols about.'

'Do you want me to go on from Rutizza straight away or should I wait for the replacement radio first?' said Pat. 'We'll see what Base have to say. If they promise a replacement on the next drop, you may just as well wait a couple of days. I should like you to see how we prepare the reception. Naturally enough it is quite exciting waiting for the arrival of the plane at the rendezvous.'

We were interrupted by a quiet knock on the door. Manfred said 'Avanti' and the door opened revealing a soberly dressed little man, hat in hand.

'Good afternoon,' said the visitor. 'May I speak to the Major?' The little man spoke with a pronounced Midland (England) accent. 'You may,' said Manfred. 'Won't you take a chair?'

Appearing quite at ease, the stranger introduced himself. 'I am Flight Sergeant Desmond.[3] I have been a prisoner of war for close on three years. Perhaps you remember that a Wellington Bomber flying to the Middle East was forced down in Sicily. We were carrying VIPs. I was the rear gunner in that plane. We made a comfortable landing but were all taken prisoner almost immediately. In September '43, most of the Italian POW camps were left unguarded. I took my opportunity of escaping to the mountains up here. Lots of the boys decided to remain in the camps thinking they would soon see the British or American armies. Most of them will be transferred to POW camps inside Germany by now. There were many rumours, the most convincing one was that they would soon be relieved and on their way home.'

'What have you been doing since your escape?' asked Manfred. Desmond explained, 'Well, for one thing, I have almost worn through my shoes. I have walked from village to village, sleeping in barns or any suitable shelter that I could find. Sometimes the odd villager has given me a bed for the night and whatever food they could spare, but they were all anxious for me to move on. The penalty for harbouring escaped prisoners is severe, and in most villages, there are still Fascists who would tip off the Gestapo. Times have been hard, but it is wonderful to be free again.'

'You may remain with us for the time being Desmond,' said Manfred. 'When there are about ten of you, we will arrange to send you to the south of Italy.'

'Thank you very much, Sir,' said Desmond, 'There is one more thing, Sir. I know where there are two more escapees who would welcome this opportunity. I could bring them here within 3 or 4 hours.' 'Whereabouts are they?' Manfred asked. 'They are living in a hut on the mountainside on the way to Clausetto.' Desmond seemed keen to bring them along. 'It's not very far, I wouldn't have difficulty finding them, for they intend to remain at the hut for the time being.'

'All right, we will send you along in the car later this evening.' Manfred said, 'They will definitely be there then, probably getting down to it for the night. Do they know that I am here in Pielungo?'

'If they don't, they soon will, for the local villagers are all in the picture. That's how I came to know that you were in the neighbourhood,' replied Desmond. Manfred looked towards Pat, his face expressing fully his conviction that we should move to another area without delay.

'That settles it, Pat, we shall have to send these boys up to Monte Rossa for the time being. It is as safe a place as any. When we have assembled a large enough party, we'll arrange for their disposal south. At the same time, we can continue as previously arranged. We'll leave tomorrow morning.'

Turning once more to Desmond, he asked, 'I imagine you could do with a meal?' Desmond, looking a little drawn, replied, 'Yes, Sir.'

'Very good, you shall have one.' Calling for the owner of the hotel, Manfred ordered lunch for Desmond, to whom he said, 'When you have eaten, remain here and I will arrange for a guide to take you to your friends. Here, there's a packet of cigarettes, you won't have seen any of them for some time and you could probably do with one.'

Desmond thanked Manfred, but refused saying that he did not smoke, but Manfred told him to keep them anyhow for the other prisoners to whom he should give them when they next met. Turning to Pat, he suggested that they take a stroll adding that I might like to keep Desmond company. To this proposal I agreed, for I understood Manfred wished to speak to Pat in private.

For the next 2 hours Desmond recalled his prisoner-of-war experiences. The Italian camps were very inefficiently administered making the life of the prisoner additionally hard to bear. At first there were no Red Cross parcels of food and the ration issued by the camp authorities was monotonous and scarce. Many prisoners died of dysentery which was aggravated by the inadequate food ration and conditions inside the camp. By stages the prisoners organised themselves, setting up proper latrines, obtaining better ablution facilities and in general cleaning up the filth into which they had been thrown. Later it was possible to work outside the camp which allowed them the opportunity of purchasing vegetables or fruit in return for cigarettes received with the Red Cross parcels. An escape committee was organised, the prisoners who worked outside the camp supplying useful information with regard to the lay of the land outside the wire. But inefficient though their captors were at humane administration, they were well practised in the art of mistake and were always prepared for any break-out attempt after which they would apply petty restrictions designed to curtail would-be escapees. I found this personal account of prisoner-of-war life interesting, little realising that I should have occasion to value the tips Desmond had described in detail. He made light of his experience, adding a few humorous anecdotes, but these incidents did not conceal the humiliation and frustration which with the passing of time undermined the morale of the prisoners.

The driver of the car detailed to take Desmond to Clausetto entered the room saying that the vehicle was ready. With their departure I went in search of Pat whom I thought would have concluded his conversation with Manfred. Questioning a Partisan, I learned that they had gone to a smaller hotel which was to provide our accommodation for the night. I found them actively engaged in conversation, but they motioned that I should remain.

'Has Desmond left for Clausetto?' Pat asked. I replied that he had. Having thus established Desmond's departure, they continued where they had left off, Manfred concluding his appreciation of the situation before our arrival.

'The discussion with Orellio earlier this afternoon brings me to a point which I have omitted to mention. It has some bearing on what he said. We have competition in the form of a gentleman by the name of "Fred", who dropped into the Province a few weeks ago. He is worthy of mention, for I have reason to believe that he may prove a nuisance, to put it mildly. He has an assistant who works his radio. A particular specimen of Italo-Egyptian origin. I have made a few inquiries about Fred which are some-what disturbing. He is an Englishman who has lived in Italy for about eighteen years, having married an Italian girl, and has settled down here in Italy living for the greater part in the Venice area. It is noteworthy that he never returned to England. I believe that he too was advised against returning by those close to him. However, all that is unimportant, what is important is the fact that he is the right-hand man of a left-wing Italian of some prominence, who may well have been his sponsor for the work he has now adopted. He is in radio communication with OSS base headquarters through whom he will obtain his stores.' Manfred clarified his concern.

'He has already contacted the Garibaldi, although he landed in an area prominently Osoppo. For some reason he outlived his welcome. The Osoppo didn't like the look of him. Moving further north he linked up with the Garibaldi. It looks to me that he is the advance party of an OSS mission. It would be unfortunate if he is, for the neighbourhood will become overcrowded, not only duplicating the work but possibly complicating it. My initial concern is that he will limit our chances of amalgamating the Garibaldi and Osoppo movements of the two Provinces.'

'Are Base aware of the fact that he has chosen to remain in this locality?' Pat asked.

'They are now, but they had no idea until I investigated the inquiry. It is a matter for Base to clarify. Naturally, all the obvious difficulties are clearly represented, and Base are aware of them as well as you or I understand them. The solution requires immediate liaison between the Base Staff and OSS headquarters. The OSS preparation effecting Fred's operation may be so advanced that it would be inadvisable to call a halt. Like ourselves, they may have equally important motives for operating within the bounds of these Provinces. We can do no more than await developments.'[4]

'It's almost 7 o'clock,' said Pat. 'I should like to assemble my kit ready for tomorrow's move, before we join Verdi and Orellio.' 'I'll see you both about 8 then,' Manfred replied. Following Pat upstairs, we went to our room, where we prepared for the early morning move to Tramonte di Mezzo.

Chapter Four

A Sermon of Special Significance

Peppino was due to make an early radio contact with Base at 5am, which would provide me with a chance of studying local conditions or at least allow me the opportunity of hearing the Base transmitter note for future recognition. Dressing hurriedly, I joined him. He was busy setting up station. 'Che ora adesso?' I asked. Looking at his wristlet watch, Peppino replied. 'Alle cinque meno cinque.'

Just 5 minutes to go. Once again, the weather promised to be fine, for the sky was a clear blue. Even at this early hour, the village was astir. Many women carrying large wicker baskets on their backs were leaving on their way to distant mountain slopes in search of fodder. During the summer months the way to the higher pastures entailed none of the problems accompanying inclement weather. It was commonly accepted that the nearby surrounding pasture would be left untouched providing an adequate supply for the winter period. Taking their lunch, the morning and early afternoon would be spent scything and turning the grass which when dried by the sun they piled high in the wicker baskets. Each family kept a goat, or in a few more prosperous cases, a cow. The fodder costing little in terms of money demanded many hours of tiresome work at the end of which remained the normal household chores after bedding down the animals and storing the rest of the fodder.

It was quiet when the patter of feet subsided. For those in the front lines to the south, the watching hour before the dawn would have eased with the light of day and the accompanying clatter of activity, perhaps breakfast-time harassing fire and first daylight air sortie overhead. For myself, and Peppino, we knew that the enemy wireless interception operators would be searching for the sound of clandestine radio activity. At 2 minutes to the hour, Peppino switched on. Running his finger lightly over the frequency tuning dial he set his receiver to the incoming signal which repeated the call sign of the Base station. Peppino answered querying whether there was any traffic. 'Nothing for you' was the reply, so he switched off. At 3 minutes past the hour the call was made. Returning to Pat's room, I collected our rucksacks, carrying them down to the entrance, while Pat finished dressing. Manfred arrived asking if Pat were ready. Soon, he too joined us. The young woman of the house offered black ersatz coffee in addition to a glass of grappa liqueur, a colourless spirit which had a warming effect.[1] We set off.

Passing through Tramonte di Mezzo, we skirted a large flat field, sown with sugar beet. 'This is the Body-Ground or Stores, as you like; it can be used for both.' said Manfred. It was large enough for a small plane to land on, the approach from the south over the Meduna valley providing an inlet to the valley of Tramonte. Following the road to the north, we left the village behind, in a small matter of minutes arriving at the house Rutizza, a small farmlet. It lay well into the side of the mountain, trees covering the slopes reaching down to the rear of the house providing a concealed route into the remoteness of the woods above. Here we were to spend several uneventful days waiting for the next drop, which Base informed us was delayed through bad flying weather conditions. Enjoying tropical Mediterranean summer conditions ourselves, we were ill-satisfied with these reports as the days passed. Our priority was high for stores delivery. What were Base playing at? While meditating over the answer to this question, we rarely considered the overall picture and the requirements of other missions, throughout Central Europe, hence we were the more impatient.

The first Sunday I attended a service at the local church of di Mezzo. Entering the church, I noticed that there was an empty place towards the front, in a pew close to the altar, and under the pulpit. Without realising what I had done, I was soon aware that I had distracted the congregation. A ripple of whispers and a feeling that I was being closely observed by many pairs of eyes confirmed my reaction. I continued to look towards the altar trying to appear unconcerned and hoping fervently that I had not committed a serious breach of Catholic etiquette. Then it dawned upon me! I was sitting among the younger women, the virgins of the community. On the opposite side of the aisle sat the un-married men judging by their youthful looks. The older members of the congregation filled the rear pews. Preceded by two small altar boys, the priest walked from the sacristy. *In Nomine Patris, Fili et Spiritui Sanctus, Amen.* The Mass began. The missal was carried by one of the altar servers to the left or Gospel side of the altar. Following the priest's example the congregation stood up, making the sign of the cross three times over their foreheads, over their mouths and finally across their hearts signifying that they would think and believe in the Gospel, that they would never speak against it and that they would love and cherish the words of the Gospel. The priest took his place in the pulpit, many seizing this opportunity to clear their throats. Passing his hand slowly over his brow, he closed his eyes patiently waiting for the people to settle down. Taking up a piece of paper, he read the church notices which ended with a call for prayers for the faithful departed. After reading the Epistle and Gospel chosen for the Sunday, he closed his prayer book and placed it on the stand in front of him. The sermon was a surprise, and not as normal, a reflection on the appointed Epistle and Gospel of the day.

'My Dear Brethren, it is a fitting time for us to consider, not the moral of the Gospel I have just read to you, but the consequences and tidings of a parable with which you are all familiar.' Pausing briefly for them to measure his words, he then carried on, 'You all have sometime during the past, heard me speak of Lot's wife and the pillar of salt. It has occurred to me that we have not seriously considered this story, at least many of us haven't. We all make mistakes, we have our failings, none of us are born perfect, far be it for me to say any more than that, we are very much a human community and this failing of Lot's wife is peculiar to most of us.'

Glancing to the left and right, I noticed that every face was turned towards the priest. They were both interested and concerned. Placing his hands within the folds of his surplice, he moistened his lips, running his tongue over them. Satisfied that his words had found their mark, he continued. 'This unfortunate woman suffered from the pangs of "curiosity", it was a temptation, but she had been warned to take care and yet she weakened! Brethren, I have already said that curiosity is a common weakness, we all suffer from its blight, it is so commonplace that we don't recognise it as a failing anymore and that is where the danger lies. Life on earth is a trial, it is so easy to commit sin, but it requires a certain amount of effort to do good. It doesn't matter what station in life we hold, this rule still applies. If you have a curious turn of mind, if you must investigate things which are of no concern to you, what happens next? Why, you have to tell someone what you have discovered and so the word goes around. Oh yes, you'll say, but if I stumble on something, I'd keep it to myself or perhaps you'll say, oh, that's common knowledge, so I'm excused if I talk about what I have seen. Be honest with yourselves now, it's true, isn't it? Most of you have this failing.' Several stirred uneasily in their seats. The priest knew that he was attacking a common practice among the villagers.

'Well, Lot's wife had a warning, so have you. What are you going to do about it? We are living in troublesome times. All the more reason for you to examine this little matter in the clear light of day. It may be that you will see strangers in your midst! That will be something to start the tongues wagging. I can picture the words as they are spoken – "Did you see those strangers with so and so the other day?" Yes, that will stir your curiosity. Brethren, this old news. The village of Forni di Sopra was raised to the ground last week, and why? Why were those poor people of di Sopra terrorised in this disastrous manner? The nearest German garrison was miles away from this village. I ask you, why was it burned down? I will tell you the answer, somebody's tongue was set wagging and the result it grieves me to inform you, came as a surprise. Take heed of my words. Be warned Brethren, guard against curiosity and idle gossip for this practice brings nothing but pain and suffering in its wake, not perhaps to the guilty one, but to someone whom you love or respect. In the name of the Father and the Son and of the Holy Ghost, Amen.'

Then the priest returned to the altar, the service continued. *Ite missa est.* Soon the Mass was ended, and the congregation filed out of the church. As I left, I noticed Pat. I walked back with him to Rutizza. 'Well, Sir, what did you make of the sermon?' I asked Pat. 'I should say that it was an incredibly wise warning. I liked his approach. Some days ago, Manfred met the local podestà and the village priest and took the opportunity of mentioning the unwelcome publicity he had received elsewhere. They were favourably impressed, agreeing that it was unnecessary and a danger to themselves.'

'Do you think it likely that the SS will get to hear of our visit here, Sir? I asked. 'We must always be prepared for an unexpected visit,' Pat replied. 'I'm certain that the Boche know that we are here in the Friuli, but not our actual strength or definite whereabouts. Verdi has a protective screen covering all likely routes of approach. At the end of the Meduna valley, for example, there is a Partisan post, who can get through by phone to the Podestà. The area is too large to encircle and though there may be many routes of approach, we must regard that as an advantage rather than a handicap. This is as secure a spot as any you will find.'

'What about when the weather gets worse, won't many prospective escape routes be inaccessible?' I re-joined. 'They may well be, but I very much doubt whether we shall be in this neighbourhood then. In any case, I hope that the fortunes of war will have advanced in our favour. What made you ask?' Pat said.

'Oh, I was just wondering,' I answered. 'It looks as though the locals have taken heed because there aren't many of them standing in the Piazza gossiping today.'

'It remains to be seen,' Pat remarked. 'It would be of interest to call into the General Store on the way back and hear the midday news. The

Fifteenth Army Group may have surprised us overnight with a further advance. The storekeeper tunes in every hour measuring the moves forward, calculating when he can expect to be liberated.'

'I'll join you, Sir, if I may,' I said.

The storekeeper had not much business, it was difficult to obtain commodities for one thing and transport was scarce. Possessing a radio, he was the local authority on the progress of the war. Wine was plentiful and his chief revenue. Most evenings a large crowd gathered to hear the news and commentary given by Colonel Stevens following the current news.[2] It was gratifying to find that the BBC was regarded as the one and only reliable source of information in the opinion of the villagers. Colonel Stevens' comments especially were well received, his day-to-day summary of the general situation providing material for prolonged discussion hours after it had been received.

Inside the store we were offered a seat near the radio, a kindly gesture much appreciated, for there were many gathered to hear the broadcast. It was a poor transmission, atmospheric disturbances drowning out in some cases complete sentences. A poor old gentleman to the rear provided another source of disturbance, frequently emitting one sentence, 'Ecco, la guerre e dura'. Frequently, he would repeat it. 'It's a hard war.' At midday there was no commentary following the news. The transmission provided no surprises, all fronts remaining more or less static. We returned to Rutizza.

After lunch in company with a Partisan named Tommasso, I returned to the village in search of a woman who would give our clothes a thorough cleaning and pressing. Hearing Tommasso say that another Englishman had joined the local 'Patria Battaglione' some weeks before, I though it strange that we hadn't seen him. I asked Tommasso why it was he hadn't been to visit us at Rutizza, he must surely know that we were there. His reply was not convincing, for he said that the Englishman had had a long spell of guard duties, but would be in the village this afternoon, probably at the wine shop. We went in search of him.

Reaching the Piazza, a small cobbled square in the centre of the village, Tommasso pointed to a group of four Partisans saying, 'Ecco l'inglese, quello le?' I looked towards the group but could not distinguish which was the Englishman. We walked over to the group.

'Are you English?' I said looking at the one standing on the right who was a little fairer that the rest, but heavier built, and a rather swarthy complexioned fellow in the middle of the group replied, 'No, but I am a New Zealander.' He was dressed very much the same as the other three and carried a small-barrelled Italian rifle which was ornately carved at the butt end.

'I'm pleased to meet you,' I said. 'If you are on your way to the wine shop, I'll join you.' His name was Henry and he said, 'We're a bit short of ackers,' I said, 'Oh, that's all right, I have plenty of lira, come with me, we can have a chat over a drink.' Arriving at the end of a narrow street we entered the shop. The building was much like other houses, but in place of a stable on the ground floor, the proprietor had placed one or two tables and chairs converting the stable into a drinking parlour. Once the drinks were ordered, I passed a cigarette case round. They were all very thankful. Over a bottle of wine Henry told me his war story which was unique. He started the tale at Tobruk, where he was taken prisoner.

'The Anzac Divvy [Division] y'might remember were engaged in the fight to relieve Tobruk. I got a packet of shellshock and was evacuated to a CCS [Casualty Clearing Station]. That's how I became a prisoner for the CCS was overrun by the Jerries.' He would have stopped there but I was interested to hear the rest of his story including what he had been doing in the Dolomites. 'What happened then?' I asked. 'Well, the Jerries packed us off as quick as they could to a hospital of theirs, some miles behind the line. After a few days I was passed as fit and we went by lorry to Derna, where they loaded us onto an Iti [Italian] ship which took us to Naples. On the way over, the RAF did their fair dinkum best to sink the ship but there were lots of Messis [Messerschmidt aircraft] which interrupted them. I spent a few weeks in a prisoner-of-war camp near Naples. It was pretty grim and then I was sent up north near Bologna. I met one or two cobbers from time to time from my old Battalion, the 18th AXXXX. When the Itis packed in I reckoned it was time to get out of the wire until I knew what was going to happen. I'm glad m'luck was in, for if I'd stayed, I'd be in Germany now looking forward to a Red Cross box.'

Henry continued his story, 'I'm a carpenter and joiner by trade, that helped, I teamed up with two Pommies who had escaped from the same camp. We stuck together until we reached a village called Erto, about 20km from here. The first night we stayed in the village, but the people who took us in got a bit scared, thinking that the Jerries might pay a surprise visit, so we found an old shed just outside the village with fodder in it. That did us for a while. A couple of nights after we'd been there the Jerries did make a raid. They scared the life out of the Itis in the village and found out from someone that we were in the shed. Having heard one or two shots, we ran into the woods. We saw the Jerries search the shed and then a section came towards the woods. The other two wanted to beat it, but I reckoned that it was safer to lie low. The other two made a run for it and the Jerries started shooting. They winged one of the Pommies in the arm, but they didn't catch 'em. The Jerries didn't follow them and they didn't notice me. Soon after that they went away.' Henry stayed in the shed and a couple of days later, the 'Pommies' came back, one had his arm in a sling. 'They'd had enough of Erto though, they thought the Itis would give them away. I never saw them again. The same afternoon that they went, a little "Sheila" came up to the shed. I parlayed with her and she recommended me to the local carpenter. The Itis in these parts needed their windows and tables mending, so I helped out. The little "Sheila" had a room with a bed and a couple of odd bits of furniture so I "kipped" down with her. It was just right for a while, I earned enough to keep the pair of us, and I didn't have to work on Saturday or Sunday. Eventually I felt strong enough to move on, the Shelia got very peeved when I told her I was getting out, and she even threatened to tell the Jerries but I knew it wouldn't be worth her while. Eventually I came over here to Tramonte di Mezzo and joined the Patria battalion.'

'How long were you altogether in Erto, it must have been quite a long time?' I asked. 'Yeah, I said a while, but it was about eight months,' replied Henry.

I asked him if he wanted to stay with the battalion or prefer to be on his way home? He replied, 'Oh, I'm having a fair time. They haven't been doing much except keeping a watch out for the SS, since I have been with them. I'm satisfied to keep out of Jerries' way until the war is over. I wish they'd have a go at Jerry sometimes though, but with the arms that they've got, its wiser to keep out of the way. Anyway, they're always arguing the toss, they haven't any teamwork, there's too much bickering among them, and when they start squabbling among themselves I wish that I could find my way down the south, to our own lines, but that's a long way.'

I told Henry that he had an interesting story and said, 'Well, keep your chin up, it may not be long before you do make a move south if you are keen. I shall have to go now, but I'll be seeing you again soon. Here, take this lira, they'll keep you going for a while.' With that I left them, making for the washer woman's house. She saw me coming along the street but closed the window shutter just before I reached the house. I knocked on the door but there was no sound of movement from within. This was funny, she had seen me making for the house, yet she wouldn't answer the door. I gave it up as a bad job and returned to Rutizza, the washing under my arm.

Chapter Five

The Action was Unnecessary

A short distance from Rutizza flowed a tributary of the Tagliamento River. The waters of the stream were icy cold, even on the sunniest day curtailing an immersion to 2 or 3 seconds. First thing in the morning, it became our practice to take a hasty bath in the stream, returning to the bank where we rubbed ourselves down vigorously, after which we felt much more awake and refreshed. The passing villagers were amused, but not amazed, after all it was a peculiar habit of the English. Halfway through the month of August, Manfred expected a drop on the stores ground at Clausetto, at the same time a party of ten escaped POWs assembled on the top of Monte Rossa was becoming difficult to feed. It was decided that they must be sent on their long walk back to the British lines via Jugoslavia. Making my way back to the house from the stream, I noticed that Manfred, normally a late sleeper, was already up, talking with Peppino.

'Any news, Sir?' I asked. 'Yes, a plane will arrive 0010 hours, the morning after next which means that Pat will miss seeing the drop,' replied Manfred.

Pat was away on a recce over towards the Ampezzo valley and would be returning to Rutizza probably late evening, preceding the reception morning. He would be too tired to continue on to Clausetto, even if it were possible to arrive in time for the drop. The nature of Pat's present tour of the northern part of the Province entailed a search for additional DZs, positioned closer to the Carnia where in the future we should work.

'I shall go over with Verdi to Monte Rossa this afternoon and make arrangements for the movement of the POWs. When I have seen them off, I'll go on to Clausetto, there's a man there I want to see named Alberto, he works for the firm. It will be necessary to convey some reason for my visit to Clausetto to the locals there. The appointment with Alberto will prove sufficient to allay their suspicions until such time as I think fit, they should know about the drop. Charles, will you wander up the hill and bring that New Zealander here. I'll take him over to Monte Rossa with me when I leave. Just tell him to bring his kit, we'd like him to accompany us this afternoon, he need know no more than that for the present,' said Manfred.

'Right-ho, I'll collect him straight away, Sir,' I answered. Taking the track to the rear of the house, I set off for the Posto di Rastrellamento, the observation post above, which was maintained by members of the Patria Battalion Partisans. Climbing the track, automatically keeping direction, for I had been to the post several times before, I glanced to the north, tracing the re-entrant in which the house was situated. At its extremity there was a saddlebacked mountain over which Pat had made his way the day before. He had been keen to be in on the first reception party that was to be prepared. It was bright one moment, overcast the next, low-lying clouds were passing overhead, temporarily shutting out the bright sunshine. The rain came down heavily for several minutes soaking my clothes, a very moist cloud, but by the time I had reached the post, my clothing was dry, the sunshine taking the place of the rain, the drops of which glistened like falling lights, as they trickled from the surrounding leaves to the ground.

Henry certainly undertook his fair share of the duties. I found him preparing the meal when I arrived, standing over a large pot which was suspended from a roughly constructed tripod. He had prepared a regular hotchpotch on which his attention was fully focused, for he was not aware of my approach until I stood opposite him. I explained as quickly as I could what was afoot, cautioning him not to mention his journey to the others. Collecting his small rucksack, he told the local commander that he was required for a few days by Manfred, whose name was respected. Walking down the track on the way back to Rutizza, Henry relaxed. 'Well, I'll go to hell, so we'll be well on the way to south Italy in three weeks' time, will we? By Christ, won't I make up for lost time when I hit the nearest sizey town! You betcha.' I had stirred his excitement so much that I wished that I had not keyed him up so. He had a long way to go yet. His long journey would demand his whole attention and energy for more than three weeks. It might take as long as three months, but if he were to exercise care obeying the guides, he would make it.

Swelling the numbers of the party at Monte Rossa, the latest members of the trek south expedition were the crew of an American bomber which had met with opposition on a return journey from Czechoslovakia, and the airmen had been forced to take to their parachutes over the Friuli. The new men brought with them valuable experience, the navigator in particular with the aid of guides would be able to lead the party. In addition, they had landed with their arms, automatic pistols it is true, but nevertheless they guaranteed certain protection in close country. I was to remain at Rutizza to explain the position and latest developments to Pat when he returned. Wishing Henry all the best, I watched them drive off for the north-western fringe and foot of Monte Rossa where they would take to their feet, the car going on to Pielungo and the driver arranging for the first guide who would take the escapees as far as the high ground to the north of Gorizia. Later they would make for the eastern border of Istria, moving in a southerly direction, ultimately making for the Mountains of Knin. While the car drove on to Pielungo, Manfred and Verdi would climb to the malga linking up with the airmen and POWs to whom they would explain the escape route as far as they knew it. As they made their way south and east towards Jugoslavia, the friendly elements with whom the guides would put them in contact would provide a picture of the local situation, an important issue affecting their navigation and choice of route. I hoped that their footwear was equal to the journey. At a minimum it would mean a walk of 600 miles.[1]

Watching the car depart I reflected that they stood a reasonable chance of getting through safely. I had heard several stories of escaping prisoners. There was the story of the two Indian soldiers, who walking fully equipped, minus only one item, their rifles, had made a journey from Central Germany eating only what they had found in the fields, a trek of more than 200 miles, terminating safely within the borders of Switzerland. In the case of the Indians warmly dressed in British Army greatcoats, they could only move with any degree of safety during the hours of darkness, choosing places of rest miles from the main highway, causing them to make wide detours. The country through which our acquaintances would travel was for the most part wild countryside sparsely populated, a factor containing both advantages and disadvantages. Food, an essential, would be difficult to obtain for a large contingent. Shelter in cold weather would perhaps prove tricky to find. The latter should not prove a deterrent for they all valued their freedom and would be prepared to suffer hardship in order to achieve their object. Their route, following the path of Partisan controlled territory, provided limited freedom of movement so that they could travel day and night, resting only when they were tired. They would certainly earn their freedom.

Pat returned to Rutizza exhausted after his recce stating that he had not found any ground suitable. He had tumbled on one interesting discovery regarding enemy methods of infiltration into Partisan localities, whereby they extracted information concerning clandestine activities on the part of the Partisans. Dressing in British battledress suits, English-speaking members of the SS wandered individually over the mountains asking shepherds how they could join a Partisan element, at times questioning the unfortunate shepherd regarding his political leaning. If he were to declare allegiance to anybody other than the Fascist regime, invariably he was shot on the spot or taken into custody as a political prisoner, later to endure indescribable torment.

After this enlightenment, I explained Manfred's future movements and his proposed appointment with Alberto with whom Pat was apparently familiar, for he nodded knowingly. I informed him that I would remain up listening for the arrival of the expected plane leaving him then to enjoy a well-earned sleep.

Shortly after midnight, I joined Orellio who was standing on the road outside the house. He had arranged his period of guard duty so that he too could listen for the plane's arrival. We were aware that an aircraft was flying over the area before we heard its telltale drone break the silence of the night, for in the distance the beams of a searchlight battery hunted the starlit sky for the invader. Orellio said that the battery was stationed around the Osoppo airfield on which the Luftwaffe kept two flights of Messerschmidts. Soon after we heard the unmistakeable harmony of a Dakota's engine. It was harmonious to the members of our operation for this plane was bringing stores which would bolster our dwindling prestige.

The navigator found no difficulty locating the DZ, for the plane only made one run in over the target area unleashing its load and then passing on into the distance, the way back to base. This was a tonic, but then so was sleep which I intended to get the most of, leaving Orellio to finish his guard alone. We awoke to find Manfred had returned.

'Well, Pat, what luck?' said Manfred. 'Very little in respect of DZs. There were one or two placed on the small side, but I considered them additionally unsuitable because of their altitude. In the winter months, they would frequently be covered by low lying cloud,' replied Pat, who then related the methods recently employed by the SS which he had gleaned in passing from a shepherd.

Manfred was impressed with this information and answered that Pat's discovery was interesting and worthwhile recording for future reference. He then gave an account of his last 48 hours.

'I'm sorry that you weren't with me. I've had quite a lot of fun, I joined the POWs on Monte Rossa finding them all in the best of spirits and raring to go. Briefly summing up the difficulties facing them and after generalising on their journey, I nominated the pilot of the aircraft as the leader of the group. We then set off for Pielungo where we had arranged to meet the guide and collect a supply of rations for each one, thus catering for the first part of their trek. The guide said he knew an English major over in the neighbourhood of Gorizia through which they should pass. That's why I selected from those nominated by Verdi. In your absence we received a message referring to last night's drop. It was a pity you missed it, Pat. However, I hope we'll have more drops now that the weather is suitable. For some reason apparent only to Base, they decided to use the Clausetto DZ, so I killed two birds with one stone, seeing the POWs on their way into the bargain. I walked with them until our ways were divided. They're in capable hands, the pilot and the navigator were sound chaps.'

Manfred continued his story. He had wanted to talk with Alberto who had been killed the day Manfred had met him in a cafe and talked over a coffee. Manfred had wanted to publicise the purpose of his visit in the hope that meeting with Alberto all lines of thought would be trained on the meeting and that only. At that moment, a Partisan reported that a small convoy of Wehrmacht lorries were making their way up to Clausetto from the direction of Spilimbergo. Manfred quickly ran off to observe the approaching convoy from a vantage point overlooking the escarpment, it looked like a supply column probably en route to Tolmezzo. There were four vehicles and Manfred felt they would be easy to deal with should it be necessary. Manfred continued, 'The local Partisan commander is a fellow called Marco, I hadn't seen much of him before. I suggested we should allow them to enter Clausetto. There they would have been easier to ambush in the narrow street. He readily agreed and I watched them take up positions after a short briefing. If it were a supply column, I hoped that the bulk of the stores would contain food. I went back to the cafe but found Alberto had vanished into thin air. The next 5 minutes proved too hectic for words, and did not go according to plan.'

The Partisans, instead of waiting for the column to enter the village, had opened fire too early. It transpired the supposed supply column was not as it appeared, each vehicle contained ten SS soldiers who immediately got out and took cover. Then the SS opened fire using heavy mortars, the bombs falling in the village. Supported by a couple of machine guns, they moved towards the village. Marco had sited his Partisans well because, despite the weaponry of the SS, they managed to hold them off. The battle lasted an hour and a half, after which the SS withdrew carrying off a couple of dead and some wounded.

Checks were carried out on the buildings in the village. Several had been hit but were repairable. One bomb had found its way through the window of a house in which Alberto had taken cover. He was a ghastly mess and it was a case of shovelling him up. He was buried straight away. In addition to Alberto, there were two or three wounded and two killed.

Manfred felt he should contact Base and cancel the next morning's drop, but they were desperate for arms and ammunition and he decided to let the arrangement stand. Fortunately, the navigator of the aircraft knew his stuff, he flew straight in over the target area, dropping the packages directly on to the fires. They were transferred to two new safe houses, as suggested by Verdi and the arms were to be distributed the next day.

Manfred said, 'There are very few men left in Clausetto. They have taken to the mountains until this little fracas has passed over. It will be a place to avoid for some considerable time to come. The SS will scour the village for information, you can bet your last dollar. I'm sorry that it should have worked out like that, deeply sorry for Alberto, he was a brave chap, and had worked extremely well. I shall have to inform Base immediately. They will wonder why he hasn't answered their signals. God! I wonder where he kept his radio, I should hate the SS to find that. We'll have to get it. I think that Peppino will have to go back. I hate to send him for the moment, he would have to be very careful. I'll have a word with Verdi, he may be able to produce two sound men to accompany Peppino while he has a look round Clausetto. They could notify him if the Boche appear; tomorrow will do. Well there it is, Pat, the whole story. Oh, dear, pardon me, but I have a lot of sleep to catch up with.'

'I'll have a word with Verdi while you are resting if you like. I could arrange for Peppino to make the journey back by car to Clausetto this afternoon. That will give Peppino time to get some shuteye, while Verdi finds two suitable men,' replied Pat.

It was imperative that the radio should be found very soon before the SS discovered it.

Chapter Six

More Friends Arrive

The principle item which Pat and I had hoped would arrive with the next drop was not apparently included; when the packages were opened it was not to be found. A replacement radio had been demanded and in fact was notified by Base as sent. The case of the missing radio would be solved later, meanwhile we were still without. Peppino went back to Clausetto and covered every likely place where Alberto may have deposited his wireless set, but the cache containing the missing instrument was not discovered. If Peppino could not find it, it was thought to be secure and not likely to be found by the SS, should they search Clausetto, this put Manfred's mind at ease. It was debatable whether Pat and I should move without one, but the situation, unpredictable as it was, weighed against proceeding minus radio means. If the position became untenable, perhaps cutting our lines of communication with Manfred, or worse, if Manfred was eliminated and contact with Base terminated, Base may conclude that the whole operational strength was a write-off! Our work and progress in that event would be valueless. All points considered it was essential that we obtain a radio before we left the Friuli to go further afield.

As time passed the bare cement floor and the whitewashed walls of the room we occupied accentuated a sense of confinement. The view through the small window which at first enhanced the flavour of adventure, once more became a living picture of poverty and meagre living, a broken outhouse and muddy yard, door in the shade of the nearby mountain. Our enthusiasm was restrained, the plans and purpose of the operation could only survive with a steady intake of supplies from Base. Dash and drive temporarily succumbed, the fundamentals of a Partisan fighter in keeping with any infantier demanded more than these qualities. Weapons were the key which would release the principles now dormant, with sufficient arms they could display initiative and the confidence showed by their leaders would be reciprocated by the Partisans. They could then stand up to the enemy and dictate the form and progress of the battle on ground of their own choosing, the final principle they would learn easily for the nature of the ground controlled their movement. Having engaged the enemy, they were forced to change locality; the Partisan fighter must continually exercise discretion, the seeds of his valour ever alive in the knowledge that he is fighting in his own backyard.

The turning point came on 31 August, approximately a month after we had arrived. Peppino had a schedule at midday. I sat by him while he worked to Base. 'Have you any traffic,' deliberately he manipulated the key in typical Marconi style. Yes, there was a message, a long one, which promised well. The call finished, we deciphered the message together; when we had it in the clear, we ran to Manfred.

Manfred took the message and read it out aloud to Pat:

FOR MANFRED. ONE PLANE TO YOU 1 AUG. REPEAT 1 AUG. LOAD CONTAINS 32 REPEAT 32 PACKAGES. 12 BRENS, REPEAT 12 BRENS. 3 MORTARS REPEAT 3 MORTARS, 12 STENS REPEAT 12 STENS, 20 RIFLES REPEAT 20 RIFLES. 1 TON AMMN. PREPARE RECEIVE ROYAL PARTY OF SEVEN, REPEAT SEVEN. GEORGE TO EXPLAIN ON ARRIVAL. ALSO 8 REPEAT 8 JOHNNY WALKER MEDICINAL PURPOSES. ETA 0145 REPEAT 0145 HRS. ENDS.

Manfred said, 'A very cleverly worded message, starts and ends on a good note! What the hell are we going to do with the Royal party? There is little or enough room here for ourselves. I can understand there being four of them, but who are the other three? George certainly will have a lot of explaining to do on arrival.'

They noticed the consternation on Manfred's face and Pat remarked, 'They haven't mention the DZ to be prepared.' Manfred explained that he had notified Base that after the Clausetto episode, that DZ should not be used until he notified them. Thus, the next plane should use the Tramonte DZ. At least it was not so far for them to walk!

Manfred told Peppino to bring Verdi. He should be informed of the drop immediately; with little difficulty Verdi had soon learned the requirements of a reception party. With the aid of a mechanic he had produced a system of lights which were portable and quickly assembled, eliminating the need of wood fires, a recognition method which was laborious and left telltale evidence on the ground. Verdi entered the room, 'Siamo fortunato Verdi,' said Manfred.[1] 'But we also have a problem which you may be able to solve. A plane will arrive tomorrow morning at 0145 hours. Arriving with this plane are seven other Englishmen.'

Verdi was then asked if he could suggest where they could be accommodated. It was at this juncture that Pat made a suggestion, 'I'm sure that the radio will arrive. In that case there is no reason for Charles and I to remain here a moment longer. We could set off first light, that would make room here for two of the party.' Manfred nodded his agreement and waited for Verdi's solution. After some deliberation Verdi remarked, 'I will clear the barn below and send my men to a house in the village. I would still maintain a guard here, but they will be quartered a little farther away. I will arrange for fresh fodder to be laid in the barn. Would that be satisfactory?'

Manfred nodded his approval. He hoped that the newcomers would not remain for too long and that they would be keen to get on with their business further north.

The afternoon was spent discussing future plans, Pat suggesting that he should use a courier to arrange a meeting when he had progress reports to make. The point was who? It was finally decided that we would transmit a message via Base enclosing a rendezvous. That settled, where was Pat to make his temporary headquarters in the Carnia? As yet we had established no safe house or for that matter any useful contact in that area. Manfred suggested that Primus would probably offer accommodation. Timau was rather close to the frontier, and Pat was not happy that it was secure. We should wait and see what Primus offered. Timau was more than two days' journey on foot. Manfred suggested that we set off at 3 in the morning using the car which should find the roads clear at that hour. The route was then considered, Manfred suggesting the most direct route via the Ampezzo valley immediately to the north through Enemonzo to Comeglians and then west to Paluzza.

'This drop calls for a small celebration, Pat. I'll send Orellio to the Inn at Tramonte di Sotto just before midnight. We'll have the best meal that they can provide and plenty of wine,' said Manfred. In view of our early start the following morning, we settled down to some rest. The local Partisans gathered round a small fire and sang folk songs, one little man playing a concertina. The favourite song was 'Stella Alpini', the refrain was popularly used as a form of recognition at night.[2] The intruder giving an answering whistle, taking up the refrain where the challenging guard left off. The atmosphere was completely changed, petty bickering and short tempers absorbed in happy contemplation of the impending thrill of yet another long-awaited drop, the pill of resistance.

The hours of waiting pass slowly, temptingly suggesting a check and re-check of one's watch. Pat had a solution to this; taking a piece of paper he would write small compositions in a neat hand, making a careful study of each sentence. Having satisfied his powers of description he would destroy the paper which had helped him review the past or perhaps refresh his memory on some obscure incident of ancient history. I heard someone enter the room which was in darkness. Then Manfred's voice broke the silence, 'Pat, Pat, come along wake up! It's time we made a move! Are you awake Charles? Come along, get dressed.'

My watch read 35 minutes after midnight. Manfred had left his torch in order for Pat and me to get dressed, we were then to meet him on the road in front of the house. The cold air of morning penetrated the warmth of the room through the door that Manfred had purposely left ajar. Tucking my trouser bottoms inside my socks I was then ready, all but one thing. Searching near my pillow (an old duffel-coat) I picked up my revolver secured inside a holster attached to a belt which I fastened round my waist. A defensive ornament affording some moral backing. We joined Manfred.

He offered his flask which contained whisky before we set off. The DZ was 10-minute walk from Rutizza. Preceded by some twenty Partisans, we made our way there. Billowing shrouds of high cloud passed the partially formed moon providing an intermittent veil, and a forecast of wet weather. The breadth of the valley would allow the plane to pass low over the DZ, the present breeze would not appreciably affect the descent of the visitors or carry away stores, scattering them over a wide area. We should be able to clear the DZ inside 10 or 15 minutes. At the DZ Manfred indicated where the centre light should be placed, leaving Verdi to arrange the other two, making one line of three lights. The boxes containing a single car headlight were laid on the ground, one man paying out a thin cable connecting the three boxes up in a series to a large Fiat battery with switch attached. When these arrangements were made, we lay among the sugar beet, waiting for the arrival of the plane. No one was allowed to smoke. Verdi moved between detached elements arranged as an all-round protection party.

A quarter to 2, the scheduled time passed by – 5 minutes, 10 minutes. Then, the murmur of dissenting voices carried from a distant outpost. In the distance, intermittent at first, we heard the warning drone of an approaching aircraft. 'Lights!' cried Manfred. Three pencil beams shot heavenwards brilliantly indicating the DZ, which must have been visible 10 miles away. The plane closed in over the valley, losing height as it cut one engine. As it passed on into the distance, we counted the floating cargo it had left in the wake of its slipstream. One, two, three, each of us on the ground counted the billowing dirty white inverted saucers gently lowering their packages or bodies. The plane had gone for good it must have released the whole cargo in one run over the target. The first man was down. 'Lights off, Verdi, we shall not need them anymore by the look of things,' cried Manfred.

A tall figure loomed up, closely followed by another equally tall. The first one said, 'Where is George?[3] He was the first out of the plane.' Manfred replied, 'Haven't seen him yet, is that you Bill?'[4]

The man replied it was indeed himself. The stores were quickly gathered in and despatched on their way to Rutizza. Eventually George put in an appearance, he had landed near one of the outposts, who had returned with him to the centre of the DZ, where we waited for him. George assured himself that all had arrived safe and sound and then we made our way to the inn at Tramonte di Sotto, everybody talking ten to the dozen, completing introductions as we moved towards the village.[5] This really had been fun, equally enjoyed by the new boys. In the light of the taproom, the names mentioned in the course of introduction while we had made our way into the inn became less formal. The thrill of a safe descent into enemy territory was developing for them, their expectations were being fulfilled, the spirit of the reception was a memory that they would carry with them into the future and, for a few of them, the beginning of a long-awaited revenge. Cigarettes were produced, soon the air was filled with rising smoke and newsy conversation. The Royal party included George the commander, Bill, Georgiou and Arthur their radio operator.[6] The remaining three constituted a separate operation. George, having seated himself, explained the purpose of their visit. As soon as it was possible, he said, they would move to the Silian area on the Austrian frontier to the north of the Cadore Province, more than 50 miles to the north-west as the crow flies. Once there, the reason for their visit should not take long to accomplish. He confined their instruction to that.

I sat with Arthur, from whom I learned more about the intentions of Operation Royal. He explained that George had been acutely aware of the time factor. He had remonstrated with the staff at Base stipulating the urgency of their departure, in view of the fact that with the arrival of October and the first snowfalls, the way over the frontier would become increasingly difficult, and eventually impassable except by the main highways which, of course, were not to be considered. Manfred had been more than eight weeks in the field without finding a route over the frontier; it was now the end of August, they would prefer to set off, although the route over the frontier remained a problem, they could at least become acclimatised during September and be at hand when Manfred's party had established a safe route. It was conceivable that they could outwit the frontier guards, but combatting the elements presented a problem which only he, an expert skier, and possibly Georgiou were prepared to consider, but since Bill and Arthur would be largely responsible for the execution of Operation Royal, they must cross before the snow fell.

Arthur carefully bypassed the military intention of their operation, a matter which I did not enquire further into. Putting two and two together I thought that their object would be in pattern, much like our own, apart from our desire to find a way for Operation Royal into Austria.[7] Another point occurred to me. Once that they were established over the frontier, their work would not be complicated by a divergence of political opinion, an obvious drawback to more rapid and cohesive action in this locality.

The best meal that the inn could serve was a warning of austerity, but our new colleagues attacked it with relish. Fortunately, there was no shortage of vino rosso, a liberal number of bottles of which were placed on the table. Casually I asked Arthur if they had brought a radio for me. He confirmed that they had not, but thought that one had been despatched with the previous plane. I said that we had not received it. Arthur had surmised correctly, for several days later the radio was found discarded in a cabbage patch extremely near to the Clausetto DZ.

Verdi approached Manfred reminding him of the time and quietly mentioning that the inn keeper was a little concerned, it was 4am and it had been a long day and although he desired to be of service, he wished to retire. Leaving the inn, we returned to Rutizza making our way by the road passing through Tramonte di Mezzo where the guard now maintained a post and, taking no chances, sharply called for the password, on receipt of which we were allowed to pass. Arriving at the house I noticed the car and driver awaiting to take Pat and I to the Carnia. We were late.

'You will have heard that there was no radio for us, Sir,' I said to Pat. 'Yes, I learned that from George, but we shall take the car, nevertheless. If you'll collect the rucksacks and put them in the car, I'll have a word with Manfred, do you mind?' replied Pat.

By 4.30am we were off!

Chapter Seven

Cleulis and Treppo Carnico

'Have you got everything Charles?' said Pat. I replied that I had and that I had put his rucksack in the back of the vehicle.

We set off with the grey light of dawn creeping over the mountain tops and down into the valleys, the scene brightened with the rising sun which brushed away the mist, revealing in its place dew-freshened pastures and hedge-growth, a passing film of a late summer morning. Soon we reached the Ampezzo valley and the town of Enemonzo where the assortment of chimneys guided an equally varied selection of tinted smoke, evidence of recently lit fires and the preparation of coffee. As we entered the town the engine died out, the car taxiing silently to a halt in the main street, just outside a cafe, where the proprietor was in the process of unlocking the door. The driver got out and lifted the bonnet cover and having ascertained the root of the trouble, said that we should have to obtain the services of another vehicle for the fault would take a long time to repair and a spare part would be required which would probably have to come from Tolmezzo.

Giacomo, who had joined us for the period of the journey, jumped out of the car saying as he went that he would see what the chances were of obtaining another vehicle. He disappeared around a street corner.

I found that we could get a coffee in the cafe, and while we were drinking the jovial cafe proprietor passed the time of day, casually mentioning that Enemonzo wasn't healthy at this time of the morning, for a German Infantry Company accompanied by armoured cars was due to pass through the town in the course of a daily security march along the valley. A company passed between Tolmezzo and Ampezzo each day. The local Partisans had mined the road today so the visit should prove interesting. Fortunately, Giacomo returned saying that the replacement vehicle would arrive later, so we waited patiently, but the wait was hardly comforting. Eventually, it arrived. The new driver had been a chauffeur to Marshal Bagdoglio, and we were extremely glad to see him. He certainly made up for lost time once we were underway, driving extremely fast with more imagination than skill.

We made a second halt outside Paluzza, a town on the main highway north and into Austria. On this road a Wermacht infantry company passed each day, a warning to Partisans that there were still troops available other than those at the front to be used more effectively if the occasion demanded it. An old peasant walked by, we asked him if the way was clear. He affirmed that it was, so we proceeded to Timau, a miserable sprawling village of grey stone buildings, just off the main highway reaching up the lower slopes of a mountain that overlooked the Austrian frontier. We halted outside the village according to Pat's instruction. Getting out, he told the driver to turn the car around so that it faced south. 'You remain here Charles with the driver. I'll go into the village and find Primus. I'll stay long enough to make another appointment with him and discuss where we can spend the night, then I'll return.'

Pat walked off with Giacomo, I followed their movements until they had disappeared among the buildings of the village, I offered the driver a cigarette which I'm sorry to say he took, for my reserves were running low. Two young people driving cattle ahead of them along the road passed by the car, taking stock of us as they passed and whispering to each other. What happened if an armoured car and jack-booted infantry came along too? I hoped that Pat would not be long. The countryside either side of the road was as bare as the village and the road ran too straight. I looked at my watch – 5.45pm, it was past bedtime and I felt like sleep, but so did the driver so I kept awake.

'Ecco, gli'altri vengono!' exclaimed the driver.[1] He spoke so suddenly that I pivoted not knowing what to expect. Pat and Giacomo were on their way back, walking quickly towards the car. The driver leaned over the front seat and opened the rear door. 'He wasn't there and won't be back until late tonight,' said Pat, referring to the movements of Primus. 'Giacomo knows the people in a trattoria, 2km down the road in the village of Cleulis. We'll stay there for the time being.' Giacomo ordered the driver to move to Cleulis.

Turning off the main road, we made towards the village, which was several hundred feet above the road, a small community of not more than twenty houses but probably sheltering many more than that number of families. The vehicle pulled up outside what appeared to be the general store. Getting out, we passed through the door of the store ringing a bell which warned the keeper. He answered, a little man dressed in dark, coarse trousers and waistcoat, a dirty white shirt minus collar, open at the neck. Standing behind the counter, he looked ill at ease, curious, even frightened, Giacomo set his mind at rest for a moment when he had introduced Pat. He agreed to give us a room suggesting that for his good and ours that we remain under cover during the hours of daylight. This was our intention. When Giacomo and the driver left, the keeper led the way to a room on the first floor which contained a bed with a mattress and two chairs. His wife joined him in the passage clutching a baby to her breast, both equally scared. He apologised for there being no blankets on the bed but these days there were many shortages.

Pat looked out of the window, muttering more to himself that it bore little resemblance to the Grosvenor but had to do.

I asked Pat, 'When do you propose to meet Primus then, Sir?' He said that he would allow Primus to get some sleep first after his expected late return and Pat would leave at first light around 4 o'clock for Timau.

I asked, 'Shall we have to remain under cover?' Pat responded, 'Yes, it's too close to the frontier and it will be under observation; we can't afford to take any chances. I suggest we rest all afternoon and have a scout round after sundown. In the event of trouble, we must move further up the mountainside, the route is covered and the safest.' I said, 'The storekeeper was very scared, Sir.'

'Most of the people are. The Garibaldi crossed over the frontier in some strength a few days ago and rustled nearly a hundred head of cattle from Austrian farms. A very well-executed raid, they had re-crossed the frontier and scattered the cattle among the peasants this side within 24 hours. The villagers expect the SS will make a thorough search of the neighbourhood. From our point of view nothing could be worse than to stir up trouble along the frontier at this time. It will be difficult enough to cross without putting the Gendarmerie on their guard.'

'How long do you propose to remain in Cleulis?' I said. 'A lot depends on Primus, we've got to eat and I don't think for one moment that the keeper will be able to provide us with food. But in addition to that, the village is too close to the frontier, we shall have to find a place about 10km south of here.'

Both my mind and my stomach agreed with Pat. I hoped the move would come soon. I looked through the window at the rear of the house and saw a watermill and behind that, in the distance, the main road sweeping like a question mark around the town of Timau, disappearing behind a mountain bend. 'It looks as if they have a flour-mill here, I wonder if it's producing anything?'

Pat responded, 'It will be used for a similar purpose. They grind the seed which finally looks like flour. In actual fact, it is the substance you thought so tasteless on Monte Rossa, polenta.'

The trattoria keeper brought some soup in the evening. Pat asked if he would call him at 3.30am. Reluctantly, the man said he would, he had a permanent air of dejection. His wife was having trouble too, the baby screamed, painfully aware that it was bedtime. I thought to myself, 'Bloody nuisance, this baby!' But I smiled at Pat who tried unconcernedly to interest himself with his writing, eventually the baby's sobbing subsided, peace reigning once more.

I heard Pat get up and leave the building, following his receding footsteps as he made his way through the darkened street. He probably arrived at Timau before I had settled down to sleep again, it would be about a quarter of an hour's walk to Timau. I got up at 5.30am to have a look around the area. There was not much to look at. I had left the village after 3 minutes' walking. Standing beside an old barn, I looked at the western approach to the village, a bare patch of meadow stretching a hundred yards and you would be lost in the trees. The musty old room had left a bad taste in my mouth, so I stopped by the communal well and drew myself a mouthful of water. It was cold and refreshing. I got back to the trattoria just before Pat.

Primus had told Pat he agreed that to stay in Cleulis was unsatisfactory and arrangements would be made for Pat and myself to be accommodated at Treppo Carnico, a village 10 or 12 kilometres south and due west of Cleulis. There was a post of armed Partisans in Treppo Carnico where some protection can be given.

'What was Primus like?' I enquired.

'Reasonably well informed. A man about 45 years of age, average height, wiry. He is one of the senior members of the Garibaldi movement in this part of the Carnia. A commissar. He supplies the active members of the movement with funds and food. If there are any local problems, he will try and supply the answer.'

I said, 'I suppose he was surprised to see you?' 'No,' Pat replied, 'I imagine that he is used to early morning calls. I kicked at the door of his hotel and within 2 minutes he had let me in. He poured me out a glass of grappa and excused himself while he dressed. Apparently, the frontier guards pay frequent visits to the town of Timau but haven't yet been here. He was rather proud of the cattle-rustling operation but wonders what repercussions there will be. After mentioning this incident, he suggested that we could be well advised to fall back on Treppo Carnico. We should at least get adequate warning if the SS were on the warpath.'

We decided that was a fair comment and we decided to move that afternoon. 'We are to meet Primus on the other side of the main road opposite

Cleulis. He will put us on our way. He has arranged for a guide to meet us on the track and introduce us to Giovannino, the local Garibaldi commander at Treppo Carnico who has made quite a name for himself of late. His speciality is shooting the sentries at the roadblocks surrounding Tolmezzo.'

We were to meet Primus at 3 so at 2.50pm we set off. Primus had sent some food to the inn keeper for our lunch. We wasted no time reaching the main road. On the opposite bank a man dressed in a grey plus-four suit waved, beckoning us to join him. Pat said the man was Primus and we climbed the bank to where he was waiting.

'Come stai, il signor Capitano?'[2] said Primus, to whom Pat introduced me. We shook hands; I thought for one moment that Primus was flattering me, for as we pumped each other's hands, he said, 'E tanta bello cosa.'[3] I replied sharply, 'Bon giorno.' We climbed up the bank until we were astride a mule-track which for some 300yd ran parallel with the road below.

Primus spoke with a pronounced Carnese accent. He conversed with Pat as we walked, 'L'appuntamento l'ho fatop. Uno lei inconttaremo sulla mullatierra giu.'[4]

We moved from the close proximity of the road, the track running in a south-westerly direction passing along the edge of a small escarpment and, later, over wooded slopes. When we had covered half a mile, Primus left us, returning to Timau. Not long afterwards we met the guide as promised. He carried a short Italian carbine and wore a vivid, red-coloured scarf which was draped around his neck. Walking towards us he shouted, 'Arrivederci, Vittorio', a greeting and introduction all in one breath. We returned his greeting, Pat, in a more formal manner but nonetheless pleasantly, gave him our rank and Christian names. He was a talkative fellow, immediately engaging Pat in conversation asking many questions which Pat good humouredly parried, not in the least damping the Partisan's spirit. He was no ordinary guide; our young acquaintance whom we had yet to meet at Treppo Carnico had seen to that. Giovannino apparently wished to know what sort of characters he was due to welcome and had trusted Vittorio with the task of finding out.

Vittorio looked healthy enough; if the remainder of the Garibaldini looked like him, they were well rationed. We made a halfway halt at a malga where several Partisans were cleaning their weapons, while a young woman brushed down a table on which they had recently been served a meal. She was dark, bright-eyed, with a compact figure. It may have been my imagination, but I thought she looked up with more than usual interest when we arrived. I am no judge, but I thought too that she spoke with a cultivated accent. The remainder gave way to her when she chose to speak. She addressed herself to Pat in English. 'Good day Captain, welcome to the Carnia.' 'Good morning,' replied Pat.

Pointing to two chairs she continued, 'Prendate. [Take the chairs.] What news, when are the British Army going to liberate us?' I sensed that her words were tinged with sarcasm. 'We hope that it will be very soon. I'm sure that they are fighting hard to achieve that object,' Pat answered.

'Osterica [Austria], we've waited a long time!' she paused, carefully choosing her line of approach. 'The Red Army has marched a long way from Stalingrad, why are the British and Americans making such slow progress? Is it because they are frightened of Russia and want the Germans and Russians to weaken themselves while they remain strong?'

This was a blunt statement, carefully calculated to hurt or extract a hasty reply. Pat evidently thought it was a fair question and gave her a satisfactory answer.

'The Germans have lost a large number of men during the past few months. They are finding it increasingly difficult to fight on an extended front. On the other hand, I think that the Red Army have made wonderful progress. I also think it was essential that the Germany Army shortened its lines of communication. In the East they could afford to give ground under pressure, whereas in the West, we are already at the German frontier. The British and Americans have commitments in the Far East in addition to Europe. Japan and Germany have similar motives. I honestly believe that the Allies are working as a team, all pulling their weight.'

'Maybe you are right, Captain,' the young woman was not impressed. 'Here, some wine, we'll drink together for liberty,' she said offering two cups of red wine.

'Sono pronto, Capitano, andiamo adesso?' Pat answered for both of us saying that we were ready to continue. Having said goodbye to Maria and the other Partisans, we set off walking at a steady pace without exerting ourselves for it was warm in the sunshine and there remained but an hour's journey ahead of us. The mule-track wound its way around the mountainside at a height of 1,000ft and from this height we looked down on to Treppo Carnico, a straggling village with two clusters of houses connected by a narrow street. The eastern portion was grouped around the church and main piazzas, the church in the centre, its steeple tarnished green through years of rain and snow. It automatically attracted one's eye for it was Eastern rather than European, though it was not out of place among the remainder of the gaily coloured houses which gave the place an air of prosperity and charm.

The western end of the village centred around a smaller square, the most prominent building being the Albergo di Cicilias. Leaving the mule-track, we followed a trail steeply down towards the back gardens of the houses situated on the northern fringe of Treppo Carnico, finally entering the narrow street along which we proceeded to the di Cicilias.

Vittorio asked to wait while he went in search of his commander, Giovannino. He left and entered a walled building on the extreme west of the square. We didn't wait long, Vittorio returning in the company of his youthful commander, a chubby, rosy cheeked, broad-shouldered person of not more than 22 years, dressed in short trousers, dyed battledress jacket and brown Africa Korps cap with a red scarf draped around his neck and shoulders. On the cap he had stitched a red star. He carried a carbine of Italian origin and from his belt hung two Mills grenades and a Belgian grenade. He was attended by three or four other Partisans. 'Salute,' he said smiling while his eyes covered us from head to feet. He invited Pat and myself to join him. They were about to eat. Pat thanked him for his cordial invitation and accepted gladly. We all returned to the walled building which might have been a small monastery at one time and entered a large refectory where a long table had been set for the meal. Two daughters from the nearby albergo had cooked the food and as the Partisans took their place at table, they put a plate of minestrone in front of them which they drank amid the uproar of voices, engaged in multiple conversations.

Before asking Pat our business he gave account of his recent activities, stressing their readiness to take the field against the Boche, adding tactfully that they were handicapped by a shortage of arms and ammunition. Pat took his cue, saying that he might be able to arrange for a supply of arms in the near future when we received the means of communicating with Base. Giovannino was elated and in return promised that we should receive adequate protection while we remained within the bounds of his com-mand. Pat asked where we could be accommodated. Giovannino's second-in-command who had until now listened carefully to the conversation, spoke up suggesting that we try the trattoria situated in the narrow street through which we had passed. Having ascertained this information, we excused ourselves and made our way to the trattoria. It was small but offered accommodation. The proprietor was sitting listening to the radio, a news broadcast from London, he was a tall, upright old man of 65 years, who had one time served in the Savoy Grenadiers. He still retained his curling military moustache, now grey with age. He was dressed neatly in a suit of worsted material, trousers cut short at the knee, plus-four style, with a belted jacket and stockings. He remained seated listening attentively until the news bulletin finished. He then became aware that we required more than the minute summary of events and soon showed us the way to a room on the first floor, overlooking the street, as we climbed the stairs shouting to his wife to bring clean linen for the beds. He left us within the quiet of the room.

When he had washed, Pat said he was going up to the Albergo di Cicilias to have another word with Giovannino. I told him that I was going to have a walk around the village for an hour or so. I had soon walked round the eastern limits of the village, so I continued down the road towards Paluzza. The sun was setting as I made my way back. A young girl cycled up behind me dismounting by my side. She greeted me in Italian and asked if I was English, she was an inquisitive little thing. She asked what I was doing in the Carnia, was I an escaped prisoner of war and was that why my clothes were so dirty? Was I staying in Treppo Carnico the night and was I hungry? I told her that I wasn't a prisoner of war. I wasn't doing anything in the Carnia except seeing the sights and I was going to remain in Treppo Carnico for a short while until I felt it was time to move on. To which she replied that she was one of the three daughters living in the Albergo di Cicilias and if we wanted our clothes cleaning, she would only be too pleased to be of service. As we entered the village, she mounted her cycle and peddled away ahead of me up the street. I joined Pat at the albergo.

He was sitting in a small parlour with two civilians who were visiting the village for the evening. They were man and wife. He was a vet from Arto, a village 16km to the south towards Tolmezzo. They were an attractive couple with engaging conversation. I noticed that he was referred to as 'Doctor' and in fact he dealt with the ailments of all the villagers from Timau to Arto, a widespread practice for a man whose sole means of transport 90 per cent of the time was a bicycle. We all left the albergo together, Pat arranging to meet them again and the Doctor and his wife cycled home.

It was a humid night, so I threw the blankets back over the end of the bed, only using the sheet to cover me. Reflecting on the day's events, I fell asleep. I had a vivid dream in which we were both cut off in a village surrounded by the SS. I could even hear the shots as they closed in on the village covering every exit. With that I woke up to find that indeed the sky was red with the blaze of some nearby fire. Voices and shots filled the air.

Pat raced to the window as some women passed underneath and inquired what was afoot. He learned that an old man had dropped a cigarette in a barn below his house in which was stored the Partisans' supply of ammunition. Everyone was busily running between the well and the blazing house carrying water to drench the flames. The building and most of the ammunition were saved. In half an hour, the village was restored to quiet and sleep.

Chapter Eight

A Radio and a Route Discovered

We were forced to remain in bed an extra 2 hours next morning. The youngest Cicilias daughter, true to her word, paid us a visit, bringing with her two bowls of hot milk and a request that we should give her our clothes which she took away to wash and press. She returned them having repaired all tears and hoped that we would ask her again should we need our clothing laundered.

Pat set off for Timau in the hope that he would meet Remus. He thought he would be away for two days and if he met Remus, he would have a shot at crossing the frontier. He told me that if Manfred paid a visit, I should tell him that Pat would report to him directly upon his return. I should make note of any time and place of rendezvous.

I said that if Manfred should bring a radio, had Pat any traffic for Base, he may like them to know what was happening here. Pat then wrote a short message on a pad and handed it to me. I read it back to him, 'For Darling; from Pat: Staying Treppo Carnico. Hope to find safe route over frontier 4 repeat 4 Sep. Propose cross near Timau with the help of one named Remus repeat Remus. Full report on return. Ends.' Pat told me to send it at the first opportunity, if Manfred did not bring a radio, I was to give the message to him for onward transmission.

Pat had borrowed a bicycle for the trip to Timau. It was amusing to see him set off, nodding 'Good morning' to the passing villagers. As soon as he had left, I commenced putting the message into cipher and later, once more, I set off for Paluzza to pay the barber a visit. Pat had had his beard trimmed and mine was now worthy of a visit to the barber as well. Paluzza was larger than Treppo Carnico and the main road from Timau to Tolmezzo passed through it. The SS had at one time quartered a company of infantry in the now empty barracks, which the Partisans had stripped of all internal fittings. Manfred arrived by car at 2pm. 'Pat has gone off in search of Remus and hopes to find a way over the frontier tomorrow,' I said.

I told him that Pat would report his findings on his return and if Manfred would suggest a rendezvous, Pat would join him there in two days. Manfred continued that he had some news for Pat. The Royal party had found a secure house only 4km from the frontier in the western Carnia in a village called Forni Avoltri. Manfred said he had arranged one or two parties in the Friuli which would keep him occupied, he expected a couple or more drops and then he felt the Osoppo would be ready to tackle some targets that Manfred had in mind. 'The best thing then is for Pat to join George and Bill and hand over whatever information he has direct to them. They are rather anxious to make a move and if his information is satisfactory there is no time like the present. You will find them in a hotel called the "Sotto Corona".'

I said that I would inform Pat as soon as he returned. Manfred then gave me some good news; they had found a radio. It was in a cabbage patch near the Clausetto DZ. Someone thought he had got away with something and finding that it was my radio discarded it. Fortunately, it was in working order, Peppino had tested it.

We then spoke about messaging Base to tell the Royal party when Manfred could be expected to arrive in Forni Avoltri, he declined to stop for a meal, he had to see some of the local commanders in Rutizza later, and he left saying that he hoped to see me in Forni Avoltri.

It was news time again, the old man tuning in the radio to which several of the locals had come to listen. After the bulletin the announcer stated that there were several special messages. I listened to him slowly reading odd sentences – 'Francesco e giovane' – 'Adesso Andiamo a mangiare' – 'Ho ricevuto una letter che aspettavo.' The announcer read perhaps thirty of these sentences which fascinated the locals, who would wonder what the meaning of the transmission could be. Perhaps one of the sentences was meant for Manfred! He was expecting another drop.

5 September

I was in bed when Pat returned. He brought with him a young man called 'Henry'. Pat then described his mission. He had met Remus at Timau. Initially he was not keen to make a journey over the frontier. He had run into a spot of bother on the last occasion, but anyway, he decided to accompany Manfred and set off directly when it was dark. It had been a difficult climb, but good time was made. Once in Austria the going became dangerous. They had passed within a mile of the frontier post when they had seen the light in the check post. Remus had mentioned that he had a young friend in a village close by. Henry [real name Rudolf Moser] had been an NCO in the Wehmacht but had lost a finger in action and had been released from the service. He had served on the Finnish Front, most of the Austrians were sent either to Finland or to the Russian

Front with a purpose. He had recently received call-up papers, an indication that the Boche were finding it difficult to find reserves. Henry had had enough of the German Army and had fled his village, hiding out in one closer to the Italian frontier. He wanted to move into Italy and join the Partisan movement. It was obvious that Henry could be of a great help and in particular to the Royal party. Pat remained outside the village while Remus went in search of Henry. They hid in a small wood all day waiting for the cover of darkness before they returned to Italy. In 24 hours, they had been over the frontier and returned with an addition to the strength.

Pat asked if I had heard from Manfred. I told him that he had been and gone and had brought a radio with him. I said that I had transmitted his message to Base and that the set was not a good one, I thought the night in the cabbage patch had probably not done it much good.

I told Pat of Manfred's intentions and his instruction that we should move to Forni Avoltri and meet with George and Bill.

With much enthusiasm Pat exclaimed 'I see! That settles it. Remus said he knew of a much quicker route over the frontier behind Sappada and looking at the map I should say that it wasn't more than 5km due west of Forni Avoltri.' He continued that he would snatch a couple of hours sleep and then set of for Timau, pick up Remus then take the mountain route direct west for Forni Alvoltri.

Pat instructed that I should remain with Henry, get a good night's rest, and then join the others at the Sotto Corona, it was a distance of 35km, which could be covered in a day. Pat would not arrive until the following day so I could give George advanced warning of his arrival.

He then gave me a message for Base saying that he had made a crossing safely but not satisfied it would suit the purpose. He had another route in mind and was arranging contact with Royal.

Pat and Henry laid on the beds. By the time I had put the messages into cipher they were both breathing regularly, fast within the realms of sleep. Looking out of the rear window I noticed some apple trees. I saw that some fruit had fallen on the ground. What the eye does not see the heart doesn't grieve over. I ran down and gathered a few. It was almost 1.30am when I woke them, they had slept deeply, the sleep of the exhausted. Within a few minutes, they had washed and hurried along to the hotel for some food before setting off for Timau.

6 September

The old man of the trattoria was very thoughtful. Knocking gently, he pushed the door ajar, 'Bon giorno, siete fame, ho portato mangiare?'[1]

He entered the room carrying a small tray on which there was bread and two eggs in addition to a bottle of wine. The radio transmission had been difficult, atmospheric conditions unusually bad, so I had only transmitted one message. Both messages were of equal importance, but I felt that the information concerning the frontier was the more important as far as Base were concerned. The second signal would have to be sent via the Royal wireless link.

By midday we reached Raviscletto, a village halfway between Paluzza and Comeglians, a long wearying climb all the way for best part of 12km. The road and sloping pastures either side of it were deserted except for one person who was going the opposite way. It was Primus coasting on a bicycle; he would have stopped but I think that the machine was without brakes, so he waved his recognition as he flew past. Henry was equal to the climb, but my legs were feeling the strain. I suggested a rest, we had made fairly good time, it wasn't yet noon. As Henry did not understand English or Italian and my knowledge of German was nil, we had left Raviscletto behind us before we established an understanding, by which time we had reached the crest and were proceeding downhill. I felt better then and agreed with Henry that it was better if we kept plodding along, recommending that Comeglians should be a well-earned halt.

Comeglians was at the bottom end of a downhill stretch of 6km. The thin shoulder straps of the rucksack were cutting the muscle part of the shoulders, changing what was once a pleasant walk into an endurance test. Henry was smiling cheerfully enjoying every minute of the march, walking with a springy gait, and reminding me of perpetual action in the flesh. Comeglians remained hidden from our sight until we had caught up with the last of the 6km, which added to my incentive for I wished very much to see the town. In true competitive spirit we stepped up the pace having entered the last straight of the final kilometre. My feet were burning.

Seeing the first cafe, I was not to be trifled with; I thought to myself 'this is it', thinking more of a sit down rather than food. Masking my face with a beaming smile, I tapped Henry on the arm and pointed to the brown bread in the cafe window, suggesting that we have something to eat.

Using my best colloquial Italian, I asked the proprietor for bread and cheese, we sat facing the window watching the street and passers-by. Hungry though I was, I found it difficult to eat for the bread was as dry as my throat was parched. I called for water which the waiter placed before us on the table. Henry pushed back his sleeve showing a bare wrist; I uncovered mine letting him see the time. He nodded motioning that he was ready to continue. Walking to the centre of the town, we turned right at the road junction, heading in a northerly direction and once more uphill. The mountains looked less and less attractive and the kilometres seemed more and more like miles. The first kilometre stone indicated that we had 15 more to go and one more village to go through before we reached Forni Avoltri. We carried on in silence for though I would have liked to have broken the monotony with a little conversation, trying to find a sign that would fit a word was tiresome. We were walking much slower and it was after 6pm when we reached Rigolatto.

In the main street we saw several Garibaldini. They eyed us with suspicion but chose not to hinder our progress. I was thankful we were not questioned because military minded civilians can be very depressing, especially if they are peasantry. It becomes not a business to ask questions in the interest of security but a malignant pleasure. I think I would have been impolite if we had been waylaid for the thoughts of a warm bath and a bed with clean sheets took the weight of my feet, whereas questions put to me at this moment would have been mere verbal barriers, crushing this wonderful picture of incentive which I should be forced to brush angrily aside.

However, they did not annoy us. The last few kilometres produced no spurt or enthusiasm to increase the pace, rather we could be likened to a couple of wise, old tortoises, realising that what was ahead would be there in another hour, and so it was.

We entered the village of Forni Avoltri and asked the way to the Hotel Sotto Corona. As we neared the hotel, an elderly woman walked towards us as though she had recognised old friends said, 'Good evening, if you hurry, you will find the water still warm and you can take a nice bath! I'm the Countess *Sausage*, how do you do?'[2]

She had spoken the very words I wished to hear and without realising my mistake, replied rather more warmly than I would have in my more alert moments. 'You must be our guardian angel! How do you do? My name is Charles and this is my friend Henry.'

She told us that the others were waiting for us in the hotel. It was strange that the others should have been expecting us. I thought the Countess must have been making conversation. We were rather dirty and perhaps she felt sorry for us, it never occurred to me that someone had passed us on the way.

Entering the hotel, I saw Arthur sitting with the Silian 'Op' boys. I asked Arthur how he was and he invited me to sit down and asked me if I wanted some wine, topped up with a bit of grappa. He asked who Henry was and I briefly told him the story.

Arthur told me to put my kit in a room, and he would show me the way. The group had more or less taken the place over for the time being. There was an empty room next to Arthur's which I took and Henry got one at the end of the corridor. It transpired that George and Bill were out on a recce but would be back for dinner. Arthur said the proprietor was an American woman who married an Italian about eighteen years ago and she looked after the group very well. 'There is an English lady here as well, she is a paying guest, she's a bit of an old so and so and she has a "Pash" on George.[3] He won't wear her at any price and is quite rude at dinner sometimes, but she natters happily away about the good old days, while we all in turn fade away.' I thought if she was the lady who had met us in the street, she seemed quite pleasant. We had a bath before we went to the parlour, during this time I reflected upon the village. Forni Avoltri was built either side of a 'V'-shaped bend in the main road which led to Sappada. The apex of the bend curved over a bridged tributary of the River Piave at the mouth of a re-entrant leading from the Pierebeck Pass.[4] Three mountains rising to a height of 6,000ft with formidable granite peaks dwarfed the village emphasising its toy-like appearance. Not far distant to the north was the source of the Piave. A tiny trickle of water growing rapidly as it ran down the valleys, fed by its tributaries until reaching the plains, 30 miles to the south it became a river of importance.

Feeling very much refreshed, I made my way to the parlour. In one corner was the bar behind which were a limited number of bottles containing highly coloured drinks. A large portion of the floor was covered with a cement stone, about a foot in height on which burned a charcoal fire, the fumes being collected by a curtained vent hanging from the ceiling. Together with some of the locals, my colleagues sat with their feet resting on the stone. It was time that George and Bill should have returned, they had gone up to the Pierebeck Pass which looked down into Austria. They had felt that they would have been able to judge the time of a frontier crossing better on the ground rather than relying on the map. 'They won't need to bother so much now,' I ventured. 'Pat has found a couple of guides. Henry knows at least one way over and the other man knows of a route up behind Sappada, his name is Remus. Pat and he will be arriving some time tomorrow.'

Two tall figures dressed very much like tourists on a mountain holiday entered the parlour, looking very wet and tired. Bill dressed in army breeches and windjammer waterproof jacket, George similarly clad with his legs covered in short plus-four trousers made from army breeches, in addition to a US Army windjammer jacket and ski cap. Despite their obvious fatigue they were cheerful, their conversation woven with successful threads. George addressed the party first. 'Don't wait for us. Go ahead and have your meal, we'll join you when we are ready. Hallo! We've a guest, what news from the east?'

I started to tell him, but he said he would change first and listen to me later. He felt it was a reasonable excuse to evade after dinner conversation with the Countess and her inevitable reminiscences, but on the other hand, he was wet and in need of dry clothing.

Maria treated us very well as though we were all part of one happy family. She cooked each meal and helped serve at the table. She was quiet and rarely entered into conversation unless she were addressed directly. Her son was an officer in the Italian Army and had been taken prisoner early in the war during the Western Desert Campaign. She had a photograph taken when he had first joined the service. He was a handsome young man resembling his father. She liked to talk about him, wondering what his life in the POW camp was like. He had been sent to a camp in India. She had imagined that Indian soldiers were very wild, but we were able to reassure her on that score and confirm what he had written about his good treatment. Today was a feast day, so Maria had made a large chocolate cake with a cream centre, but it was the Countess who cut the cake, reserving the largest piece for George!

The Countess was in good form at dinner, at times she was very amusing and could tell a good tale. Seeing Arthur leave the table, she called to him, 'Don't forget to send my message Arthur. I would so much like to know how my husband [the harbour Master in Naples] is faring.' The Countess continued, calling to mind the good old days in '22. 'We've always lived in Naples you know, in the Corso Santa Lucia, with a wonderful view of the Bay. I shall never forget my early afternoon teas. I used to entertain a lot in those days.' She recalled an invitation to visit a well-known Neapolitan family who had an old family house above Vomero. She and Alberto, her husband, were shown into the drawing room along with other guests, the maid brought in a silver tureen and a number of plates, the lady of the house nearly died; the maid ladled the tea leaves out of the tureen and put them on the plates! She had never before made tea.

George had more serious issues on his mind, he excused himself saying he had urgent matters to attend to, he left the table and made a hurried exit, not wishing to partake in such dallying conversation.

Bill also excused himself, saying he would bring up the material. The Countess was not to be put off by these departures. She still had the attentions of Peter, Clarke and Symon who were attentive listeners.[5]

She went on to say that she had spoken to members of the Garibaldi and she was convinced that they felt they would all become generals in new Italian Army after the war. They had dissuaded her from walking to Sappada, it was dangerous to go there. They were going to attack the German post in the town. It was tiring because they must have mounted a dozen attacks in the last six weeks, all of which had been cancelled. The German Garrison is of little consequence any way, she retorted, it is staffed entirely by Austrians and the youngest must be well over 50 years of age.

At this point, Arthur returned to the dining room, 'Charles, the Major wishes to see you, will you go up to his room. It's the second floor up. The last room on the left of the corridor. I'd better come up with you.'

I bade my farewell to the Countess Sausage and made my way upstairs.

As I entered the room, I nearly tripped over a flagon of Pesita. 'Good Lord! Mind the material!' said George steadying the flagon.

This room was the private lounge where business was discussed in complete privacy. George then asked what news there was about Pat and Manfred. I told him that Pat was due to arrive the following day and would be able to put George in the picture. I told him that on the night previously, Pat had crossed the frontier near Timau. The going had been tough and Pat had not been satisfied with the route. However, when he learned that George was here, he had decided to locate Remus, the man who showed him the way across, and bring him to him. Remus knew of another route which was quicker and easier. This route was behind Sappada. The little man I had brought with me was called Henry. Pat had brought him back from Austria. He had served in the Wehrmacht. I then told George that Manfred would be visiting soon. There was a discussion between Bill and George who deliberated whether to use Remus on the new route in the original plan, meaning to send Georgiou over, but give him Remus to guide. It would be better than sending Georgiou over blind and if he had luck and decided to stay in Austria, Remus could come back with a message. It would save a lot of time. Georgiou, a powerfully build man with a large moustache, clad in Tyrolean dress, had been very thoughtful during the discussion. Bill finalised. They would speak with Remus first, look at the route he proposed, ascertain what sort of person he was. If he fitted the bill, he could become a permanent courier.

We would wait to see what Pat reported the following day.

Chapter Nine

To Points North and West

'Lord, you like your bed don't you? How about shaking a leg? Your boss has arrived, he came along about 6am. The man he brought with him is a queer little runt isn't he?' said Arthur.

It was 7.30am and breakfast time, Arthur told me that the Silian boys were leaving the next day and I could move into his room when Clarke moved out. It would be ideal because we could keep all the radio equipment in one room, just using the one set.

I complained about there being only cold water to wash with, Arthur said they only heated the water in the evenings to conserve fuel. He continued that the hotel was being paid 30,000 lira a week for our accommodation and food. I said I felt this was a bit steep but Arthur remarked that there were eight of us to support, most of the food came from the plains. All being bought in Udine. It became a bit tricky after that because the old man who transported it had to be paid, and all his purchases came from black-market sources. This made it all a bit clearer to me and I washed in the cold water before going downstairs. George was deep in conversation as he had already made two visits to Pierebeck. He was describing the first recce that he had made with a section of the local Garibaldini. He was speaking to Pat for the others had held account previously. George said, 'These militant civilians haven't the faintest conception of fieldcraft. We had reached the peak and I was employing my limited knowledge making use of every conceivable bit of cover. I had crawled on my stomach for nearly 300yd and reached a spot of scrub. To my horror, I saw a Boche company of infantry digging positions about 400yd further down the slope and to my left. I froze where I was, my first thought was to get back over the frontier, I mean in broad daylight, what else was one to do? Naturally, I thought the section would be under cover. With this passing thought I looked towards the enemy and to my amazement, one rested on his shovel and was looking straight towards my position! Releasing one hand from his shovel, he waved and then putting his fingers to his mouth, whistled. Looking back towards the crest, lo and behold the whole bloody section was sky-lined, they hadn't seen the

Boche![1] The whole blasted lot were arguing the toss gesticulating with their hands and having a whale of a time. With my heart in my mouth I got up and raced hell for leather, I have never done a faster 300yd in m'life. I rushed towards the section and over the frontier before the Boche or the "Ities" knew what was happening. I heard a shot and pandemonium was let loose. The complete section was hard on my heels. It's a wonder they didn't release an avalanche of rocks on top of me. We were well the other side before we caught our breath. The damn lot had passed me, and it was some minutes before I caught them up. They were a bit sheepish and fortunately, my sense of humour came to my rescue or I should have completely buggered our relationship with our dear friends, the Garibaldi!'

George had served with a distinguished cavalry regiment on Crete which had been equipped with light tanks. Towards the end of the campaign they, who had been the hunters, became the hunted. German airborne reinforcements reached the three battle areas of Souda Bay, Retimo and Heraklion daily. The enemy having complete mastery of the air, British naval strength was at a low ebb. From the opening of the German invasion of the Island of Crete, the Royal Navy incurred serious losses supplying the soldier defenders. After a fortnight's bitter hand-to-hand fighting, though most positions remained intact, it was obvious that soon the German force would mount a large-scale attack which the ill-supplied garrisons were not equipped to withstand. The order to withdraw and fight another day was the only possible answer. The British Empire had fulfilled an honourable agreement with our gallant ally Greece at a time when we ourselves were in peril. George had his tank destroyed and fought on as an infantry man, eventually making the long march over the mountains to the point of evacuation and shipment to Egypt. He was therefore a most experienced soldier and his opinion was valuable.

After breakfast, I walked with Arthur to the rear of the Sotto Corona where there was a bowling alley. I was interested to hear more about his superiors. I asked him if George was in charge of his party. Arthur said that nominally he was, but Bill and he shared the decisions. Bill had an exceptionally good knowledge of Germany and the language and together they made for a very good team.

I asked Arthur if he knew what the Silian boys' plans were, and where they were headed for immediately. He said he thought they were going to a place called Aurunzo by the Lake which was nearer to their target area.

We then joined the conference that was to take place at 10 o'clock in the lounge, Georgiou, Pat, George and Bill were already seated. Bill opened up the conference.

'I've had a word with Pat's protégé, Remus. We are still agreed that he will be extremely helpful. The plan, as far as Operation Royal is affected, will be as follows. Georgiou with the assistance of Remus will make the initial crossing and try to establish safe houses, or rather a safe house. He will then send Remus back over the frontier to collect George and Arthur. I shall follow a day or so later. It is advisable to make the crossing collectively for obvious reasons. That's phase one. Now for phase two. I think it is generally realised that progress is bound to be slower in Austria. The chances are that we will not be able to establish a DZ over there for some time ahead. Pat will therefore maintain a firm Base here at Forni Avoltri and once we have organised a body of resistance, we shall obtain our supplies through Pat. This is not the most satisfactory solution, but until such time as we have secured a DZ, it is the only solution. Any questions so far?'

There were no questions, but George enlarged upon phase one. 'I would like to interrupt Bill and add one thing. Georgiou, having secured a safe house, will carry on with his infiltration, moving further north. Most of his time will be spent reconnoitring. He will then be able to put Bill and I fully in the picture by the time we arrive at the safe house.'

Bill continued, 'Pat will leave this afternoon for the Friuli to contact Manfred and put him in the picture. Manfred has control of a limited amount of transport which will bring our drops to Forni Avoltri. Pat will then return here. While Georgiou is making his way into Austria, George and I will spend our remaining days this side, trying to find a DZ within the immediate neighbourhood. If we are successful, the problem of transporting stores from Tramonte to Forni Avoltri will cease. The same night they arrive, they can be shuttled to wherever Georgiou manages to establish a safe house the other side of the frontier. I hope that I am not complicating the issue. You realise everything depends on Georgiou's immediate success. That's all I have George; will you carry on?'

George spoke of the dangers awaiting the Royal party who were to infiltrate into Austria, when making the actual crossing and later; they would have a guide who would show them an unfrequented route but at the same time, two pairs of eyes were better than one and not that they were about to take the plunge, it would be well worth every member's while to consider the points he had in mind.

'As Bill said, there are two phases. I'm going to deal largely with phase one and the minor points one is inclined to overlook and which may affect our personal security. We are going over in three parties; any one of these points, if overlooked, may prompt the Boche to watch the route. Firstly, the movement. We shall travel best part of the way during the hours of darkness. You should make frequent halts, your ears will be of more use than your eyes, listen carefully, if you hear something, a voice or footsteps and you think your travelling companion hasn't heard them, catch hold of your friend's arm and point it in the direction of the noise or noises. Never raise your voice above a whisper, try not to speak at all unless it is absolutely necessary. Secondly, your choice of route. Make use of foot-paths, the way is easier to follow and less noisy. It will prove quicker. There is more danger of meeting someone on a footpath, but you will make an unholy noise if you use the woods, trampling down on leaves and twigs. If you hear somebody passing to your right or left, if they are more than a hundred yards away, freeze. If they are closer, lay down. We must avoid fighting at all costs, there'll be plenty of that when we are ready.'

He continued saying that it was possible they would not make the cover of the safe house before daylight. If the worst came to the worst, they might lose their way, prolonging the journey and making it necessary to complete it without the cover of darkness. They were to make use of every bit of cover. They should walk just within the shelter of the trees rather than through the densest part of the wood, even if it meant adding to the distance. They were to weigh up the round and choose the next bound, ahead of the one they had just sighted. After reaching the vicinity of the safe house, they were to bide their time, look around, familiarise them-selves with the lay of the land and local landmarks. 'Think of the future and the possibility that you may have to run for it. If they way is clear, one of you walk to the house, the other covering his movements. The first should signal back to follow on.'

George continued with this important briefing, 'Pat and Remus have provided me with certain information about the crossing in daylight. The Gendarmerie patrol in pairs, walking about 100 or 200yd apart, one covering the other. They are very cautious, remember you are entering a country that is in a state of war, unlike here where the people have had enough of it and would help you throw the Boche out, given half a chance.'

George took a breath and continued, 'Some days ago, the Garibaldi raided farms over the border and stole cattle. The Gendarmerie therefore at the moment will be more than ever cautious. At various vantage points they maintain lookout posts, scanning the ground with high-power binoculars or telescopes. You will see the Gendarmerie, but the lookout posts will be 2 or 3 miles away. I cannot impress on you enough how important it is to make use of cover, and if you can, try to value it as the enemy scan it. They will be looking at the obvious cover, paths leading from one wood to another. Straight lines attract the eye; they will follow the hedgerows or perhaps stone fences. It will pay dividends to plan your movement in stages.' George was coming close to the end of his especially important briefing. 'Finally, if you have to move near the safe house, avoid arousing suspicion. For example, curfew is at 6 o'clock. There will be no movement after that hour except by the local police or those appointed by the police or Wehmacht. It will be necessary to ration food. The Austrian farmers have to deliver crops, eggs etc., to the local cooperative branch who know just what they are capable of producing. Living off the land therefore will be extremely difficult. If there are no further questions, that is the lot, thank you gentlemen.'

The Countess had set off for Trieste to pay her daughter a visit, leaving us in full control of the dining room for lunch, the last we should have with so many sitting at the table, for at 2 o'clock Pat was to set off for the Friuli and Georgiou, in company with Remus, was to make his way over the frontier, giving him at least 4 to 5 hours of daylight, ample time to reach the Pierebeck Pass, the point at which Remus suggested they make their crossing.

Maria had prepared a meal for Remus and Henry in the kitchen, so that we were free to speak openly at the table. The topic of conversation was the priority of receiving supplies in the field. George confirmed what Pat had already surmised. There were some other operations in Central Europe the priority of which was high and with the opening of the 'Second Front', aircraft were at a premium.

George said, 'We shall be lucky if we receive more than one or two plane-loads a month from now on, Pat. Shortly before we set off from Base, they had commenced dropping stores to the Poles in Warsaw. One day they sent a complete squadron of aircraft, dropping little about 300ft, right on top of the houses. At the moment, the Warsaw boys are first priority. A pretty close second are the Czechs for they are building up a strong Partisan element near the Ostro Gap. If the Czechs can keep control of that neighbourhood the Ruskis [Russians] will be saved a great deal of trouble.' He went on to say that the Poles would fight to clear the west bank of the Vistula, in the vicinity of Warsaw. There was talk also of arming 250,000 Partisans. By December, the Russians should be able to cross the river without firing a shot.

'It will be a wonderful feat, that is if it comes off, and there is every reason to believe it will be successful. The Boche Garrison in Warsaw have their work cut out. They have no reserves at the moment, and they have had a difficult task finding able bodies for the front line. They can do nothing about the supply question.'

Pat ventured that Austria was new ground and that when established, our group would receive a higher priority. George agreed but did stress the point that over the next month the weather would deteriorate, flying conditions would worsen and in mountainous country such as that in which we operated, the best of weather was needed. Our group could do with the higher priority *now*.

Remus returned early on the third day, as promised; they had no difficulty getting through safely, the weather, which was a hindrance physically, gave them a clear passage. They saw nobody on the way and reached a little village which Remus had visited before. Friends at one house gave them food, but would not consider at any price giving them cover, and during the meal their hosts' worried countenance prevented conversation. They were hospitable but glad when Georgiou and Remus had left their doorstep. The time sped by with no safe house or even barn being found. Georgiou then decided to send Remus back with the message that he would continue to search for a safe house and return when he had found one.

He was never seen again.

George said, 'It is abundantly clear to me, Bill, that these people on the other side need inspiring, they're so dreadfully scared of the Gestapo and Nazi informers, what are we going to do? I have one solution, it is a hairbrained scheme but the more I think about it the better I like it.'

Bill asked what the idea was.

'I think we should hang the Gauleiter of Leisinger.[2] No, seriously, I think we should leave him hanging from a lamp post in the main street. I have been speaking to Henry who knows the village quite well. The Gauleiter's house is on the outskirts of the village. There is a small wall surrounding the grounds and the house which is in the middle. With a small party, say eight men, we could lay under the cover of the wall, while two went straight up to the door and asked for the Gauleiter. With any luck he may answer the door himself. If not, we will have to brush our way past the servant or whoever answers the door, get hold of the Gauleiter and tie the remainder up. Next, we hang him in a remote spot not too far distant from the village and when he is 'kaput' carry him into the centre of Leisinger between the two of us, giving the impression that he is drunk.

From the first lamp post, we leave him swinging. If that does not rouse them into action, nothing else will. We must break down this fear of the Nazis. We could observe the result from a safe distance. Let the word get around for a couple of days and then send Henry over to the village near to Leisinger to listen to the trend of local gossip. If it does the trick, Henry will be able to tell us the result.'

Bill responded warily, he was not impressed saying that it sounded like Edgar Wallace![3]

This did not perturb George, he continued with his diatribe stating the group could do with some additional reserves. Five or six British soldiers to boost the numbers but who would also be handy in any confrontation. The Partisans could be used but George wanted men who would react immediately to orders or to any circumstance.

Bill was still not impressed. I then ventured to tell them that I had met a Partisan that very morning who had come from the Cadore. He knew the whereabouts of six POWs who were hiding out in a barn near the village of Santa Lucia, a village 14km south of Cortina D'Ampezzo. He was still here in the village visiting the local commander of the Garibaldi. He said that one of the party was a pilot and another an infantry officer. I said that I was at a loose end at this time, and I could go over and bring them back.

George said, 'What a strange coincidence, the very thing. When is this fellow returning to the Cadore, do you know?'

I told him that he was going back that very afternoon. He had a motorcycle and his name was Fischio.

George agreed that I should go telling me to offer them two alternatives. They may not wish to return but I was to tell them there was a British officer here, not to mention the village name but only the area of the Carnia. That he would like them to join the group. I was not to mention the nature of the work but only that it would help the resistance movement. If they came back with me, we could pay them a closer look and maybe take them on. The alternative was to tell them that we were in a position to return them to their own lines within ten days. George added a rider stating that the POWs were extremely cautious, a spell in the bag made them that way, I would have a job persuading them to return with me.

I said, 'I fully understand, Sir. I'm quite certain that Pat will not require me to perform any duty for several days, certainly none that Arthur can't cope with. The journey there and back will probably take eight days.'

George decided he would speak to the local Garibaldi commander; he felt that I should have a guide on such a journey, but I was confident that

I could find my way by map, but a guide would help me to obtain food and cover. 'I'll get him to sign a letter proving that Charles is a British soldier and requires every assistance in the form of guides, accommodation etc., that will solve the problem.'

Fictitious names were widely favoured in Partisan circles; it disassociated the user from his family and relations and established for him a more peaceful frame of mind, essential if his morale was to be of the first order. In the case of Fischio, his associates gave him his name which was a natural choice. He was young, always cheerful and very fond of music. He was forever whistling popular melodies and it was for this reason he became known to all as 'Fischio' or 'Whistler.'

Fischio's ancient machine was an Auto-Guzzi and of reputable manufacture but it remained nevertheless temperamental, for he took some time coaxing it to go. Maintaining his stance and dignity, Fischio eventually had the engine running and easing the motorcycle forward off its stand he allowed me to take my place behind him on the pillion. Releasing the throttle too quickly, we jerked uncomfortably forward in ever diminishing bounds until finally we travelled smoothly, the engine turning over at an even tempo promising an uninterrupted journey to Campolongo via the town of Comeglians. Gaining more confidence in Fischio's ability to ride, I relaxed my grip slightly and concentrated on the passing scenery which was assuredly looking its best. The road ran alongside the Piave River crossing it several times over small bridges before we reached Comeglians and then turning west. Without mishap or consideration for the passing pedestrians, who seemed to prefer the roadway to the pavement, we travelled through the narrow streets of the town, following the sign marked, 'To Pesaris', a small village on the way to Campolongo.

On more than one occasion I had discovered it inadvisable to place much faith in the peasants' judge of time or distance, but for the sake of making conversation, I questioned Fischio asking him how far Campolongo was from Comeglians. He thought it was about 25km, which in fact was not far wrong. Fischio was a hard task master, each gear literally screaming its annoyance until he changed down when climbing the steeper gradients. The old engine, regardless of the mismanagement to which it was being subjected, staunchly caught its breath downhill and chugged on. But misfortune was only a pace ahead of us! Pesaris amounted to forty or fifty houses running either side of the road. A mile past the village, and without warning, the rear wheel left us, its frame scraping along the road surface, bringing us to an abrupt halt.

Fischio was not dismayed, examining the rear frame he quickly decided that we should have to walk the remainder of the journey and without more ado, hauled the motorcycle off the road, hiding it in some shrubs.

He said that it was no more than 8km to go. The road veered north at the base of Monte Terza and Terza Grande, sloping for the better part of 8km to the valley containing the towns of Campolongo and San Stefano di Cadore. The route was deserted, the bare precipitous slopes, gaunt sentinels of the way, were ominously quiet, brooding over all they surveyed and steeped in a thousand memories of the past.

Fischio pointed to several black mouthed cavities, gun emplacements of the Great War, which faced what were once the southern frontiers of Austria, Fischio said they were monuments to a futile past. Reaching the outskirts of Campolongo, he advised caution. The Germans maintained an outpost in San Stefano, 200-men strong. They made patrols along the road which ran to Sappada, passing through Campolongo.

A cold wind carried ripples of reflected moonlight over the quiet flowing stream and set the branches in motion, a whispering ran through the nearby woods, the incidental music of nature effectively muffling our footsteps. Halting at a small bridge, the entrance to the western suburb of the town, Fischio left me, slipping silently away in the shadows of the nearby buildings. Checking my bearings, I judged that San Stefano was 2km to the west and Campolongo was roughly in the centre of the valley.

'Psst.' Fischio stood on the other side of the bridge waiting for me to join him. We walked quickly through the street over another bridge in the middle of the town, turning first left and then right until we stood before a four-storey building, outside which a weather-beaten board advertised 'Trattoria'. The door was unlatched; Fischio pushed it open, closing it quickly behind me.

The lights were very bright inside the room where two Garibaldini Partisans sat, nursing glasses of wine. They stood up, throwing a clenched fist in the air, a recently acquired Eastern form of greeting which momentarily confused me for their uniforms which were devoid of Fascist symbol once clothed Mussolini's legions. They had been studying a map which one carefully folded and placed inside his pocket. I was asked to sit down and offered some wine which I accepted. I then produced my letter of introduction, Benedetto, the storekeeper, brought another two glasses of wine. While reading the letter, they nodded approvingly from which I gathered we should receive adequate attention on the first stage of our journey. Fischio, although not an inhabitant of the town, was a member of the local Partisan movement. They were asking him if he knew the way to Aurunzo on the Lake, a town a further 20km to the west. Fischio told them that he knew his way over the 'Comelico'.

Both Partisans were elderly, simple men, who had worked most of their lives in the surrounding fields. They were brothers, and for simplicity's sake their parents had chosen to call then Prima and Seconda. Prima satisfied himself that the letter was genuine and informed me that Fischio was free to take me as far as Auronzo, but no further, there I would have to obtain the services of another guide.

'Why do you make the journey into the Cadore?' Prima asked. 'I wish to help some of my comrades,' I replied.

'Well, you must start early in the morning, at 4 hours. The German Post will be asleep then, which is good for you must take the road behind San Stefano and then climb the mountain up over the Comelico. They keep to the road nowadays, so you will have no trouble until you get near the town of Auronzo. Then you must let Fischio go into the town. They will find a way. I hope that you will have no trouble,' said Prima.

With that he called out, 'Benedetto, a room for the Englishman, and call him at 4 hours, remember!' Having made good his promise to help, Prima and his brother left the store, he had another appointment to keep. The old storeman apologised, he could only offer us bread and cheese, our rooms were ready! Preparation is half the battle, we retired early for the march, the next day would be strenuous.

Chapter Ten

Auronzo and the Second Stage

We walked quickly to the small bridge where I had waited for Fischio the previous night, following the path leading through the woods, keeping sight of the road which led to San Stefano. When Benedetto had roused us it had been dark, but the grey light of dawn uncovered the ground over which we travelled revealing the town wherein our enemies slept. A road from the main highway led to a large building, Fischio pointed, saying 'Ecco, la Caserma'.[1] It was larger than the other buildings, but there was nothing to indicate it was any different to them, there were no sentries posted, the whole life of the town was dormant. My guide was visibly disturbed, there was no doubt that he had experience of the occupants of that building, he murmured more to himself than to me, 'I Tedeschi sono bruto!'[2]

Leaving the town behind, we ran for the cover of the woods and crossed the main road, scrambling up a small track which rose steeply from the highway. Without warning he had commenced running, but now that we once more were in the cover of the trees, he paused and looked back. Along the road was a round pillbox, another remnant of the Great War. Fischio said that sometimes the Germans manned the post but not today, there was no sign of any occupation. We continued. The trail may have been the dried bed of a small stream, it was uneven with mossy banks either side, the bed was covered with stones, making it difficult to obtain a sure footing. After climbing a thousand feet we left the path for a mule-track which wound more evenly through the trees making the going easier. By 6am we had broken the back of the mountain and left the closeness of the woods for more open ground, rolling green pastures, damp with the early morning dew. This was the Comelico, a summer grazing ground used by the lower lying villagers during the months of May to September.

Standing in the shade of a copse, we observed an old man who had walked from a long narrow barn. Fischio recognised him, but before proceeding, he looked right and left for further signs of movement before we moved towards the barn. He greeted the old man warmly, shaking his hand vigorously. Turning to me, Fischio winked slyly and asked if I would like some milk; the old man had just finished milking. Inside the barn there were ten head of cattle. While we drank our milk, they were led into the pasture.

Following the mule-track, we descended the northern slopes which took us to the neighbourhood of Auronzo on the Lake. Fischio once again issued a warning to take care and listen. From the cover of the trees he showed me the route he would now take, eventually out of necessity crossing a large bridge on which there were two sentries leaning against a stone wall, the near end to us.

Fischio told me to lay at this spot and wait, he would be about an hour, 'You must remain alert and await a signal to join me.' With that he ran quietly down towards the bridge. I watched him pause where the woods met the road near a bend in the highway. Stepping onto the road he walked casually in the direction of the bridge. The sentries looked up and as he approached, they asked for his identity card. He pulled the card from his pocket and offered it to one while the other ran his hands over Fischio's clothing searching for weapons. They allowed him to pass.

While I waited the sentries were relieved. It was a slack changeover, the old guard leaving their post without passing on any instruction, the new sentries lighting cigarettes having propped their weapons against the wall. The hour passed and still no sign of Fischio. The sun was bright, and the rays drew a smoke-like steam from the road's recently wetted surface. An hour and a quarter; what was the trouble? He should have been back by now. He was! I heard his unmistakeable whistle. Riding his bicycle, he took the road on the opposite slope which led to Candida; when he was out of sight of the sentries, he waved but continued on his way, eventually passing from my view. Now what? Within 2 minutes, a motorcyclist followed the same route dismounting where Fischio had waved. Looking in my direction without seeing me, the newcomer also waved and then bent over his machine as though he were carrying out a minor running repair. Leaving my cover, I clambered down the bank which had concealed a river, noticing stepping stones ideally placed for a crossing.

Half expecting a challenge from the sentries, I ran gingerly over the stepping stones and on all fours up the opposite bank to the stranger. As soon as I had joined him, he took a mackintosh and a scarf from a satchel, 'Here, you must wear these, hurry!'[3] When I was ready, we rode off into the town. The sentries watched us but made no move to stop us.

Auronzo was a pleasant town with almost every other house a hotel, another Cortina in a wilder setting. Turning up the driveway of one such hotel we came to a halt and for a second time, the stranger spoke introducing himself. 'Good day, I am Larry, you must come this way.' I followed him into the building where there were twenty or more Partisans. A young woman who understood English came forward and introduced me to the local commander, another Marco.

I explained my business and handed my letter of introduction to the commander, who dropped his official mask and invited me to join him at a table where food was about to be served. Via the interpreter, we made conversation.

'And what brings you to the Dolomites, friend?' I thought I might ask him why he carried a gun, but decided against that and replied more courteously, 'My commander has a mission helping the Partisan movement.'

He was a robust man and his choice of vocabulary blended well with his rough work-coarsened hands. 'Pig out of misery, are the English helping the workers now? Ah, I see it, they have discovered fresh fields of fodder and they are supplying them with the means to destroy themselves and the Fascist swine, they're clever ones these Capitalists!' The girl was embarrassed, but Marco was enjoying his repartee which his men found amusing. 'Never mind, we need you, you need us, so the hatchet's buried until the end of this war and we thank you for your help.'

The girl excused him saying he was bitter, but he was a good man and a worthy leader. I thought I understood. Marco pinched the girl's buttocks and continued.

'Come and see a friend, we caught him the other day. He won't last to see the light of another though, he says he knows nothing. His mouth is closed with fear; here, this way. We couldn't understand why our plans were going wrong, but now we know, we've caught the informer.' Leading the way to the cellar, he pushed open a door, I followed two of his Partisans. A youth stood in the corner of the room. He had recently been crying. He was about 20 years of age, clad in a dark, coarse suit, a dirty shirt minus collar. The two Partisans punched him in the stomach and drew blood from his face and another flood of tears and cries of mercy. His cries encouraged them to punish him still further until he collapsed, a sobbing heap on the filthy floor. 'A Fascist spy, he sold his countrymen for silver to the German swine, we shall not dirty our hands on him much longer, his head will rest on a pole, a warning to any other scum that may hover in the neighbourhood!'

We left the foul interior of the room for the sun-filled parlour above. It was arranged that I should return with Marco to his Posto di

Rastrellamento, situated, he explained, nearly 20km west on top of the Marmerole.

A foot bridge crossed the lake over which we went in single file, the guarded bridge was visible at the southern end of the lake but was out of rifle range. Marco set a fast pace until we were well clear of the town among the safer cover of the firs which reached down to the western border of the lake. I lost interest in the scenery, the morning walk had tightened all my leg muscles and it was a case of mental strength versus physical as I concentrated every effort into the saving of energy. The climb was arduous, but Marco never relaxed for one moment, glancing around frequently to see that everyone was keeping close behind him.

On the summit we arrived at a large, grey stone building, an old Alpini outpost. Marco held more than a hundred prisoners of war, old Austrian men wandering despondently in pairs close to the building which was their prison. They were all over 50 years of age, clothed in ragged field grey-green uniforms and soft peaked caps. Most had forcibly traded their boots with the Partisans, some retained no footwear at all. They were a taciturn crowd, the miserable dregs of a country's last reserves.

Close to the large stone building were several wooden barns, filled with recently cut fodder, Marco pointed one out to me telling me that was where I was to spend the night. 'But first, you come and eat,' he said.

Entering the headquarters of the 'Battaglione Marmerole', we joined our fellow travellers who had commenced eating. Taking my place at a roughly constructed table, I was passed a roll of weavel bread and invited to dig into the communal tin of marmallata, a jam conserve prepared with a generous vegetable content which ruined the fruit flavour, it was a thick gelatinous substance. The long walk had whetted my appetite.

Before darkness settled on the camp, curtailing all movement, I made my way to the barn to find my next day's guide comfortably dug down in the fodder. Digging myself a hole, I pulled a blanket of fodder over me, it was warm and comfortable. My sleeping companion lay awake speaking of the past and future. I listened for sometime but my eyes were heavy with sleep, it was difficult to concentrate on what he was saying. I fell asleep, his voice trailing off, becoming an indistinct mumble mingled with the wind which whistled through the cracks in the warped roof.

My guide was talking about how hard a struggle Italy had gone through. He never wanted to fight for Fascism but had to. He joined the Alpini and the regiment was sent to Albania. It was a tragedy, they were annihilated and what was left of them were sent to Istria, and in 1942 it was a new regiment that marched into Jugoslavia. Their 'perfumed' officers were too busy enjoying themselves to notice if the troops were being fed sufficiently but, by the Grace of God, he had not been sent to the East where many men were killed. He said he would have deserted. Why should he have to fight a cause that wasn't his? Finally, it was the officers that deserted the men. I was fighting sleep, but he continued on, it was in 1943 when 'that Fascist' Bagdoglio assumed command and surrendered, most of them fighting with the Partisans for a while and then returning to Italy. He asked the question: 'Why do the English support Mihailavitch and Tito? They are scheming here in Italy too. They supply the Garibaldi with arms, but I'll wager the so-called Democrats get more. It is to the East that the workers should look for help, not the Capitalists of the West. But we are learning, we'll accept your guns and we'll use them again when this war is over, it's a peculiar game this life. Here we are under the same roof now, but who knows, in two years we may be on opposite sides of the fence.'

He had become too complicated, I had to sleep I murmured goodnight and drifted off to sleep. The night passed swiftly. My guide was already up. He shook me by the shoulder, 'Hey, Sergeant, come on, wake up!' For a moment I wondered if he had been talking all night.

He opened the door of the barn saying that we had to start off now, we had a long walk ahead of us. For two days we walked together, spending the nights in barns, similar to the one on top of the Marmerole. On the third evening, the close of a sunny day, we wandered lazily down from the slopes of Pelmo and into a valley and the village of Santa Lucia. Here, the guide was on holiday for two days but would be returning part of the way to Selva and offered to accompany me if I wished him to the following day. His conversation was morbid but apart from that we got on very well together. I thanked him for his offer but thought that I would be able to find my way without difficulty.

He then pointed out two men who he said were English prisoners. Two men in civilian dress approached us in the opposite direction. They were conversing quietly as they walked. They would have passed for members of the locality with ease. As they got nearer, I bade them 'good evening' in English. They glanced slightly in my direction casually answering, 'Buona sera.' I watched them continue on their way, they never looked back, I thought that rather odd, they certainly were not taking any chances.

I told the guide I would stay the night in the local albergo and asked if he would let the English POWs know that they could find me there. The hotel was small and dimly lit, the old lady was not surprised to see a soldier in uniform, asking no questions she booked me in. That was fairly simple procedure; the handing over of a liberal number of lira; for a bowl of soup a few more lira. I soon had several visitors, the POWs arriving in force at 10 o'clock. Two entered the hotel first, I was sitting in the kitchen having just finished my bowl of soup.

'Good evening for the second time!' I said. 'We heard that there was an English sergeant in the village, so we came down to have a look for ourselves. I'm Davis and this is Williams, there are four more outside, they will join us when we are satisfied that you are what you say you are. Have you any documents to prove that you are an English sergeant?'

'I have some letters which were sent from England three months ago and my pay book, is that sufficient evidence or would you like to ask me some questions?'

Williams said, 'What are you doing in this neighbourhood, I mean in the north of Italy?'

I told him that I was not prepared to answer that question in full, I said that I had two propositions for them to consider. I could take them to an English officer who was working in liaison with the Partisans, he would be prepared to send them to the south of Italy to their own lines or offer them a job working with him. I told them I was the officer's assistant and that I worked a radio and that we had already despatched several ex-POWs, the last about one month before.

Davis handed back the letters and my pay book and asked if I had any other proof of identity, 'You see we have been on the run some time now and we don't intend to be caught. The Germans have been working a dodge just lately, wandering around in British uniforms and they have been successful in clearing up a number of Partisan gangs.'

I told them that I had no additional proof but ventured that my guide would not have accompanied me to this place if I was a Boche in British uniform. 'I have travelled with him for three days right through Partisan controlled territory. Oh yes, I have a letter here written by an Italian Partisan Commander, read it, you understand sufficient Italian I take it?'

They read the letter together. David remarked, 'We don't trust these Communist Partisans, they have no love for the British. They'd shop you as soon as look at you if it suited their purpose.'

Williams left the room and called the remaining four who had lain in a field on the opposite side of the road. They were similarly attired. They weighed up the proposition I had made having decided that I was to be trusted. Williams was the chief spokesman.

'When will we leave with you? Three of us are prepared to stay with the officer, the others want to be sent to southern Italy.'

I said, 'Good, well I plan on starting back first light. I want to reach Selva di Cadore by evening, that's getting on for 35km from here, can you all make it in one go tomorrow?' Williams replied, 'I can, so can Smith and Jones but Davis, O'Leary and Forsythe are all wounded and they are not feeling fit enough to march far or quickly, that's why they wish to be sent straight back to our own lines.'

I made a decision and told them that we would leave the guide with the three sick men. He could bring them on slowly, but they were not to tell the guide where the ultimate destination was. He'd probably take them as far as a town called Auronzo. From there they should make for a town called Campolongo, only a day's march from Auronzo. From there it was one day travelling to their destination, Comeglians. I told them I would arrange for them to be met there. I gave them a thousand lira. I added that they would have to sleep in mountain malgas, but they had probably slept in worse places anyway.

I then addressed my travelling party, 'We'll follow the same route, I would like to keep to the valleys and pass through Lorenzago, but there has been some trouble between the Boche and the Partisans in that locality lately, so we'll have to keep to the mountains. It's pushing it a bit, but I would like to get back within four days, I suggest that we all meet here at 6 in the morning.'

They all filed out together, it had taken little more than an hour to persuade them to join me. Shortly after 11pm another visitor arrived, a young man of 25 years.

He told me he had heard I was an English soldier and that his father had a villa not far from the hotel. He had sent his compliments and would I like to spend the night at his home? He introduced himself as Vittorio Tedeschini.

I immediately agreed and we left for the villa, the old lady locking the door behind us.

We walked across a field immediately behind the albergo to a house 200yd from the village. Several lights showed from the windows. As we crunched our way up the gravel footpath close to the villa, the front door was opened by a middle-aged man who held a pipe to his mouth, the smoke and aroma blew towards us as we climbed the steps. Vittorio's father welcomed me enthusiastically and ushered me through the front door and into the lounge where his wife and eldest daughter were seated, busily engaged with their knitting. They stood up, the mother offering me a chair. The room was comfortably furnished with pictures, flowers, cushions, a modest collection of books in a case, a cheerful atmosphere.

I felt awkward for a moment, conscious of my filthy clothing and dusty boots. Sensing my attitude, Mrs Tedeschini put away her knitting and set about making me at home. 'We have very little to offer in the way of drink, allow me to make you a warm cup of coffee, we usually have one at this time.' Her daughter left to comply with her suggestion. Signor Tedeschini relit his pipe. 'We are short of tobacco, I make my own, this is leaf I have prepared myself, had it cut down on the bacon machine at the local store. It's strong, but a little goes a long way. I met your guide earlier this evening, that is how I discovered you were here to meet the boys. We have helped them as much as we could you know, giving them clothes and a little food.'

He went on to say how he had the villa built just before the war, 'It was as well I did, for my home in Venice was requisitioned and we would have had nowhere to go. We are a large family, seven altogether. The young ones are in bed. My only son Vittorio is a member of the local Partisans, commanded by Emilio, he's a Christian-Democrat; we have no Garibaldi hereabouts, I was the manager of the L-- Shipping Line at Venice, of course since the war, there has been no work for me, another reason why we came up here to the Cadore.[4] Now we have the opportunity of helping the Allies, that's why I am so anxious that we should have this chance of a talk.'

Vanessa brought the coffee exclaiming there was no sugar, but it was warm. Father continued with his story. 'Emilio has more than 200 men under his command, but as you know, men are no good without weapons. They are prepared to fight, and I have every reason to believe that they would give a good account of themselves. You are the man we have been waiting for!'

I was most impressed, but equally aware of my rank and limitations. I thought Mr Tedeschini must be fishing for information, not that I didn't appreciate the fact that the men were available and ready to do battle when they were supplied with the means. He was equally aware of the fact that I was not in control of the magic wand which produced stores from Base, but he obviously wished to find out who I was and I was sorry he had to give me a build-up as it were, in the hopes that I would give him the picture.

'I will remember what you have told me Mr Tedeschini. When I return to my Commanding Officer I will let him know that you have a Partisan movement assembled, of course you understand that we are few in numbers and are already fully committed, nevertheless, I'll make a report when I see him, he may be able to arrange something in the way of help.'

I thought that this may be a good area to bear in mind, here was a safe house and the village was no more that 40 miles from the Brenner Pass. A little more information may be useful after all. I asked if the Germans used the road very much.

'Not the one running through the village. There is a first-class road over the other side of the mountain to the west of the village which connects up with the village road 5 or 6km to the north, it leads to Cortina D'Ampezzo. Mussolini has his headquarters there at the moment, it's not more than 15km away. They rarely visit the village. On the last occasion they searched this house and tore up the floorboards, they found nothing and have left us in peace ever since.'

I asked if the mains electricity was AC or DC. He told me it was AC and asked why I wanted such information.

'I thought of a radio. This house seems well appointed and might be useful as a safe house. From here an operator could work to his Base. Tell me, can you move freely on the frontier?'

'You would have to make a wide detour around Cortina. There are many Fascist troops garrisoned there. They have a defensive circle completely screening every approach to the town and all persons approaching are suspect and are taken for interrogation. However, you could easily reach the frontier. It would take two days on foot.' I then asked if there were any suitable areas which were secure, where stores from an aircraft could be received. Both father and son had suggestions and Vittorio's seemed the better prospect. 'If it's a place away from the highway and free from observation, there is no better place than the base of Mount Pelmo. I should think it would be about 2,000ft above sea-level.' I believed that I knew where that was; the large pasture about a kilometre square surrounded by trees that I had passed earlier today.

It was after midnight when we retired. Mr Tedeschini promised to wake me at 5.30am, I bade them goodnight and made my way to a box room where a makeshift bed had been arranged by Vanessa.

Chapter Eleven

Selva di Cadore

The POWs were punctual, but the guide had not put in an appearance by 6.15am. I did not wish to wait any longer. Checking the instructions that I had issued the night before, I had said they must wait for the guide. With that we left them. Each man carried a rucksack containing a few old clothes and some food that they had purchased with the lira I had given them. Williams had obtained a bottle of grappa. They were cheerful and chattered happily for the first 10km until the strain of the pace we had maintained began to tell.

Going even slower when climbing, we doubled down the gradients keeping abreast of time, I wished to cover the greater part of the journey during the hours of daylight in order that I should be able to recognise the route and landmarks I had noticed on the outward trip.

It was dusk when we sighted Selva, a town astride the main highway garrisoned by a company of German troops who maintained an aircraft location station there. The barracks were at the southern end of the town, I hoped that we should be able to find accommodation at the other end. 'If you wait here, I'll make a recce and try and find a place to sleep, remember, no smoking, no noise and don't stray from this spot.'

The main street, in fact the town, appeared to be deserted. There was one glimmer of light on the left side of the street, halfway down. My footsteps echoed, although I stepped softly, and 10yd from the light which cast a pencil beam on the roadway, I stood still in the cover of a doorway. To the left of the doorway from whence the light issued, sat a man with a female friend upon his knee, they had heard me and were watching my next move. Stepping from the doorway I approached them, they stood up, the girl running inside the house. 'Buona sera, sono Inglesi, I miei amici vogliamo mangiare.'[1] I said. The man surprised me, 'I bin Amerika, spik Amerikan pliss, I unnerstant you!' I barely understood him, but I thought we would do better in English. 'My friends and I require beds and food, where can we find a hotel that is open now?'

The man responded, 'No 'otel in Selva for you. It is bedder you go Vinigo on the mountain, de Goddahm Hun bin fightin' 'ere t'day, iss bedder you go now.' The man said it was 2km up the mountain, and he indicated a rough direction pointing to the end of the street where I was to turn right.

Vinigo was much smaller, a village amounting to a church, a general store and a sprinkling of houses. Next door to the church, I thought we should find the priest's house. It was. We knocked for 5 minutes. The priest was either a heavy sleeper or he didn't wish to be disturbed late at night. He opened the door slightly inquiring our business. I requested a room for the night, but he wasn't keen to help. He suggested we try Selva, I told him we had just been there and had been advised to come to Vinigo. It was drafty, he asked us to go inside. He left us for a minute and returned with a lighted taper, lighting an oil lamp in a room off the main passage. The room was bare except for a wooden table. He scratched his head trying to find a solution, he was weighing us up at the same time, I don't think he was impressed. Finally, he spread his hands stating there just wasn't any room to sleep in Vinigo. I looked at the others, they were dead tired, I didn't intend to move another step tonight. I asked if there was a stable, anything would do. Seeing that we would not be put off, he said there was a stable two doors down the street; we followed him. The stable floor was muddy, but there was a hayloft with ample hay which would keep us warm. I thanked him and he left us. We slept clothed, except for our boots.

We had been asleep 4 hours when the stable door creaked open. I sat up and asked who was there. It was our old friend the 'American'. 'It's me Yohnny, you gotta come 'ere a minut – a fella want t'spik wid ya!'

'Tell him to come back at 6, we need some sleep,' I replied. The door closed for a few moments but Mr Amerika returned. 'Hey Yohnny, it's no good, 'e says you gotta come now.'

I pulled on my boots and jumped down from the loft, walking outside. No sooner was I outside the door when I was pounced upon from all sides and forced along the street and into a building, two doors past the priest's house. The room contained about five Garibaldini Partisans who were standing behind a youth seated in a chair. All carried weapons and had scarves draped around their necks, red ones. The youth looked serious and ready for business.

'What is the meaning of this surprising interview?' I tried to be calm. Mr Amerika interpreted, 'This is the boss, 'is name is Yimmie, 'e wants to know what you want round 'ere? The Padre reckons you're a spy.'

'You can tell Mr Jimmie that I am nothing of the kind, ask him to read this letter and tell him that I shall report his conduct to his superiors.'

Another Partisan entered with my revolver. 'One thing more, I shall require my weapon and right now!' Mr Amerika passed on my reply, which made an impression. 'Sure, I know you're OK Yohnny, but we take no chances, you folla?'

I thought I understood, but now that the interview was over I was going to get some sleep, we still had a long way to go, we had come a long way and furthermore we were tired and rather sick of Italians at the moment.

'Sure, you're damn right, but it's not safe 'ere in Vinigo for you, the boss say you gotta go wid him, e's gonna see you 'ave a safe passage. You go wid 'im now. 'E gotta a liddle job and then 'e take you along wid 'im.'

He explained that there had been a fight that morning and that he had to bury the dead, but he wouldn't be long.

My watch read 4.10am, but there seemed little point in arguing further. We joined Jimmie and his party after he had visited the cemetery, following him to his mountain retreat, three malgas, 2,000ft above Vinigo. He arranged breakfast for us and an escort who would take us as far as the Marmerole. We carried on almost immediately, the escorts taking a path which crossed the road half a mile from Selva, one of them suggesting stopping for wine in a trattoria on the main road, but I objected and we continued with our journey.

Our escorts were in better shape for marching than we were, we had to ask them repeatedly to slacken the pace but they weren't interested, they had to return that night to Vinigo, there was no time to be lost. We stopped twice on the way at malgas which housed families to obtain a drink of water, ultimately reaching Marco's headquarters at 7pm. We didn't eat, we were too tired. I took them straight to the barn in which I spent the night on the way out.

The rain fell heavily during the night, seeping through the roof, a monotonous drip, drip, dropping faster that the passing seconds of time when the storm was at its height, and keeping pace with the minutes towards the break of day. Our limbs ached prompting frequent changes of position, an aid to better rest, great minds think alike, even the less gifted will when the occasion demands it. We welcomed the slow approach of dawn. It was a dull morning overcast with angry looking cloud; the lower lying valleys filled with grey mist limiting visibility to 200ft. Many of the old Austrian prisoners stood bunched together under the eaves of the stone building looking as wretched as the weather.

'We'll not wait for a guide. I can find the way without difficulty to Auronzo. I would like to get on the move if you're ready,' I said.

Williams had a mouthful of grappa to aid his circulation he said, we had a mouthful each and set off. The track was very muddy and slippery, in places water flowing from the higher slopes rushed across the path, minor tributaries hurrying to join the fast-swelling streams below us. The trees which had been covered in cloaks of green were showing their autumn lustre, a seasonal change now due. An attractive picture not dispelled by the inclement weather but serving as a reminder of meagre times ahead. Manfred would receive few supplies if the barometer was low. I hoped that there would be a change.

'Roll on a long time, what I could do to a plate of eggs and bacon, I've been promising myself since the day I was taken prisoner that my chief hobby after the war will be food, are there any jobs going in Blighty as food-taster?' said Smith.

Jones responded, 'Ya don't think you'd get the job if there was do ya? Why you're all skin and grief; those kind of jobs go to the busty fellas, good adverts who don't eat a lot any 'ow,' answered Jones.

The subject of lunch arose and I told them we should arrive in Auronzo in time for lunch, we'll go to the hotel, perhaps we will be lucky I told them. We crossed the lake and entered the hotel from the rear. The young English-speaking girl was alone in the parlour and not a bit surprised to see us. She was helpful and told me that we were lucky, there was a car leaving in 2 hours' time for Candida which was in the same direction we were going, perhaps 2 hours' walk north of Campolongo. She said she knew the man well and if I agreed, she would ask him to take us with him.

'You will have to walk outside the town a short way. Sometimes they stop cars at the bridge, even though the car doesn't cross it, the road to Candida as you know, bears left near the bridge. You will have to cut across the hills and meet the car as it proceeds along the Candida road,' the girl said. This we did. The car drove straight for Candida, dropping us off in the main square where a new guide had been warned to meet us. He was a gnarled old man carrying a crook which he found necessary to help him on his way. His looks were misleading for he moved across the countryside at no mean pace. We arrived in Campolongo 2 hours later and made our way straight to the trattoria.

It was Benedetto who answered the door, peering up and down the street before he closed it behind him. He took us into his private room where he had already had company. 'Hello Charles, fancy meeting you so soon,' a voice I recognised as Clarke's came from behind a tall man in US Army dress, who he introduced as Captain Hall of the US Army Signal Corps.[2] I was invited to join them, and they were about to open a bottle of grappa but I temporarily excused myself; I wanted to get the boys fixed up with some accommodation for the night first. Benedetto came to my rescue once again, taking them to another hotel across the street. There was only room for two, so Williams shared my room.

I re-joined Clarke and Captain Hall, the latter asked me where I had been, and I told him I had been to collect the boys who had escaped from a prisoner-of-war camp who had been hiding out just south of Cortina.

'Say, that's great, I'm on my way over to size up the form, how did ya make out? You can give me a few pointers. I know the ground well enough, it was a sort of favourite holiday spot ya might say.' He smiled, listening carefully to my reply, at that stage. Clarke got up to go to bed thanking Hall for the snapshots. Williams went upstairs with Clarke, leaving myself and Hall on our own.

'What would you be interested to hear?' I asked the Captain. 'Well, one good turn deserves another, I have just given your buddy some snapshots of the Silian area, they're right up to date, taken from the air not more than a month ago. Three good shots of the bridge, gives dimensions, height, weight, breadth, the number of guards, in fact the whole works. He was sure pleased to see them. I'd like to know if you saw any likely DZs or met up with anybody who owns a safe house, you know the kind of information. I want to meet up with any Partisan movement. We have reports that there are plenty about 40 miles north of Belluno, that would be near enough to where you have just come from I guess.'

I answered that I might be able to help and told him of the large pasture at the base of Mount Pelmo, it had one set back as far as a DZ was concerned in that it was a thousand feet above sea level and it would be difficult to spot from the air and the added problem of the future weather as well. I told him of Santa Lucia, in a valley running north about 14km south of Cortina. 'There is a villa just outside the village, a rather gaily painted pinky coloured house, you couldn't mistake it. The owner is a man called Tedeschini, his son called Vittorio is a member of the local Partisans. That's it for what it's worth.'

'Very interesting, Sergeant,' said Hall.[3] 'Tell me, did ya have any trouble on the way, was it difficult to approach? I've had so many near shaves lately, I'm getting cautious in my old age. I drove straight onto a guarded bridge the other day; the Huns were as surprised as I was. This uniform is remarkably similar to theirs and before they could ask any questions, I turned my bike round and got out pronto!'

It was time for sleep. I bade the Captain good night and sat on my bed and took off my boots. What an incredible fellow the American was. He seemed distinctly out of place but at the same time very much at home, not a care in the world, his casual, almost blatant conversation was partly bluff, partly high spirits, he listened intently and I imagined missed very little of what went off around him. He was a man well chosen for the task, an obvious choice for this area of operations, his knowledge of the Cadore and neighbouring Provinces accumulated pre-war, stood him in good stead now.

It must have been close on 1 o'clock in the morning when I heard several voices in the street below, followed by a loud rapping on the front door which must surely have awakened the whole street. Next door I heard Hall hurriedly dressing. Groping in the darkness, I found the handle of the door. I called to Hall, 'Who would be paying a visit at this time of morning, Sir?'

'I wouldn't know, get dressed and be ready to follow me. We shall have to make for the cellar, through the window and then straight for the open country. There's no mistaking the guttural sound of them voices.' Hall was curt, crisp, very much alert, and almost dressed ready to go. Returning to my room I awoke Williams, briefly stated our position and required action. In my haste I dropped my revolver, causing an outburst from the Captain who spoke of discipline, accentuating its benefits with a suitable choice of adjectives. I accepted the reprimand without acknowledgement, I appreciated his point of view only too well.

Bendetto made his way down the stairs, we watched him, he seemed calm and not in the least disturbed. We heard the door open and several minutes of animated conversation, but 5 minutes later the visitors left us in peace. Hall whistled quietly, expressing his relief. Bendetto tramped back up the stairs, seeing us he mentioned that there was no cause for alarm, it was a party of Partisans in search of petrol, they had conversed in a dialect he explained. 'Buona note.' 'Goodnight,' Hall answered pointedly, and we returned to our beds.

Chapter Twelve

Opportunity Seldom Knocks Twice

'This is the parting of the ways, Sergeant. There is one thing more you might do for me. My colleague, another US Army officer, will expect to see me a lot sooner than will be possible, I hadn't visualised going right the other side of the Cadore immediately. I have a letter here that I would like you to deliver to him, it explains my future movements and present intention. You'll find him in the village of Artis, it's not far out of your way, about 2km south of Comeglians. I would like him to have this information as soon as possible. I'd be grateful if you'd carry it.' He handed me the letter.[1]

I told him that I would deliver the letter that same evening. I wished him the absolute best of luck and told him I hoped we would meet again under better circumstances. We shook hands and went our separate ways. Hall northwards, taking the steep climb above Campolongo, a more direct route to the Comelico than Fischio and I had taken previously; the POWs and myself proceeding in the opposite direction through the town, up the south road, the 8km rising gradient to Terza Grande.[2] Half a mile from Campolongo, we stopped a moment to look back, and we saw Hall, a tiny fly-like figure working his way left and right in easy stages up the slope.

It was fresh, sunny, not warm but a nice walking day, everything looking bright after the heavy rainfall of the recent past, the gurgling streams carrying the waters more placidly to the river. A cart had rolled along the road ahead of us leaving clearly defined impressions on the road's surface, with each kilometre covered the tracks dried off and gradually become less obvious, until there were none and we reached the top of the gradient and turned east for Pesaris and Comeglians.

'Blimey, 'ow much farther 'ave we to go yet?' exclaimed Davis suddenly and in contrast with our silence, and intimate reflections. 'My feet are killin' me.' I told him that we were at the top of the hill now and the worst was over and that it would be much easier now. I suggested a halt at noon, the ground was dry, and we could take the weight of our feet for half an hour.

Williams retorted, 'I always told yah, yah should have taken more exercise when he was in the bag, it's a real treat to be out, just you think of them eggs and bacon we're going to 'ave.'

Davis felt that bacon and eggs were as far away as the indecipherable Italian place-name to where we were headed; but said it with a twinkle in his eye.

A short distance west of Comeglians, Jones pointed to a road sign which indicated a rough cart track to Artis. The track wound for 2km between high-banked grazing pastures entering a wood, the other side of which we found a scattered group of houses, the hamlet of Artis. One house, larger and more modern than the others, was situated in the middle of an orchard. From the rear of the house we heard the dull, regular thud of steel on wood, the sound of a person busily engaged chopping logs. I felt this was the sort of house they would choose to live in.

It was the wireless operator wielding the chopper, as we rounded the corner of the building he stopped work and called to us, 'Well, what d'ya know, more Limeys, we'd heard there were some in the neighbourhood, making a social visit eh?'

'Kind of, I have a letter for your OC from Captain Hall, I met him yesterday,' I replied after introducing the others.

'Pleased to meet you, my name's Gray,' he answered, 'The Major has gone along up to Forni Avoltri to meet your party, we heard you were there, anyhow, I'll give him the letter when he arrives.'[3]

We discussed in brief the progress of the war and activities closer to our own scene of operations. Gray had an attractive easy flowing collection of humorous anecdotes, his catch retorts were automatic, drawing a successive flow of smiles from my compatriots.

Williams was particularly interested in the Colt automatic which Gray carried slung in a cut-away holster hanging from his waist, cowboy fashion. The butt normally of brown Bakelite was made of transparent thick Perspex, underneath which he had placed a picture of a young woman. He asked Gray if it was his girlfriend, he replied that it was, sort of! It was his wife, 'I've always got her in the palm of my hand!'

I thought it time to move on with quite a long way to go, I was hoping to arrive before the others went to bed, before 10pm. We took to the main road that led to Comeglians. I thought that Hall would have passed through Auronzo by now and probably commenced the long climb up the Marmerole, at least we were on a road, even if we had further to travel tonight. Davis, truculent by nature, soon felt the strain and in good old army fashion aired his complaints. 'If I ever get back to Blighty after this war, I'm going to get a job as a bus conductor, no more bloody walkin' for me,' he said. We were too tired to laugh, amusing though his comment was. Williams was sometimes a thorn in Davis' side, encouraging him to additional remarks even more descriptive. 'What beats me is how you got into the infantry with feet like that,' he jibed.

'Some of us had to hold the enemy back, but you wouldn't know anything about that.' Davis felt satisfied he had made his point.

To avoid the argument, which was getting out of hand, I abruptly changed the subject. I told them at Forni Avoltri they would be sleeping in a hotel in a bed with sheets, with the opportunity to have a bath and be comfortable. There was the question of what they would have to do when they met the officer. I told them that it would be nothing out of the ordinary, he would tell them soon enough and if they didn't like it, they could always refuse and join the other three.

It was closer to 11pm when we did eventually arrive at the Sotta Corona, but the others had not retired, at least not George and Bill who were sitting in their lounge. I left Williams, Jones and Davis sitting in the parlour while I reported to George.

'The prodigal returns, we'd almost written you off!' I told George that I thought that myself at one juncture. I told him three POWs were downstairs and the other three, less fit, were still on their way. They'd had a bad time of it over the past two years and I felt they ought to take it steady.

'What have you told them? Are they keen to work with us?' George queried.

I made my report as briefly as possible, confining the details to the first meeting with the POWs and the incidents at Auronzo and Selva di Cadore.

'Very interesting, Charles, at least you have found the chaps, although God knows what we're going to do with them now. Georgiou sent Remus back but we haven't heard a word from him since. They reached a small village just the other side of the frontier and were able to obtain a meal in a house known to Remus. The young woman would not consider putting up our two friends at any price. They slept in a disused barn that night. The next day they moved on to two other villages, but the people just wouldn't entertain them.' It was at this stage when Georgiou decided to send Remus back to put the boss in the picture while he continued the search for a safe house.

George said that an American officer had visited that afternoon and had brought information that the Boche were to make a clean sweep of the Carnia and the Friuli, concentrating their efforts along the immediate frontier region and the main roads. This same intelligence had come from another source as well. The Germans were going to use Caucasian Cossacks, thousands of them crossing the border via Pontebba from Austria with more on their way. Most of them were on foot and had families with them. Hitler promised them the Friuli and the Carnia as a happy hunting ground with possibly us being the game.

It was believed the Cossacks were badly equipped and most certainly not front-line troops, which George believed pointed to one thing; they would bolster the security formations, their plan being to break up the Partisan movement which meant that we would have to think of some-thing pretty fast.[4] George had sent Pat to Sauris to recce the area, it lies about 20km to the south above the Ampezzo valley, we could not stay here. Forni Avoltri was bound to be one of the villages on their clearance list; if all of us left, however, and Georgiou returned, he wouldn't know the details and most likely fall into the trap being set.

'Bill will therefore remain in Forni Avoltri. I would like you, Charles, to remain as well as his radio link. All movement will shortly be curtailed, Arthur has drawn up a lateral system of communication so that we can communicate with you from Sauris and use Base as secondary means of keeping in touch with you.'

He continued, 'If the worst comes to the worst, we will be in a better position to make a get-away from Sauris. If the scent gets too strong, I shall inform Base that we are going to make our way out. From Sauris the going will be easier, there is a good covered exit route to the east, at night under the cover of darkness, we could do it without difficulty.'

George could see no alternative; if Base refused to send supplies, the Partisans would lose faith and would be unable to offer any resistance without the means. He had decided that he would leave the following day for Sauris taking Arthur, Peter and Symon with him, there they would meet Clarke. George had had a phone call from Clarke that morning, he had met Pat at Comeglians and he had some interesting information. Pat had decided to return with it rather than proceed into the Cadore, his original intention. Accommodation was sorted out for the POWs, and we arranged to meet in the lounge at 8am the following day.

I retired to my room where I found Arthur fast asleep. The room was warm so I opened the window, voices carried from the street below as Williams and his fellow escapees left for the smaller hotel across the village. The parlour lights illuminated the glistening cobbles, their lengthening shadows swallowed up into the darkness through which they made their way. Arthur was having a restless sleep, his breathing was heavy; he had packed his radio and rucksack, leaving them handy on the table. George's appreciation of the situation had been delivered with candour, stressing our changing fortunes; the scales which balance our success or failure lay in the hands of the two factions. Base, which controlled the aircraft and stores, and secondly the Partisans, whose support we needed. Additional elements that would turn the scales were the enemy and the weather. It was of primary importance that we receive supplies regularly and thus ensure that the Partisan movement flourished.

As arranged, we assembled in the lounge at 8am. The new developments demanded a complete reorganisation, which Bill now explained. He spread a map of the area on the table.

'In order that you understand the complete picture, I shall reiterate certain points that we discussed yesterday. To begin with, the Boche have enrolled mercenaries in great strength with whom doubtless they will attempt to clear the area. We have learned that they are Caucasian Cossacks, ill equipped and are travelling with their families, we must assume that they are not front-line troops therefore but will be used to secure their lines of communication on which we are not sitting. These troops are at present concentrating in the Friuli below Tolmezzo and along the road to Udine. We can expect them to commence their drive northwards through the Friuli and the Carnia at any moment. So much we know, but we must be prepared for a drive from over the frontier. They will certainly secure the frontier before they commence their drive. At the time being, we can depend upon situation reports. We shall know when they start and their rate of progress.'

Bill continued his briefing stating that the Partisans were short of ammunition and the means of maintaining resistance. The Germans had deliberately chosen this time, it was thought, because the weather was deteriorating, and they would know the Partisans could not hold out for long. If they did capitulate and cease to become Partisans, they would return to their villages and mingle with the population, in short there would be no Partisans and our group had to make plans for that contingency.

Bill turned his attention to the German situation, 'They are concentrated south of the lower foothills. Their first objectives are within the area of the Friuli. We can rest assured that they know we have been receiving supplies from the air, and I think that bit is safe to assume and that they have a pretty shrewd idea where those drops were made. When the Boche roll up the carpet, Manfred will be nearest to the end that they start rolling.[5] Apart from Monte Rossa, there are few places he can retreat to. He would not be able to remain up there long, he must eat and drink.'

It would be difficult for Manfred to get away. It was thought that one suitable place of retreat would be Sauris; equidistant between our group and Manfred and a feature the Germans could not contain. That meant that we would have a reasonable chance of escaping to the east if we considered our aims to be unobtainable.

Bill continued this long but most necessary briefing. 'We have warned Base of the enemy's intention and as the issue is made clear we shall keep them informed. The problem confronting them will be can they afford to send sufficient arms, and can it be done before we lose our DZs to the weather. We will have to try and find DZs in the neighbourhood of Sauris, a resort which may jeopardise our future. It's just as much our problem of course for upon it will decide whether we shall stay or evacuate. Have you any additions, George?'

'I've very little to add, Bill, just the immediate future. Manfred will remain for the time being where he is. Directly the Boche make a move, he will sabotage the communication system, tearing down telephone lines and destroying the bridges in his area, falling back on Sauris. Pat is already at Sauris, securing our accommodation and reconnoitring the locality. All of us, with the exception of Bill, Charles and Remus, will now join Pat. Remus and Henry will act as runners, although we have arranged lateral communication by radio and via Base.'

Bill added that he hoped providence was just around the corner for unless the group had a little charity soon, our combined operations would amount to nothing more than a topographical interlude at great expense to the public.

Bill asked if there were any questions. I asked what the POWs would do, Bill replied that he had spoken to them the night before, Davis had changed his mind and wished to join the sick trio. They were to be sent off to Gorizia and south to Italy via Jugoslavia.

It was still hoped that Georgiou would return, but this was a forlorn hope, he would never be seen again.

Bill walked down the road a short way with George and his party. The hotel seemed odd, strangely quiet with their departure. Maria and one of her daughters watched them as they went, standing with clasped hands in the doorway of the Sotto Corona. When they had disappeared from sight, Maria's eyes filled with tears, she waved vaguely, a delayed but final goodbye, seeing them still in mind, intuitively feeling that this was the last time. The Countess was still in her room, she would be surprised to find that her favourite had left without saying goodbye. No matter what happened there remained the household chores, Maria and her daughter left the doorway for the kitchen.

There was just the two of us for lunch, Remus lived nearby. I looked at Bill closely over the table; he was eating without tasting his food, his mind occupied, his eyes fixed while he thought about the future. When he had finished his meal, almost automatically, he lit a cigarette, blowing a cloud of blue smoke into the air and raising his head he appeared to search beyond the limits of the room. His cigarette burned low, leaving a grey deadened ash which broke off, scattering over his hand and on the table-cloth. He reached a conclusion, stubbing the end of his cigarette on a plate. He asked for a coffee, and Maria's eldest daughter returned pouring two cups before she left the room.

'I'm going to have another shot over the frontier tomorrow, Charles. I shall take Remus with me. If I leave in the afternoon, we can reach a farmhouse Remus has spoken of about 4am. It is a mile, not more, above Leisinger. I must find out what the feeling is over the other side and have one last attempt at finding a safe house. I should arrive back here by the morning after next. It's a long shot at this stage, but I have a feeling I might succeed.'

When at lunch, I had the opportunity of studying Bill for the first time. I was more interested in what he had said earlier in the morning than what he was.

His face was usually set in a serious mould but when he smiled, which was not often, his expression reflected an acute sense of humour. His eyes were misleading, they were kind, passive perhaps would describe them. They were, however, those of a man who looked at all sides of a picture. He was tall, broad-shouldered and not a person to be trifled with. We were to learn a lot about each other in the ensuing months.

Chapter Thirteen

Austria Remains a Closed Book

It was after 2 o'clock on the following day, Maria was anxious to provide a meal, I knew the Major wouldn't be too much longer, so I asked her to wait a little while. It seemed as if he had been away for a week. The character of the village had changed, perhaps it was my imagination, but everything was too peaceful to be true. The war was a long way off and time stood still. I had been for a walk to Frassenetto during the morning; there were few people about, and those I saw were working. The feeling was strange, as if I were on a holiday that I couldn't afford. I didn't bother to walk into the village, I could see all that there was to see from a hundred yards away. The Province was dotted with places such as this one. The people seemed to spend their life gathering fodder, feeding it to a goat or a cow, and waiting for the animal to produce the milk from which they made cheese and butter for cooking. That was the curriculum during the hours of daylight anyhow. There were a surprising number of deformed creatures; the women worked extremely hard.

The church was opposite the hotel, its ponderous bell sounded the half-hour. The belfry had a marked place of importance in village life. It set the people to work, it rang the Angelus, reminding them of their spiritual duties, I thought it odd at first when they paused for a moment's reflection, it marked the end of their daily labours.[1] On Sundays it called them to church. Very few villages could boast of a municipal building, but the smallest contained a church around which its existence seemed to focus. Life was simple but very much in earnest. Bill returned.

He had a quick wash and asked Maria to wait just a moment longer before serving food, Bill wanted Remus to eat too. Lunch was not a success. The meal was well cooked, and we were hungry. There was a lack of diverting conversation. I saw that Bill was disappointed but not prepared to admit it, at least not just then. We had a glass of red wine with the meal, good wine, it was Pesita, made locally and fortunately very plentiful, at a price! It occurred to me that life around us wasn't as simple as it looked, there were a great many shortages. We had taken to rolling our own cigarettes, using the leaves from nearby trees. With the arrival of autumn, they too would be scarce. Remus wiped his mouth on the back of his hand, eased his chair away from the table and excused himself, he was in need of sleep.

Bill asked if there had been any traffic from Base, I told atmospherics had been bad, but I heard them transmitting there was no traffic. 'I would like to prepare a message for Base. You may as well hear the result of my reconnaissance.' Bill wondered if George's proposition would have borne fruit. He was sure that Georgiou would not turn up and Remus, although a brave fellow, beyond crossing the frontier there was nothing else he could be used for. He wouldn't stay over the border for longer than 24 hours, not that he could be blamed for that, the people had such a dread of the Gestapo and the Gendarmerie. No one would give him cover under their roof, so we had a problem. He had to have time to compose his message to Base, he wanted it to go in sequence as things had taken place, and he had to consider the context of the message that would be interpreted 300 miles away.

Bill gave a rather detailed view on Austria saying that it was incalculable with a background that differed from all other countries in Central Europe. It had been the first to be overrun by the Nazis and the seeds of Nazism. The German regime was not going to take any chances of failure of those 'seeds' to grow to fruition. They introduced a flourishing period of brutality and recruited most of the youth of the country into the Wehmacht, hastily despatching them to Finland and when the Eastern Front opened up under the 'Crusader Guise' appealing to the faithful to take up the cross against the Communist menace, and so the greater part of Austrian manhood was conscripted. Needless to say, those that remained were the aged and the Nazi faithful. The rural areas and agricultural districts had a preponderance of women, very few men, and an active system of policing. The few industrial centres which were largely in the capital and Wiener Neustadt were not possible to penetrate and, in any case, were largely operated by inducted labour. The areas open to our group contain only womenfolk and aged men who have to maintain a productive target or else!

Austria had remained a closed book for the past five years, any transmissions that we sent to Base will be studied by men who probably had an intimate knowledge of Austria pre-war. Bill emphasised that he did not make a bland comment when saying this was a drawback, on the other hand one could not help remembering Vienna and Salzburg before they were overrun, the people were the atmosphere, kindly, humorous, stimulating, old-fashioned, not old-fashioned, perhaps clinging to their gay past; their outlook and that of our own had much in common, it was anything but totalitarian. It is difficult to understand that all that wonderful atmosphere, so very much the people, had been temporarily banished. Bill continued saying that we were the mirror, he did not wish to give them a distorted image, and that he could only report what he had seen, his report would be based upon recent experiences and he asked that I should hear it first, he wanted a second opinion.

I reflected on this as Bill continued his tale; before proceeding to the frontier, he had looked in at Pierebeck, George and he had visited the chalet there once. They had plenty of time and Bill proposed to make the crossing in darkness, it being shortly after midnight when they crossed over and were into Austrian territory. They hadn't intended going near Leising again, but, unfortunately, they lost their way. They thought it best to wait for daylight so they could orientate themselves. This they did by laying in a copse. It was just as well they did, if it hadn't been so damp, they would have fallen asleep. Just before dawn a slight drizzle fell, and Remus suggested that they sought the cover of a barn. They were about to move when they saw two Forestry Gendarmerie emerging from the cover of a wood about 300yd beyond them. Bill thought their movements were a little cautious, otherwise he may have risked a conversation with them. Instead, they watched them pass. When they reached open ground, one stood still, while the second, carefully observing his front, walked slowly forward for approximately 200yd. Bill was intrigued by this, but progressively wary. Finally, they both stood still, listening, and again surveying the area. They waited 5 minutes after they had passed from view before they risked moving on. Glancing at the map, they realised that they were well off route and near to Leising.

The village had many small farms close by. After half an hour's walk they had observed one farm after another. They were all typical of each other with a large building, a farmhouse and a barn for tractor or cattle combined and a couple of smaller outhouses with a dilapidated low, stone wall surrounding them. At the time of their arrival at one, they saw an old woman walk from the house carrying a milking bucket. Hearing their approach, she stood still. At first, she was curious, wondering who they were, then she put her bucket down and walked quickly back to the house. Remus called to her it must have sounded reassuring because she halted again. With restored confidence, she joined them at the stone wall.

Living in a remote spot such as this was, one soon becomes familiar with the everyday passer-by; the look in her face conveyed to Bill a certain anxiety, coupled with the knowledge that Remus and Bill were strangers and perhaps not to be trusted. There was little point in beating about the bush; in addition, he wished to sound her reactions, Bill told her that he was an English officer and was in need of rest. She wasn't disturbed, at least not at first, she studied Bill closely, her eyes covering him from head to foot. She saw their clothing was wet, she abruptly terminated the examination and invited them into the farmhouse. This looked promising.

The kitchen was warm. Bill and Remus took off their coats, placing them on chairs near the fire. The walls were covered with shooting trophies, antlers, small and large. The woman busied herself preparing a hot drink. While the milk heated on the stove, they heard her climb the stairs. Returning shortly, she made them a steaming hot cup of cocoa, placing an additional cup on the table. Her husband, a man very much older than his wife, made his way laboriously down the stairs, he walked with the aid of a stick. If anything, he was the more worried of the two. Gruffly he greeted them, 'Grüss Gott!' Sitting at the table, he pulled open a drawer from which he took his pipe and tobacco. Remus took a lighted twig from the fire and offered it to him. The old man seemed content to sit quietly without making conversation, a simple indication of his reluctance to sit with them. Drawing on his pipe and blowing small puffs of smoke out of the corner of his mouth, he watched them speculatively.

Bill continued, 'Several times I tried to draw him into conversation, but he had made up his mind not to encourage our stay any longer than was necessary and within the bounds of courtesy. He would simply nod or curtly voice agreement. Hopefully, I persevered waiting for the appropriate moment to bid for accommodation, but he remained adamantly opposed to offer the slightest sign of encouragement. He finished his smoke and knocked the pipe on the stone floor; I felt we had outlived our stay. His wife had managed to remain in the kitchen putting the room in order and now she too waited for us to proceed on our way. It was futile putting the question to them, they wanted no part of us; I hadn't made the purpose of our visit clear and without doubt they were shrewd enough to contemplate our reasons.'

Bill realised that the time was not ripe for them meddling in subversive activities or harbouring those who would. They got their jackets and prepared to leave. The old couple did not breathe a sigh of relief, but the accompanying thoughts were there. Leaving the farm, they made their way back to the frontier.

Bill said there was not much more to tell, they saw nothing of importance on the return journey, a long way off, they saw two other Forestry Gendarmerie, it may even have been the same pair they had seen earlier.

If the two had visited a hundred farms in the area, Bill felt the result would have been the same. Satisfied with having told me his tale he said, 'It is the essence of this recce that I must now precis. Have you a message pad handy? I think we will set to work.'

I went to my room and brought back a message pad. 'What did you make of my tale, Charles?' Bill remarked.

'Well, Sir, as you say, I think that your chances would have been the same wherever you had stopped over there. There just are not the men for one thing and if there had been, I think we would have heard a lot sooner from Georgiou,' I said.

Bill said the signal must convey the atmosphere all too clearly prevalent at that farmhouse. Base must accept it as a general consensus of the prevailing conditions here. 'Got your pencil ready, Charles, here it is then.'

THIS SITREP BASED ON PERSONAL RECCES STOP CONVINCED LOCAL AUSTRIAN OPINION SYMPATHETIC BUT IMPROBABLE THAT THEY WILL GIVE ACTIVE SUPPORT STOP JURGO STILL ABSENT CONSIDER HE IS NOW PRISONER STOP SAFE HOUSE AS YET UNOBTAINABLE STOP WILL CONTINUE TO OPERATE FROM AVOLTRI UNTIL POSITION DETERIORATES WHEN WILL MOVE TO SAURIS. ENDS.

I asked if he had anything to include for Manfred or George, he said that he had not and that I should get to work on this message with no alterations to its content. Bill then went off to get some sleep with the instruction I should wake him at dinner time.

In contrast with the warm bright morning when the peaks of Mount Tuglia and Chiadin were sharply defined against a background of pale blue, the afternoon winds brought rain and cloud, limiting visibility. Evening was in consequence premature, an inclement shroud of darkness falling over the whole district aggravated by white flashes of fork lightning, following which were giant peals of thunder, rumbling with perpetual ferocity like a continuous bombardment. I ran to my room to close the windows. The torrential rain beat a metallic tattoo on the roof and rebounded off the windowsill into the room; already a small puddle lapped at the carpet.

Returning to the parlour below, I found Pat discarding his sodden ground sheet. He had reached Rigolato when the storm started, he had run almost all the way from there. He looked to hang up and dry his ground sheet. He said, 'The Bosch have commenced their clearance drive. At least they have assembled in two large groups, one at Tolmezzo and the other around Spilimbergo. It looks very much as though they will march up the road via Arta and Paluzza to Timau, fanning out east and west from Paluzza to Comeglians through Raviscletto to the west and towards Pontebba in the east. The other arm from Spilimbergo will make firstly for the Meduna valley, following it to the Tramonte and thereafter parallel to the Tolmezzo force, northwards.'

This looked as though the Germans planned to occupy all the villages along the main roads. Pat replied, he thought there were enough of them, their objective would be to corner the Partisans within certain areas, drive them into the woods. Having thus cleared the roads, the approaching winter would force the Partisans into activity if only to obtain food. The Germans would be on the lookout for odd stragglers intending to wander back to their villages. By the end of October, winter will have made its presence felt; the Bosch would increase their vigilance and try to eliminate the movement. In short, the Germans would clear the roads, contain the Partisans and mop-up.

I asked Pat if he thought Manfred would move to Sauris. He felt Manfred was enjoying himself, impeding their progress. With what explosives remained, he would destroy bridges and telephone systems, falling back on Sauris as a last resort. Another major and wireless operator had landed at Tramonte two nights before to help in the formation of the Garibaldi-Osoppo Partisan Division. The Partisan leaders had met Manfred and the new major, verbally co-ordinating their future liaison. It remained to be seen if the combination would co-operate in action. I suggested that it was a bit late in the day to send another team into the field, fewer talks and lots of stores would ease the Division's birth in my view. Pat said that was true to a degree, but he felt Manfred had sold the idea to Base before the Boche had concentrated his security forces. His intention was sound enough and he would have required additional help. They would need more stores otherwise they would be doomed to failure. As soon as the weather cleared, there was to be a high-level delayed drop, about seven plane loads. They were intended for George, but should they arrive, Manfred would distribute them to the Division, the new DZ near Sauris being used for the drops.

He spoke of this new DZ; it was extremely high up and had been permanently covered in low cloud. As the planes would fly over in formation, it was suggested they use the delayed drop method. The load being deposited 3,000 or 4,000ft above the DZ. It had been tried before with successful results. I thought this would be great to observe and if the locals saw it, a tonic to them, there would be more than 200 'chutes in the air at the same time.

It was time give Bill a knock and retire to the lounge, Maria had arrived, and dinner would be imminent. Pat asked me for the loan of soap and a towel and would join us shortly.

Chapter Fourteen

We are Taken Prisoner

The next fortnight were days of expectancy and dual anticipation; although it was now apparent that Georgiou had fallen foul of trouble, we wishfully cherished a faint flicker of hope that he would, like the prodigal, return. Meanwhile rumours spread through the villages, paces ahead of actual events, each more wildly exaggerated, carried on a crest of fertile imagination, forcing us to produce the map and plot and replot the clearance drive through the Provinces, which was now three weeks old. The consensus of opinion now circulating Avoltri alternated considerably. The inhabitants had remained shielded from the fortunes of war in the personal sense, mildly speculating its progress on the various fronts. Individuals who suffered the loss of a near relative were naturally awakened to the utter futility and horror of war and mourned the loss accordingly. But the Partisan picture for them was more exciting and very much alive, a new phase of warfare more directly affecting the people and places in close proximity to themselves. German counter action against Partisan activity, the destruction of villages was a subject of serious and general contemplation. It was expected therefore that the latest developments would arouse their interest in no mean fashion, since Forni Avoltri now lay in the path of the SS, who from all accounts were rapidly spreading northwards. What would they leave in their wake? Several villagers, including our acquaintance the Countess, evacuated, seeking shelter in the nearby mountain malgas. Such was their fear that they were not leaving anything to chance or the last moment. Studying their plight made us conscious of our own. Pruning successive rumours, we calculated that the SS had cleared the main road running between Tolmezzo and Timau, while, as anticipated, they had fanned out east and west from Paluzza, taking in their stride the town of Comeglians, 17km south of our present location. Within the past 24 hours, local Garibaldi had successfully captured the German post at Sappada, killing two German officers and taking more than a hundred Austrian prisoners. This action would certainly determine an SS drive north from Comeglians, an indication we fatefully accepted. Jubilation that accompanied the victory over Sappada, long awaited though it had been, was to be short-lived. We watched the Austrians as they were herded through the streets of Forni. I remembered a remark the Countess had made; the prisoners were assuredly a collection of bewildered old men, finding the march extremely tiresome. It was difficult to decide which of the two elements were the more pathetic, these conscripted degenerates or their proud custodians. We had had almost the exclusive use of the Sotto Corona parlour until now, when the conquering Garibaldini filled it to capacity and the wine flowed freely. Frequent toasts were called amid the swim of boasts and banter even the Allies remembered in passing, a toast to the successful prosecution of the war was washed down with the dregs of one of many glasses. It was a memorable occasion.

Awaiting the early hours of the new day, I listened to the hubbub and celebrations peter out, the wine had lost its sparkle, its flavour growing stale in the mouths of most, leaving a village drowsy with sleep and contemptuous of the morn, come what may. Arm linked in arm, by twos and threes, they staggered to their homes, boisterous with the potent alcohol inside them and temporarily forgetful of the encroaching enemy, 'for today we live and tomorrow we scamper,' I thought, as their receding footsteps filtered into the silence of the night. Completing my radio appointment with Base, I packed ready for a hasty withdrawal and so to the warmth of bed and the realm of dreams, paying little heed to my own forecast.

Bill's hurried movement through the passage awoke me. 'Be as quick as you can, the SS have reached Pierebeck; they've crossed over the mountains from Timau, there's not a moment to lose. Meet me downstairs when you are ready. I'll be at the main entrance.'

His news was more effective than a cold shower, I was very much awake, but a trifle confused as I listed the items to carry with me. Rucksack, radio, do not forget the cipher pad on the table, any scraps of paper lying around, haven't got much time. At Pierebeck are they? That's 10 minutes' walk from here at the most. One last look-around. Oh, yes, my pistol and belt, ready? Now to join Bill.

Stepping out into the road, Bill was nowhere to be seen. Putting my radio and rucksack down, I waited, then remembered my wallet and diaries which were in the table drawer of my room. I rushed back to retrieve them, returning to the road to find Bill in the process of taking up the radio. 'I'll carry this for a start. Come on, this way!' he said.

We ran up the main street and turned left, there we saw two old women frantically waving and pointing to an alley, at the entrance of which they stood. Following their instructions, we hurried on, finally passing the last house not far from which ran the River Piave. A plank lay spanning the narrow part of the River, on the other side stretched 200yd of pasture.

There was a mule-track we had to follow. Bill had been this way before. It led up the slopes of Mount Tuglia. Once on the track we would be under cover and able to relax. A final spurt, Bill clarifying the route in between each breath of air, changing the radio from one hand to the other every 50yd. 'This radio is a damned weight, who the hell would have designated it portable other than the designer?' The track rose steadily, we had reached the cover of the woods. We could afford to walk now. For the best part of an hour we climbed in silence conserving both breath and energy, occasionally snatching a hasty glance at the village which now appeared in miniature below us. We hadn't noticed any sign of the Boche entering the village. We decided we would stop and have a look further on. Bill said, 'At a time like this I would have a bout of the "squitters", it will be a case of having to stop shortly, I feel another spasm coming on.'[1] I replied that it must be the water as I was having some trouble in that direction too. Bill couldn't wait any longer and choosing a site with suitable scrub, we relaxed for some minutes. We observed the village through swaying branches of foliage. The place appeared to be deserted, ah, but wait a minute, we looked behind the village on the road leading to Sappada and there was a group of twenty men or more wandering along the road. We could not see if they were carrying arms and then, at that moment, we heard the excited barking of dogs on the track below us. Without bothering to pull our rucksacks on our backs, we broke from cover and ran on along the track. A further 300yd brought us to a stream which crossed the mule-track. We walked through it, finally reaching the bare heights of Tuglia. The radio was hanging heavily, a terrible weight pulling my arm painfully. 'I think we shall have to hide the radio if we are to run for it, Sir, it's a handicap.' We now climbed steeply the last few hundred feet over the crest, the tip of the saddle-shaped feature. The barking of the dogs had ceased.

From this point it was possible to see Sappada, a town with as many houses as Forni Avoltri but covering a larger area. Our interest was not focused on the town, however, we were more interested in the route over which we had recently passed. The weather was mild, a recurring gust of wind sweeping the grass flat, still no one appeared below us. We decided to stop and have a bite to eat at a malga that was snuggled into a hollow of the saddle. We were hungry, we had been on the move, at times quite strenuously, for 2½ hours.

The malga was a long, squat, grey stone building. Recently it had housed cattle. Interior and exterior were soft with mud. A brook crossed the hollow, we sat down near it. Bill took out the map. There were several routes we could take, we deliberated over which one. I had noticed a red cross, painted on a rock just over from where we were. I told Bill and said, 'On this map, if you look closely you can see a series of red crosses passing over Mount Entralais. They finish about a mile from the village of Pesaris, that's the most direct route if we are heading for Sauris.' Bill examined both the map and the rock. He gave me a piece of barley sugar and said that we would follow the crosses. Pesaris was about halfway from where we were to Sauris, we would cross the road and climb Mount Pieltinis from where we could see the village. We decided to deposit the radio near the rock and then carry on.

Three-quarters of an hour later we had reached Entralais; the southern slopes were precipitous. We eased ourselves down on our rumps, paying little heed to the slow progress thus made, following the lines of least resistance, and making use of every hand or foothold. In the space of this circuitous descent, I lengthened the distance between us, finding a narrow ledge and path which led to a grassy slope some 20ft below. I had reached the slope before Bill found the ledge. Farther down, perhaps 300ft away, was a small hut. Still farther in the distance, near the base of the re-entrant, into which we were descending, I could see another group of three wooden buildings. Thus occupied, I had paid little attention to Bill. Turning, I was just in time to see him miss his footing and fall off the ledge 20ft above, landing a short distance from me with a hollow thump. He lay face downwards, obviously in great pain.

I turned him over and asked if he could feel anything broken. 'I think my ankle is broken, take off my boot,' he replied with difficulty. Taking off his right boot; I felt his ankle, which was sound enough, although it had already started to swell. 'Nothing wrong with the ankle, nothing serious that is, Sir, it has started to swell a bit, any other pains?'

He complained of pain in the small of his back but added that he would be alright in a minute or two.

I stood up and looked towards the three small buildings at the foot of the mountain, they were about 3,000ft below. 'If you can make your way to the hut at the bottom of this near slope, Sir, I'll go on down to the village and enlist some help, we'll have you down in no time.' Bill remained flat on his back, one hand resting on his forehead, his face reflected the pain afflicting him, 'Yes, yes, alright, I'll manage, you go ahead. I'll wait at the hut for your return.'

I was glad I had suggested this policy, for reaching the end of the grass slope I found there was yet another steep rocky descent and then a sheer drop. Looking right and left, I noticed a water chute, I slide with the water into a pool several feet below. The rest of the way was easy going. Within the hour, I had reached the huts.

Eating their evening meal, were four Garibaldini. I explained in brief what had occurred and two of them set off to collect the Major. The others offered me a bowl of soggy polenta. In less than 2 hours they carried the Major into a hut, where they placed him on an ill-kept bed. He looked faint, his face a sickly white. As he was placed on the bed, he managed a weak smile and murmured, 'Well, I made it.' He refused the polenta preferring to sleep, he was badly shaken.

The Garibaldinini settle down for the night in the next-door hut. To begin with a wood fire burned in the grate casting a red glow, the shadows licking the interior of the hut feverishly as the flame played on the wood disintegrating in the grate. Bill slept more peacefully. Sitting in front of the fire, I passed over the day's events, such as they were, wondering what had happened in Forni Avoltri after we had left. We were as helpless as two flies in the bottom of a pail, here we were at the base of a valley just as devoid of help. The night was hollow, deep, with only one disturbing movement outside, the flowing stream behind the huts. The last ember died; the night without was a shade lighter than inside the hut. Apart from the fleas which had a particularly venomous bite, we passed a comfortable night. Bill still lay very still when I awoke next morning, the memorable 13 October. The Garibaldini had left. Standing outside the huts surveying the road, I judged it to be about a thousand feet below us. Pesaris must be round the west bend, roughly a mile away. Sauris must still be 15km ahead, and a stiff climb at that. Interrupting these observations, several staccato bursts of light automatic scattered echoes wildly up and down the valley. The shots issued from the direction of Pesaris. I returned quickly to the hut. Bill did not feel too good albeit he was now awake, he enquired about the shooting.

I concurred that was the case, I decided I would speak to the family in the hut across the way, I would find out what was happening.

Inside the hut were two people, they also had heard the firing. The man sat in a chair near the table, where he had recently partaken of a meal, the woman stood behind him. They had heard my approach and waited with a forlorn expression. I may have been the hangman inviting them to take a last walk. The man, his voice shaking with fear, hesitatingly bid me good morning, his whisper barely reached me, they waited for me to speak. I said

'Good morning, I am an Englishman. You have no reason to be frightened of me.' I hoped that my words were decipherable.

'Why do you remain here? It is not good for us if you stay,' the man replied. 'Leave us quickly.' I said, 'Have no fear, my friend is injured, he can't walk. I need your aid if I am to take him to Sauris, otherwise we are forced to stay here.'

'No, I can't help you, it isn't possible to cross the road. The Russians are patrolling it, you would never be able to get across. Leave us, Mother of God! Hide in the woods, they will come here soon, and you must not be found with us, please go.' The man was sullen, in normal times I visualised that he was a disagreeable character, overcome as he was now, by fear, I was wasting my time talking to him.

I returned to Bill telling him that we could not expect any help from that family, they were scared stiff. The old boy had said the road was patrolled by Ruskis, they had already occupied Pesaris and he was of the opinion they would pay a visit here very soon, and it sounded like someone walking to the huts right then.

I looked out and saw three Partisans wearing green scarves, making their way along the path that led to the huts. They were of the Osoppo movement. They entered the hut. I hadn't seen them before, but they recognised the Major. 'Ah, the Major, what is wrong eh? He looks bad.'

Bill who had recovered sufficiently after his night's rest eased himself into a sitting posture and questioned the newcomers, the effort was painful, and he subsided while they gave an account of their experiences.

They had been forced to flee from the Tramonte valley and then finally from Sauris. Everything, they said, was finished. 'Pig of misery, how we have walked this week.' Their morale was sadly shattered, each in turn added to the commentary, an excuse for the general disintegration of the area Partisan movement. Having hidden their weapons which were useless to them without ammunition, they were now returning to their native village of Forni Avoltri. 'Your friends have left the Friuli. One Major intends to leave by aircraft for southern Italy, the others are on their way to Jugoslavia, everyone must go into hiding.² What else can we do? There are thousands of Russians commanded by the SS, they are pouring into the valleys and villages. Mother of Mercy, what are we to do? We have nothing with which to defend ourselves, perhaps we shall find that we cannot return to our native village. The Germans are hard, certainly. It is a hard struggle and the winter is nearly upon us.'

There was only the SS at Sauris, it was difficult to know where to go. At this stage I perceived that we could expect little assistance from these

1. The Castello Ceconi at Pielungo, the team fled from here during an SS raid shortly after parachuting into the Friuli. The castle was destroyed by the Nazis and rebuilt after the war. (*Shutterstock.com*)

2. The Coroneo prison, Trieste. Barker was held prisoner here. (*Carlo Larosa*)

3. Fr Cortese. (*Barker family*)

This certificate is awarded to

Cortese, Padre

as a token of gratitude for and appreciation of the help given to the Sailors, Soldiers and Airmen of the British Commonwealth of Nations, which enabled them to escape from, or evade capture by the enemy.

H.R. Alexander
——————————
Field Marshal,
Supreme Allied Commander,
Mediterranean Theatre

1939-1945

4. Certificate awarded posthumously to Fr Cortese in recognition of the assistance he gave Allied prisoners in escaping. *(Barker family)*

5. In 1946 Barker gave the Allied Screening Commission details of the treatment of Fr Cortese by the Gestapo. They considered the assistance rendered by Cortese to British prisoners and this document forms part of the evidence. It is unclear who the recipient of the posthumous commendation (handwritten note at the top of the document) was. *(Barker family)*

Recommendation for POSTHUMOUS COMMENDATION (Cert 17) sent to W.O. Ref ASC(s)/Aw/5/BM/5.6.7. on 12 Nov 46. MD.

ALLIED SCREENING COMMISSION

CLAIM SUMMARY

	CHECKED BY:
	Date
	A) Rome Org
	B) App. "A" 8/8/46
	C) P.W. List
	D) Orig. Docts.
	E) Other 26/1/47

CLAIM No. 52974
see also 53044.

CLAIM REC'D 21/1/46

CLAIM SETTLED

CLAIMANT'S NAME CORTESE PADRE

CLAIMANT'S ADDRESS CHIESA San Antonio PADOVA (Padova)

PRISONERS ASSISTED

No.	Name	Rank	Unit	Period		
62467	SCOTT H.W.	P/O	✓		A) B) C) D) E)
2379	IRETON G.O.	P/O	✓		A) B) C) D) E)
	BARKER E.C.	Sgt.			A) B) C) D) E)
2687	BROWN W.	Sgt	✓		A) B) C) D) E)

(Continue on page III of cover)

See Swiss helpers book.

VALUE OF FOOD AND LODGING SUPPLIED . . . . .

VALUE OF CLOTHING SUPPLIED . . . . .

	Claimed	Recommended	Paid

6. (*Opposite, above*) Garibaldi and Osoppo commanders, 1944. Left to right: unknown, Alfredo Berzanti 'Paolo' of the Osoppo Command, Candido Grassi 'Verdi', Commander of the Osoppo, Colonel Emilio Grossi 'Vincenzi' of the Garibaldi-Osoppo Unified Command and Lino Zocchi 'Ninci', Commander of the Garibaldi del Friuli Division Group. 'Verdi' was, among others, one of the group which assisted Manfred Czernin and the SOE team.
(*ANPI Archives, Udine, Italy; FFANPIUD_1006*)

7. (*Opposite, below*) The members of the National Liberation Committee of the Province of Udine together with military commanders of Garibaldian and Osovan formations, Udine, 5 May 1945. Back row, standing, left to right: Melchiorre Chiussi (Action Party), President of the Province, Colonel Emilio Grossi 'Vincenzi' of the Garibaldi-Osoppo Unified Command, Giovanni Cosattini, Mayor of Udine, an unidentified person, Aldo Cuttini (Italian Communist Party), Vice Prefect, Giacomo Filaferro (Italian Liberal Party), Alfredo Berzanti (Christian Democracy), Candido Grassi 'Verdi', Umberto Zanfagnini (Christian Democracy); squatted, left to right: unidentified person, Carla Cosattini (Action Party), Agostino Candolini (Christian Democracy), Prefect of Udine; seated against the rock: Lino Zocchi 'Ninci'.
(*ANPI Archives, Udine, Italy; FFANPIUD_1280*)

8. (*Above, left*) Squadron Leader Manfred Czernin, DSO, MC, DFC. (*Battle of Britain, London Monument*)

9. (*Above, right*) Captain Roderick Hall, OSS. (*CIA Online Archive*)

10. (*Below*) General Vlassov. A Russian, he had several divisions of Russian and other nationality soldiers, including Britons, organised to fight against the Red Army.
(*Online: Vlassov and Russian Liberation Army*)

11. Major Barker with 'Barry'. (*Barker family*)

12. Mary Barker, wife of Major Charles Barker. (*Barker family*)

13. The Barkers' two children, Sarah and Charlie. (*Barker family*)

14. Captain Smallwood's father's letter to Mary Barker. (*Barker family*)

Trieste, August 29th, 1945.

Dear Mister Charles,

A few days ago I have received with the greatest pleasure your kind letter of the 13th of May last, for which I have to thank you very much. I feel very happy indeed seeing that in spite of time, distance and many sufferings I am still remembered by you. I always remember you too and it couldn't be otherwise, for I shall for ever keep in my mind and in my heart your personality and your character which I have been able to know so well during your stay in the prison of the "Coroneo". I remember your gay disposition even among so many grieves, your deep piety and your desire for a frequent Holy Communion. You have, therefore, always lived near the Lord and that is why you are to-day allowed to enjoy the reward of freedom and of your being again restored to your family.

In Trieste we have gone through very bad times indeed, but now we hope that thanks to the Allied Nations we shall be able to look forward to a satisfactory conclusion.

During the weeks when the Jugoslavians of Tito held the government of Trieste, I was not allowed to continue my work as chaplain of the prison, but now everything goes on as before. Unfortunately, however, all the sacred materials for the Service have been stolen from the chapel. We must bear patience.

If you have an opportunity of seeing your three fellow-prisoners, please remember me to them.

To you, dear Mr. Charles, I send my very best wishes for happiness and prosperity in the name of the Lord.

With kindest regards I am

yours affectionately

Sac. Luigi Carra
Trieste, Via 30 Ottobre 13.

15. Fr Carra's letter to Charles, 20 August 1945. (*Petra Vide Ogrin*)

...greatness, may not I grant first you

Pleased to say I am fairly fit. It seems that the cold
weather has passed on and therefore conditions are
more bearable. Don't think that I shall ever get
used to the caged up atmosphere of prison life, but
I guess there is consolation in the fact that it
can't last forever. I try to keep the brain active
reading and studying Italian, I trust I shall
have a few interesting tales when we next
meet. How is life at Bournemouth these
days. Do you find the days slip by quickly?
Strange to say I do, they simply fly by! The
reason being I pass so many hours in the
company of the "Sandman" (I still remember
my Grimms' Fairy tales). I think of you
every day, along with Mary & Bernard. 'Twas
a happy day we spent together, but all too

short. Still I have made plans for another
weekend at Bournemouth, that is if your still
at Bournemouth by the time I attain my
liberty! Have you made any plans for the future
- its difficult to encourage ideas for the future
in these dark days; I find pleasure in it though.
Well, cheeryho, lots of love, Your loving uncle. Charles.

16. Letter written in Stalag XVII A by Charles to his niece, Ann Lane. (*Barker family*)

Dr.Carl Bobleter,
at Present SALZBURG-Maxglan, Schwedenstrasse 7 bei Schäfer

to the British FSS-Officer (FSS 300) Lt.Barker. 2323541

Salzburg, July 22 1945.

Dear Lieutenant Barker,

Since our last talk and shake-hands on Holy Easter-days evening at Kaisersteinbruch the events ran very fast end took a very happy end. Francis and Walter White, all your friends and myself reached the American lines the 4th of May. According to the instructions by Major Smallwood F.White handed me over to the proper American authorities. I saw very thankful for it towards Major Smallwood and you. By this way I got again the opportunity to continue - now quite openly - my work for the Allied and so for a f Austria. At the moment I am employed as Austrian Legal Adviser to the USA.-Military Government at Salzburg(Land Legal Office).

Unfortunately that is very difficult in the American zone here. About 6 weeks ago I met a British Officer, Lt.Maynard, T.Force, at Salzbu to whom I handed over the personal diary of Brigadier Davies. The other diary you saw I gave to the British Major Robinson at Braunau I told to Lt.Maynard about you and the other Fsns-Troop-Officers who were at the "Hotel Kaisersteinbruch Apartment 13" He was very interested in you because you came in the Russiänhands. The evening he saw me again and told me that you had the others are back in England. I was very glad about it. About one weeks later he came back to Salzburg and wanted to see me in my office.Unfortunately I w not present. He told the American Soldier in my office that I can write a letter to Brigadier Davies through the CIC. I had the impression he cabled my name to Brigadier Davies and got some good information about me. Now, there are British Officers at Salzburg, one of them was so kind as to forward this letter to you.

I dont know where you are at the moment. If you are I would be so happy to see you. It would be very nice. We both are living under quite different circumstances as we did when I made your acquaintance. If it is settled as you told me that Major Smallwood and you will operate in your Service in Vienna, I would appreciate very much to work with you what you made me understand your service too. I am sure that the brothers White and Duguid wrote you about our adventurous journey to Braunau. I will never forget what the Both and Capt.Hyman habe done for me. I can say onl Frieds in need, friends indeed.

At the beginning of June an American Officer took me along in a Jeep to Feldkirch. I found my whole family in good health. And you? How are your parents and your fiancee? About my friends in Vienna and Mrs.Dr.Bodenstein I have no news. Others news about Vienna I have enough. It would be very kind if you could go and see her, when you are in Vienna before me.(Wien, I., Bartenstei gasse 13/III/13). When I am in Vienna, I wanted to introduce you and your interested Officers to some Austrians who were all this time really great friends of England, above all in the financial world.

I would be very pleased to see you one day at Salzburg for a long talk or let me know how you are going on.If you could arrange it to call me to your service in Vienna I would be very much obliged to you.

I beg you to extend my best wishes to Major Smallwood.

Yours sincerely

PS.
If you write to England, would you be as kind as to send my best greetings to Capt.Venables, Francis and Walter White and Duguid.

17. Letter from Dr Bobleter, aka Dr Briefe, to Charles Barker, 22 July 1945. (*Barker family*)

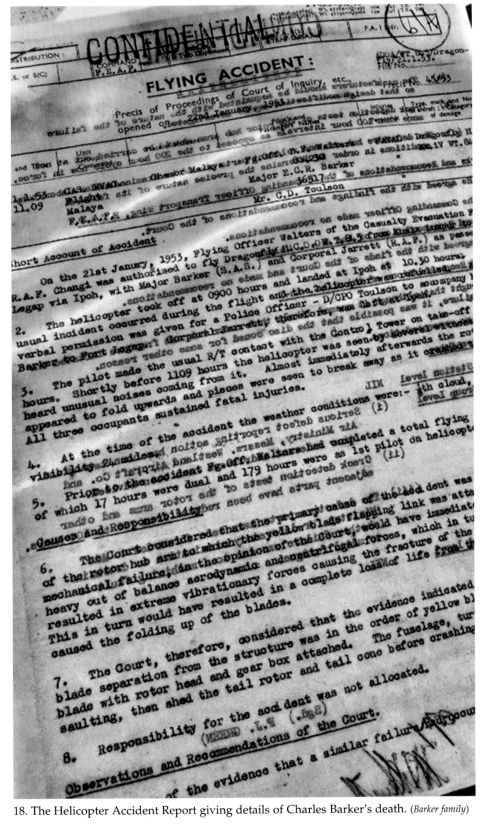

CONFIDENTIAL

FLYING ACCIDENT:

Precis of Proceedings of Court of Inquiry, etc.
opened on 22nd January, 1953.

Command F.E.A.F.	

11.09	Flight Malaya F.E.A.F.

Chemor Malaya
Major E.C.R. Barker
Mr. C.D. Toulson

Short Account of Accident

On the 21st January, 1953, Flying Officer Walters of the Casualty Evacuation Flight R.A.F. Changi was authorised to fly Dragonfly and Corporal Jarrett (R.A.F.) as passengers to Legap via Ipoh, with Major Barker (S.A.S.) and landed at Ipoh at 10.30 hours.

2. The helicopter took off at 0900 hours and landed at Ipoh. The helicopter was refuelled. Verbal permission was given for a Police Officer – D/CPO Toulson to accompany Barker to Fort Legap.

3. The pilot made the usual R/T contact with the Control Tower on take-off hours. Shortly before 1109 hours the helicopter was seen by several witnesses heard unusual noises coming from it. Almost immediately afterwards the rotor appeared to fold upwards and pieces were seen to break away as it crashed. All three occupants sustained fatal injuries.

4. At the time of the accident the weather conditions were:-
(i) visibility
(ii) Walters had completed a total flying

5. Prior to the accident F/O Walters was 1st pilot on helicopter of which 17 hours were dual and 179 hours were as 1st pilot on helicopter.

Causes and Responsibility

6. The Court considered that the primary cause of the accident was mechanical failure, in the opinion of the Court, would have immediately of the rotor hub arm to which the yellow blade flapping link was attached. This in turn would have resulted in a complete loss of life from the heavy out of balance aerodynamic and centrifugal forces causing the fracture of the caused the folding up of the blades. resulted in extreme vibrationary forces

7. The Court, therefore, considered that the evidence indicated that blade separation from the structure was in the order of yellow blade with rotor head and gear box attached. The fuselage, turning, then shed the tail rotor and tail cone before crashing saulting.

8. Responsibility for the accident was not allocated.

Observations and Recommendations of the Court.
... of the evidence ... that a similar failure ...

18. The Helicopter Accident Report giving details of Charles Barker's death. (*Barker family*)

19. Grave of Major Barker, BEM, Cherras Road New Christian Cemetery, Kuala Lumpur. (*Barker family*)

20. Medals belonging to Major Barker, BEM. (*Barker family*)

Major Barker, BEM. (*Barker family*)

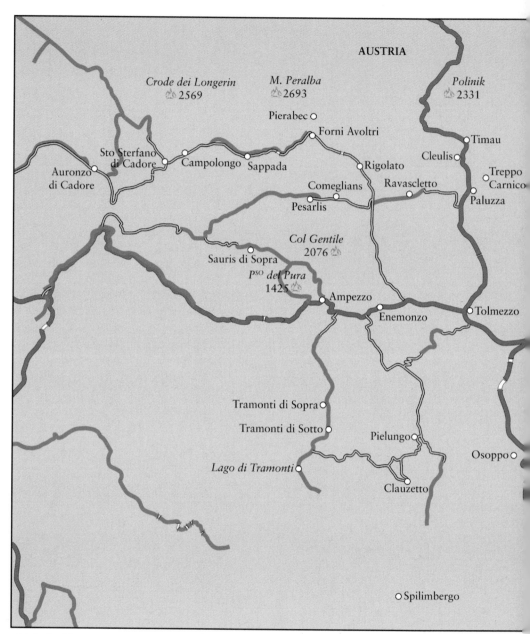

AUSTRIA

Crode dei Longerin 2569

M. Peralba 2693

Polinik 2331

Pierabec

Forni Avoltri

Timau

Cleulis

Sto Sterfano di Cadore

Campolongo

Sappada

Rigolato

Treppo Carnico

Auronzo di Cadore

Comeglians

Ravascletto

Paluzza

Pesarlis

Col Gentile 2076

Sauris di Sopra

Pso del Pura 1425

Ampezzo

Enemonzo

Tolmezzo

Tramonti di Sopra

Tramonti di Sotto

Pielungo

Osoppo

Lago di Tramonti

Clauzetto

Spilimbergo

22. Italy. The Province of Friuli. (*Michael Kelly*)

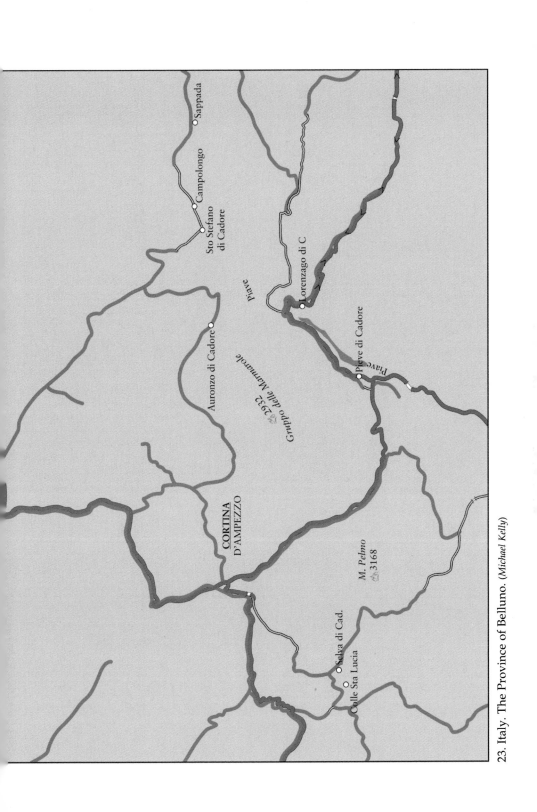

23. Italy. The Province of Belluno. (*Michael Kelly*)

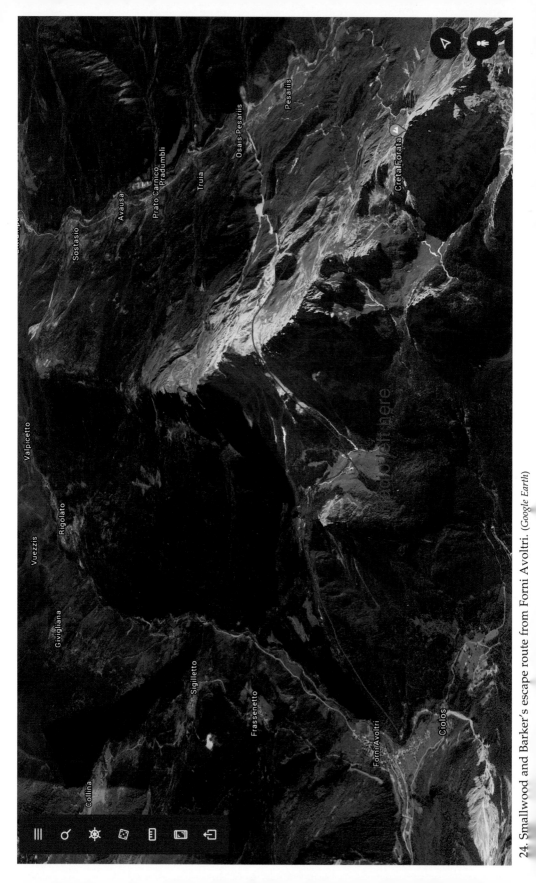

24. Smallwood and Barker's escape route from Forni Avoltri. (*Google Earth*)

fellows either, as far as they were concerned, it was very much the old adage, 'Blow you Jack, I'm in the lifeboat.' The conversation faltered for a moment, they looked at each other and then in chorus announced their departure. Backing out of the door, it was plain to see that they were ill at ease, for they blushed guiltily, once outside they broke away into the woods lest we detain them further.

I remembered in Greece a compatriot had said to me, 'Just you and me now Chas.' He had spoken for the sake of speaking, but it reflected his nervous state. I almost said the same to the Major at their departure. He appeared to have lost interest in them already. They were to be pitied rather than decried; it was useless feeling bitter.

'I think you had better have a shot at making your way alone, Charles,' the Major said. I was not prepared for this suggestion. He continued, while I sought an answer. 'It's no use, I can't walk, I shall be a handicap to you. On your own you stand a good chance of getting away. This map will enable you to find your way to the eastern parts of the Friuli. Lay low during the day and keep near to the road when you move at night; it shouldn't be difficult.'

I wanted to think, to try and find a solution, there must be a simple way out. 'I'll bury my diaries and the cipher pad, Sir, have you anything?' 'Yes, take this currency.' I walked up behind the huts carrying a shovel, which had been laying on the ground outside. Leaving the path, I walked 30yd into the wood and buried the articles, padding them over with loose scrub. The war was rapidly approaching a climax. Germany couldn't possibly hold out another month. I stood a fifty-fifty chance of getting back to southern Italy, a three-month journey on foot. What would happen to Bill? Strength in numbers, that's a point. If we were taken together, our stories might ring true. What a predicament to be in, all part of the game I suppose. A good soldier would obey instructions. If I went, I would continually kick myself for leaving him behind. We would only be prisoners for a month, perhaps two, they will not fight on German soil, they will throw in the sponge long before then, they must know that they are licked. It was also a distinct possibility that having been injured, Bill would be summarily executed if found alone. Finally, I considered that there were sufficient reasons for remaining with him. I returned to the hut.

'I've been thinking, Sir. You know this war isn't going to last very much longer. I'd probably get lost on my own anyhow. I think that it is time you saw a doctor.'

'What are you trying to say, Charles? Don't worry about me. They will find me here, unable to move, and they will do something about it.'

I replied, 'I'm not sure that it would pan out that way, Sir. That old man in the hut across the way would spare no effort giving you away if he thought it would save himself and family. They might speak to him first. I'm not very good at working things out the orthodox way and I have made up my mind that it would be better for us to remain together. I have always believed in strength in numbers. Let us wait and see what happens.'

Bill agreed and then he said he had lost the remnants of the emergency rations, perhaps the family would spare some.

The hut the Garabaldini had vacated was bare, there remained the family to approach; they had nothing or were not keen to encourage our stay, for the man spread his hands pleading that they could not spare a share of their meagre ration. His nervousness affected me strangely. I didn't wish to bargain with him though I carried the means of forcing the issue.

The midday sun reached its height. The afternoon passed by slowly. On the road I saw horsemen riding furiously towards Pesaris as though they intended to waylay someone. They wastefully released bullet after bullet from their weapons, the signal for many others to join the explosive glee from points widely circling the valley surrounding Pesaris. Towards evening, machine-gun fire was directed toward the mountain slopes some distance to the west of us. Several hundred voices carried on the evening breeze choking one or two shrieks, a forlorn objection of a terrified woman, probably being molested by the Russians at Pesaris.

'Sounds like fun and games in the village, Sir.' I said, Bill made no reply. He heard me but he seemed too fatigued to make any answer. I had felt his ankle but couldn't find a break. There was more than ankle trouble wrong with him, something must be disturbed internally. He wasn't looking so good. I didn't like the pallor of his cheeks. 'I think I will have to take you down there, Sir, you're not shaping up so well, what do you think?' He looked up, his face determined for a second, then his head slowly dropped to the makeshift pillow; his breathing was uneasy, short, sharp breaths, as though he received a stab in the ribs between each. In another hour it would be dusk. If they visited the hutments after dark, they wouldn't bother to ask questions first, they would probably fill the huts with lead. I thought now is the time to move one way or the other and away from them meant moving farther away from a doctor. 'Come on, Sir, put your boot on, we are going to move.' I pulled the boot on his foot and helped him into his jacket. Supporting him he rose to his feet and we moved from the hut in the direction of Pesaris. Leaving the woods for the bare slopes above the village, we moved slowly down, resting every 30yd. Just

3 minutes after leaving the hut a voice commanded us to stop. 'Alt,' there was no mistaking the business-like command or the levelled Schmeisser carried by the SS officer, 'Alt,' he repeated. Glancing over our shoulder while he remained still, his eyes moved left and right scanning the fringe of the woods from whence we had walked.[3] Releasing his right hand from the trigger momentarily, he signalled us to discard our weapons and empty our pockets. I toyed with the idea of taking this opportunity to use my revolver but considered the officer would have been quick to react with his Schmeisser. I tossed my revolver down. Walking towards us he motioned us back away from the spoils which he gathered into his open jacket. Positioning himself on our left, he ordered us to walk towards the village. As I was turning to lift Bill, the officer challenged sharply again, Bill had to proceed under his own steam. In a sitting position he pushed himself along the ground slowly. Eventually the Russian SS man allowed me to help the Major. Finally, we reached the village, now full of Russians, a convoy of carts blocking the main streets faced in the direction of Comeglians. We mounted the leading cart amid the excited notification along the line that the commander had captured two Englishmen. The carts moved off for Comeglians, proceeding slowly. Occasionally, an old Cossack walked alongside, staring at us in the fast receding light. One offered a tin of condensed milk, another a tin of sardines. One even said, 'Good man,' then hastily walked ahead.

Formation headquarters was situated in a hotel at Comeglians. The word had gone ahead, and our arrival was expected. We were taken into the tap room, now a guard room.[4]

Chapter Fifteen

Enemies

Brigade Headquarters was still in the process of being established when we arrived in Comeglians, the centre of much activity; line parties were attempting to string a cable from a pole opposite the hotel while carts laden with stores and tired bodies rolled slowly by. Sandy coloured Volkswagens, their lights illuminating the scene, whined hurriedly past, chasing men and animals into the curb. Parked vehicles were being unloaded into adjacent buildings, idle groups of Infantry lay on the pavement, huddled against the walls. The 'Vlasov Officer', our captor, handed us into the charge of a German feldwebel, a sallow-faced man dressed in a grey-green uniform and wearing a distinctive long-peaked cap and jackboots, a Schmeisser slung from his shoulder. We waited in the tap room for several minutes until receiving an order emanating from the lounge, the feldwebel led us across the unlit passage into the room occupied by the Brigade Operations Staff; a group of eight officers and one sergeant-major, who we later discovered was attached for interrogation duties, stood waiting. The sergeant-major was recognisable not simply by his malaria-tanned skin and gold-filled teeth, but by the emblems he wore on his collar and cap, silver skull and crossbones and extended 'Z's in each collar, denoting his association with the Gestapo, a point he made sure we understood in the initial stages of the interview. His whole manner and appearance would have left no doubt in our minds, even if he had chosen to overlook this significant pointer, for regardless of his inferior rank, during the interview that followed, he stood well to the fore asking questions or making us the objects of ridicule, invariably drawing supporting laughter from the remainder who stood in true military pose, fingers of one hand tucked inside their jackets, one hand placed behind their backs.

In their haste and search for information they overlooked the fact that we still remained together. Although questions were directed to Bill alone, it allowed me to follow the course and purpose of their initial queries.

We were unusual, a valuable find, it was plain to see that our capture had crowned a successful day's operations. The Commanding Officer, bald, bespectacled, a perfect replica of the celluloid interpretation of a

German officer I had seen many times portrayed in films, realised the error, he halted the proceedings and called the Sergeant of the Guard to return me to the tap room, where I waited under the watchful eye of the feldwebel who it seemed found me disagreeable company. Another 10 minutes passed before Bill joined me; as he uttered in passing, 'Remember! Keep your mouth closed.' The feldwebel, overhearing Bill's advice, screamed for silence, a faint flush rising in his cheeks emphasising the fervour with which he addressed us. The lounge door opened, and I was called forward. The company was engaged in animated conversation which ceased suddenly as though an unseen switch had compelled them to silence, they then faced me waiting for the sergeant-major to proceed.

He spoke with an American accent, the result of his long stay in New York where he had been a representative of the German Civil Airways. Walking to the middle of the room, he looked at me in silence for some seconds, his eyes examining my dress closely.

'What is your name and rank?' he asked curtly. I gave him the information. 'You understand, naturally, that you have been taken prisoner many miles from the front lines. I must ask you what you have been doing here in the Carnia, why are you here?'

'I am not bound to answer that question,' I replied.

'Curious,' he remarked, smiling towards the officers who listened attentively. Pointing to the insignia in his collar, a small silver, flash-like 'Z', he continued, 'You may have recognised these badges, do you know what they signify?' I thought they were badges of the Field Police I told him. Translating this reply, he caused another outburst of merriment which sounded hollow though the room was small. 'Not quite right. They mean that I am from the Gestapo. You were partially correct, we are police, but we are also very special police.' Pausing so that I could fully comprehend the difference he had taken care to underline, he concluded the introduction, adding, 'And we always obtain an answer to our question.'

'Now that we understand each other, let us proceed from the beginning once again. The officer wishes to know why you are here in Carnia?' Failing to receive an answer to his question, he addressed himself to the task in hand with more pronounced seriousness. 'If you choose to remain obstinate, I can assure you, you will be handed over to the Gestapo. We like dealing with people like yourself. Where are your identity documents?'

'When we were captured the officer took charge of them.' Turning sharply on one heel, he informed the Commanding Officer who detailed one of his subordinates to bring the documents without delay. In the interval while we waited for the departed officer's return, the Commanding

Officer adjusted his spectacles and read from a notebook, referring occasionally to points on a map which lay on the table. The interrogation had apparently interrupted an order group. Occasionally one officer would click his heels acknowledging a given instruction which was duly transferred into a notebook. The identity documents were produced. 'Where are the rest of your belongings? Very well, since you choose to remain obstinate, we shall not waste any further time here. Normally, you would be handed over to a prisoner-of-war camp, but it seems you have something to hide. We shall find out. Goodnight.'

Calling for the escort, I was conducted back to the tap room, where I now found Bill, lying on a stretcher. A vacant one was placed on the opposite side of the room for my benefit. We settled down for the night. The feldwebel sat behind the single table furnishing the room, taking his ration from a rucksack, and unravelling the greaseproof paper, he used a short bayonet to spread a potent-smelling cheese on some brown bread. Eating and carrying on a conversation with a member of the guard, he lost the odd crumb which fell onto the table. Nothing was wasted, however, for he retrieved each particle, licking his fingers. His cheeks bulged with each ravenous mouthful which he chewed energetically to the accompaniment of sucking sounds and a drum-like tempo which he beat on the table with the blade of the bayonet. Once he was called for, in his haste to comply, he knocked the chair over, cursing under his breath as he ran from the room. The operation was conducted evidently on a large scale, for the clatter of movement continued throughout the night, slithering hooves, racing engines, heated shouting, the general noises and tiresome turmoil of wearied troops on the move.

In the morning, the hotel keeper brought the guard commander a canteen of steaming ersatz coffee which he condescended to share with his prisoners. Breakfast was a hurried meal rushed in advance of the impending move. Slinging on his equipment, the feldwebel prefixed our independent visits to the lavatory briefly announcing 'Abort.' Assisting Bill to his feet we were marched outside where six Volkswagens were drawn up ready to escort us to Tolmezzo. Bill sat in the second, two civilians, probably informers the third, and I was ordered to sit in the fourth. The remaining vehicles contained the escort, with the officer commanding the convoy standing in front of the leading vehicle. We moved off.

Taking the Raviscletto road which led to Paluzza, the cars wasted no time, travelling at 40mph passing odd detachments who faced the convoy, raising their right hands in salute, 'Heil Hitler.' Every bridge had been blown along the route, but hastily constructed bypasses had been prepared. Raviscletto appeared to be deserted when we passed on the new road below it. There was no evidence of civil occupation in any village until we reached Tolmezzo, a garrison town in the lower foothills of the Carnic Mountains. Making a short halt near Paluzza, the journey lasted little more than 30 minutes. The streets of Tolmezzo were crowded, although there appeared to be a limited exhibition of goods in the shop windows. A military band played in the market square, but few people stood listening to the brassy rendering. We entered a building which was Field Police Headquarters, the site of our second interrogation. Two or three Field Police stood in the passage, a metal plaque hanging from their breasts indicating that they were on duty. One interesting feldwebel spoke to us for a few moments. He was the first human looking German we had met to date; not only did he ensure that we received a sandwich each, but he was able to converse without effort or raising his voice in guttural chant. He lived in Hamburg, the people there were very much like the English. It was notable that he had spent years in Dublin working for a shipping company.

There was something familiar about the prevailing atmosphere which ultimately revealed itself in its true form with Field Police Headquarters. As we had entered the town, I was aware of it but sitting in the passage watching the clerks go about their business and seeing the visitors come and go, here too was the common practice, a typical line of communication casualness, a picture of bureaucratic, unruffled method; there was plenty of time, no sense of urgency, everything could wait. No purposeful force urging the job in hand must be done quickly or catch phrase 'time saved saves lives', that particular demand ever present at the front line.

In turn, we were called to a small office put at the disposal of our second interrogator, a sergeant-major of the Field Police who, unable to speak English, was assisted by an Italian civilian enrolled for the occasion.

They made an odd pair. The German listened attentively throughout, but was in no great hurry, allowing his assistant to conduct the examination, while he made observations in his notebook. He kept the Italian on the right course, putting the questions he felt should be answered. The interpreter was extremely keen to please, offering doubtful advice prompted by a fear within him, as though his own freedom depended on the answers we gave.

'Awh, come on Johnnie, get it off your chest, these boys are smart, they know what goes on. The sooner you answer the questions, the sooner you will be sent to a prisoner-of-war camp, they tell me it's pretty good in the camps too. Every week a Red Cross parcel, plenty of games to keep you fit, you won't know there's a war on, believe me. He only wants the answer to a couple of questions, they ain't bothered about you a great deal. You can trust me 'cos I understand you. I bin t'London. I've laid the mosaic in your churches there, had a good time too. When the war come, they tell me I gotta go 'ome 'ere. I gotta house, wife and four kids 'ere in Tolmezzo, but, times are tough with little food or money. This war ain't no good t'no one.'

The German shifted uneasily in his chair, a single movement but a warning of his dwindling patience. Slowly, he thumbed the pages of his notebook, every action was deliberate, too painstaking for a common mannerism, but justifiably a means of checking his temper which was now overtaking his to-date methodical deliberations. He vented his irritation on the Italian who followed the lead set by the soldier becoming increasingly more objectionable.

The Italian started talking, 'Say, you gotta do better than this, the German is a bad son of a gun when he is treated bad, you ain't told him nothin'. You have t'say somethin' or you get what's comin' t'ya. Awh, come on Johnnie, its OK for you t'tell, what's it matter t'you now? They gotta nasty reputation down at Headquarters, these Gestapo boys, they're rough, you don't wanna end up down there. What d'ya say?'

The sergeant-major closed the interrogation, putting his notebook away in his pocket and lighting a cigarette, completely ignoring the Italian who looked as though he could have done with one. I re-joined Bill in the passage where we sat awaiting further developments.

An open troop-carrying vehicle pulled up in front of the building, two khaki-clad SS troopers jumping from the running board, Schmeissers slung from their shoulders, reporting to the NCO who had taken charge of the interrogation. Obeying his instructions, the soldiers escorted us to the waiting vehicle, which was to take us straight to Trieste, to Gestapo Headquarters, South-Eastern Europe. The driver drove recklessly, playing on his horn, in which it appeared, he had more faith than his brakes, scattering on-coming traffic into the side of the road. By the roadside, many slit trenches had been dug so that travellers could take cover from hostile aircraft which had been active recently, for we saw evidence of their destructive visits. The escort kept a wary watch above for the RAF who now paid frequent attention to this highway which carried reinforcements and stores from Austria to the Italian Adriatic front.

Forgetting the driver's dubious ability to control the vehicle, and disregarding the company with whom we travelled, the journey was quite pleasant enough for the weather was fine and the passing countryside refreshing, flat landscape in contrast with the mountainous regions we had lately operated in. Soon after dark, the cool breeze of evening drifted over-land from the Adriatic which drew closer with every turn of the wheel. We gained access to the city through passing one of a series of road blocks encompassing Trieste, which had recently experienced a surge of passive resistance and with it a leaning towards conversation impregnated with political circumspection, as yet without definition; many seeds were being sown on a wave of popular feeling, and, among these, pro-Tito sympa-thisers realised that the time was ripe for weaving their territorial designs throughout the Istrian peninsula. The German occupation imposed on this city of mixed population observed the trend of local opinion inject-ing suitable propaganda, conceived with the dual intentions of playing one side off against the other, thus easing their security problem and main-taining, simultaneously, their overall theme and prophecy that East and West would ultimately clash. A veil of watchfulness was cast over Trieste in the form of secret police whose methods caused deep resentment among the local inhabitants who daily grew to hate their one-time ally.

The vehicle carried us swiftly through the curfew-cleared streets to the city centre, finally stopping outside a modern cement-fronted building; dismounting, we passed into the vestibule of this one-time hotel, now Gestapo Headquarters. The duty sergeant, sitting behind the reception desk, booked our arrival assuming responsibility for our safe custody and releasing the escorts who hurriedly made their departure. Drying the carefully appended entry in the visitor's book, he then led us into a nearby office.

Inside, a senior sergeant-major of the SD was busily engaged with three Italian youths, who he questioned with the aid of an interpreter, so we sat watching the proceedings.[1] The youths stood in line before his table now regretful of their adolescent prank, unaware of the connection which the German sought to establish. At this moment the air raid alarm sounded, warning the city of the approaching RAF bombers which were about to pay a strategic visit to the port installations. The wailing signal set nerves on edge and feet in motion towards the basement, a heavy shutter added to the clamber, clanging down and sealing the main entrance. Joining the queue, we followed the uniformed and ununiformed secretarial staff and other inmates down the stairs, taking a seat in a darkened passageway. Two figures groped their way along the passage, peering closely at the seated figures until they reached us. We were recognised for the first turned to his companion, saying 'Hier Hans', then ordering us to follow him to a passage well away from the main shelter which we reached, passing through two iron gates. Obeying instructions, we sat on a bench with another civilian. The three youths stood one to each corner of the right-angled passage. Our two guards who each carried a short-handled whip, stood opposite us, glowering with eyes bloodshot from the alcohol they had lately consumed and meditatively fingering their whips. One or two bombs landed, shaking the very foundations of the building and causing the lights to flicker and fade, and the plane passed on, its mission completed. A short, broad-shouldered civilian, dressed in a brown suit, entered the passage, swinging the gate closed behind him. He spoke to the youth in the corner nearest the gate, without warning driving his fist into the stomach of the youth who collapsed in agony on the ground. Not a murmur issued from the eleven cells, the civilian faced the Major, 'And who might you be?' The Major replied that he was an Englishman, remaining motionless as the visitor crashed his fist into his face, flesh on flesh, as sickening thuds sounding monotonously crisp as they echoed throughout the stone-walled passage.

The 'All Clear' relieved the situation for a message was passed to the guards who pushed us along the passage in front of them. We climbed to the fifth floor, entering a large room favourably furnished. Several officers stood around the room and a girl sat behind a desk on which lay a typewriter. We sat on two chairs near the table, facing the assembly. Another woman stood beside the desk.

The officers stiffened, their right hands shot up, heels clicked together and voices chorused ceremoniously 'Heil Hitler' when scar faced General R— entered the room, walking energetically towards a table on which he sat, swinging his legs. His forehead glistened with beads of sweat; he had apparently hurried to keep this appointment. A senior officer reported our identity stating the circumstances of our capture referring to us as 'Churchill's Bandits', glancing in our direction each time he used the description. Duly briefed, the General addressed himself to the woman interpreter. 'The General wishes to know why you are here?' Bill answered without hesitation, informing the woman that he wondered himself. The interpreter did not translate this reply for the General's benefit, instead she repeated the question to which Bill then replied that he could only give her information already made known to the General.

'But you must realise that you are not ordinary prisoners of war. You were not taken prisoner at the front line, it is for you to clarify. Please answer the question.'

'Under the conventions of war, we are classified as prisoners, is there a special type of prisoner? If so, it is for you to explain. Please convey that to the General.'

Apprehensive of the effect that it would produce, the interpreter stumbled over her words as she translated the essence of Bill's reply, praising herself for the expected abusive rejoinder which did not materialise, for the General merely smiled, aware that this was to be accepted, at first! The prisoners were not yet acclimatised to the establishment which had a reputation to maintain, the prisoners would of course appreciate this only when they had experienced the conditions of their confinement.

One of his officer's took the liberty of expressing an opinion, suggesting that the bastards should be shot. Facing the officer, the General's face expressively conveyed a rebuke which no words would so aptly have expressed; he was a man intolerant of advice, clever in a cunning sort of way, skilled in the art of extracting information without conscience if brutal methods were resorted to. He tried again through the interpreter, 'I am to inform you that the General still requires an answer to his question and in reply to your query, you are not entitled to the treatment given to prisoners of war, captured under normal conditions.'

Bill made no reply. The seconds seemed immeasurably longer as I stared back at eight pairs of eyes, darkened with accusation. Stealing a quick look at Bill, I felt slightly more reassured for he sat hands in his lap, his face unaccountably casual as though he were waiting for a train which was as yet running ahead of schedule. The General held the cards and everyone was waiting for him to make his play, as far as I was concerned, I felt he held all the trumps. Thoughtfully he decided to play one. He gave a signal, briefly nodding his head which meant that play was about to be resumed. A subordinate left the room shortly to return with another prisoner, a short man, clothed in a battledress suit, dark receding hair, pallid face, he looked as bewildered as I felt, wondering what his unannounced introduction meant.

'Do you recognise this man?' Bill replied that he didn't. 'Are you quite certain that you have never seen this man before?' Without looking in the man's direction Bill answered, 'Quite certain.' Before the interpreter continued, the strange prisoner was led from the room. 'You must think carefully; you see we have certain information, and it would be preferable if you were to tell the truth when you decide to identify yourselves, the circumstances of your capture is strange.' Satisfied that we realised our peculiar position, the General left the room, accompanied by his officers.

Chapter Sixteen

The Political Prisoners

Unlocking a cell to the left of the basement passage, 'Kraut' indicated that I should enter, giving me a persuasive push from behind. 'Herein, schnell,' he said harshly. Together with Christian, the other guard, he left the passage, returning upstairs where he locked another door, rattling it to make sure that it was secure. Some minutes passed before the other cell inmates stirred, relieved that they had not been called for interrogation.

'Pssst, ah Inglesi, listen, I want to speak with you. Stand near your door and answer through the peep-hole.' I stood with my ear against the small circle of glass, fixed head-height in the cell door. The voice continued, 'I am Neno, I am a Croat really, but my mother chose to call me by an Italian name. I have been here for six weeks. There are ten of us, including three women, do you like women? Maria here is very beautiful, aren't you Maria?' He raised his voice when he referred to the woman. 'I will call her again in a moment. Where were you captured?'

I had somehow bargained for this question. My neighbour sounded too cheerful after six weeks' incarceration, so I answered carefully, 'Oh, not far from here.' The youth was eager for news, which was perhaps natural. The cells were without light and shaped like a small bathroom containing broken beds and a bucket available if you needed it.

'I was captured over in Gorizzia when carrying a message to an English Major. I have fought with Tito's Partisans.' He may have been a Croat, Italian or Slovene, his high-pitched voice led me to believe that he was very young. 'Were you working with the Partisans?' he continued indiscreetly. 'No, I am a soldier.' I replied more curtly than I meant to.

'Ha, that's good, we Partisans are soldiers too, we have been fighting very hard. One moment Inglesi. Hey, Maria! Maria, we have a handsome Englishman with us now. He says he loves you!' I heard him laugh quietly to himself and the reply the woman gave him. 'What's his name?' The youth repeated the question, 'Hey, Inglesi, what's your name? Maria is asking.'

'Carlo,' I replied. He appeared to be amused continuing with his light-hearted banter. Coaxingly, he chided the girl. 'Hey Maria, listen what are you doing tonight. If you like I will arrange with Kraut for you to sleep with the Inglesi. What do you say?'

'She is very kind, but I am also tired. I'm going to sleep now.'

'You will get plenty of sleep here. Tomorrow you will be the first for interrogation about 8 o'clock. Every time a new one comes; he is the first to be interrogated. Me, I haven't been questioned for a week, but that swine Kraut keeps me in touch by beating me each morning. Goodnight, Inglesi.'

The youth took me at my word but continued to speak with the other prisoners. I listened to him while I rested on the broken camp bed.

'Elena, are you sleeping, wake up il Preto, I want to speak to him. Ask him how he feels, il poveretto, what do they think he knows. They carried him back to his cell this morning, he couldn't walk.' Another voice, deeper and more manly, called for silence so that he could sleep. No one felt inclined to make conversation with Neno. I heard him slump down on his bed.

The day had been a long one, but I found sleep difficult. I was forced to lay with my feet on the cement floor, so I kept my boots on. Footsteps on the floor above sounded plainly and were mingled with the tinkling of spoons and cups; there was a dining hall on the floor above, and with the increasing movement, I was able to estimate the time, looking forward to another ration which invariably followed when the guards had eaten their fill. We received three meals daily unless there was an air raid when the guards took revenge by leaving us without. At 8 o'clock each morning we were escorted to the ground floor and into a courtyard where there was a lavatory in which we emptied our buckets, sometimes having time to take a hasty wash, pulling the lavatory chain, we used the cistern water. Kraut never ceased to find this procedure amusing. We then received a small cup of ersatz coffee, that was breakfast!

At midday, Kraut and Christian brought a bucket of water which was issued independently to each cell. The water tasted foul, and I put it down to the bucket that they carried the water ration in. In the evening, about 5 o'clock, we were given the main meal of the day, a small cup of soup which we sipped slowly, making each one count. As there were only two cups between ten prisoners, the guards impatiently hurried us along. This meal was more communal for we all stood at the end of the passage waiting our turn for a second cup. If there was any soup left, Kraut would chase us all back into our cells, each individual carrying their mattress with them to the shelters on the other side of the passage. Tired, they would be led back to their cells. The women received extra bread for their services, which they charitably shared with their fellow prisoners, Kraut making the distribution, an extra 20g of bread which he offered from his filthy paws!

My cellmates were a mixed bunch, mostly Jugoslavian, with the exception of the priest who was in bad shape after his continued rough handling during interrogations.[1] He had just finished Mass one morning when three British escapees took refuge in the sacristy of his church where he was disrobing after the service. They asked for his help, but it was too late, the SS had already surrounded the church, taking the prisoners and the priest for questioning. He had been with the Gestapo (a prisoner of the Gestapo) for little more than a month. His clothes were taken from him and an old jacket, trousers and shirt replaced them. At mealtimes, Christian and Kraut used to ask him to bless the bread or the water so that they could make a mockery of him and the church he represented, but the priest looked steadily back at them with eyes that plainly said, 'Father, forgive them for they know not what they do', which infuriated Kraut who cuffed him back into the darkness of his cell. One morning when this little scene was repeated, a tall ginger bearded Jugoslav prisoner said to me, 'They are beasts and yet they would call themselves the Master Race!' He was well dressed and strongly built; he was from Dubrovnik and had been caught up in a periodic raid for slave labour. Villages were surrounded and the fit menfolk and, at times, the young women were herded from their homes and marched to Trieste where they were held temporarily in the large Coroneo prison. The same evening, they would be issued with 'Liberty Workers Passes' and packed on a train en route for Germany. Husbands, wives, sisters and brothers were separated, in many cases for the last time.

From one of these raids, the tall Slav had escaped but was recaptured and sent to Gestapo Headquarters for special treatment. The first morning they had questioned him with regard to his escape. How had he managed it? He had remained silent, so they put his hand in a vice. It was still bandaged with a handkerchief. He still had kept his silence. He seemed resigned to this treatment, he was taken away one morning soon afterwards, I never saw him again.

Their stories were much the same and they all suffered the same treatment, the women as well. I admired them for I knew that they were resigned to their fate without showing any signs of weakness. They were mostly followers of Tito and stood firmly for him, even here.

Exacting though the day had been with the journey and introductory interrogations, I could only snatch odd half-hours of sleep, for the cell was cold and my mind wrestling with a disturbing collection of dreams which, entwined with the reality of our position, were trying to close the gap between the present and the future. Half-awake, half-asleep, my sub-conscious mind was never far from the live minutes of reality and though the cell remained dark, I could feel the approaching hours of dawn which grew colder with its grey awakening. The buckets rattled and the beds creaked and the deep-voiced man repeatedly asked the hour. There was a tone of urgency coupled with each request which suggested he may have had an appointment and wished to be punctual. Sometimes, when you would rather not think, your mind urges you on, a nagging demand which you are powerless to stifle. If your position is serious, the nagging exami-nation is all the more persistent. Time actually catches up with you and with the skill of an experienced interrogator, the scenes unfold, past memories are revealed with searching clarity. Boyhood is jumping off stage and then you remember someone long forgotten, an association you would rather forget. Yes, perhaps you should have behaved better on that occasion, you should have known better. Cringing with the embarrass-ment of indecency, you know that you will do better in the future, but the future may not allow you the opportunity. The future is in the hands of your captors; time has caught up with you. The fear of the unknown had never occurred to you before. You have an urgent desire to make amends, principles really mean something because they are clearer now than ever before. Oh, for the refuge of spiritual comfort as fear plays with your subconscious mind.

'What hour is it?' Damn that man, why doesn't he keep quiet? My feet were dead, so I sat up rubbing my legs, restoring the circulation. These cells were more like tombs for the living. The man had settled down again. I wondered why the devil he kept asking for the time. I suppose he really is awake. I curled my legs up and lay back. What was I dreaming about? Principles, values, and where they got you. I must have the jitters. I remembered someone had once said 'It is better to give than to receive', and I had asked him why? 'Well, I won't give the obvious answer, but, you kind of feel good inside.' I had said in reply that if you give something, you get something in return but where does it get you? If you are good or bad, what does it all add up to?

I think this person saw in me his good deed for the day, there was something about him material and quite spiritual.

He had continued talking about the Bible, what a good book it was, a best seller, containing hundreds of short stories each with a worth-while moral. He said that I should read it someday, most of the authors were simple men, four of them I had probably heard of, Mathew Mark,

Luke and John. For all their simplicity, they were imbued with an un-conquerable inspiration, they inspired by a carpenter whose faith, hope and charity and love of all men was made plain to them because they were what they were, genuinely simple men. If you want something easy to read, I can heartily recommend this book he had said.

I said, 'If you have read it, perhaps you can tell me one thing. Does it tell you where you go from life on earth?' He thought for a moment, I thought I had him stumped. He then responded, 'Yes, I believe it does, but you have to read very closely if you really want to know that answer, it gives you an idea. Read it yourself, I can't explain it, but it's in the book, that I can promise you.'

I wondered why they had brought that other fellow into the interroga-tion. Looked as though they had been giving him a rough time. What had they done to him? Maybe he was Peter Michael or the other fellow Steven Peters, the two names I had seen hanging from the typewriter. If we were interrogated separately from now on, the questions would become increasingly more difficult to answer, and Bill had said that we couldn't remain quiet. We would have to give them a story. Perhaps our colleagues were clear of the Tramonte by now. Whatever happens, we must not give the game away until they are free. Weakening? Why open your mouth at all? Give them the cover story that Bill had hurriedly suggested, you were dropped as a recce party in front of the army. A long way in front, it's true. Suppose they ask where the radio is hidden and where we had landed and where we had been? Bill maintained, 'Just keep to your story.'

A sergeant collected me from my cell next morning. He was wearing thick-lensed glasses. He was fat and reminded me of Himmler. On the way up to the fifth floor he was talkative, a rehearsed, carefully prepared, morale-disturbing drift of conversation which failed to achieve its objec-tive, for there was an air of insincerity about it; he tripped over his words, catching up with the sentence a few words back. I listened but said nothing.

'You are a lot younger than I was led to believe,' he spoke English. 'Have you any family? A mother I suppose, it's always the mothers that suffer, wondering what is happening to you, the sooner you leave this place the sooner you will be able to drop her a line. We've been having a lot of trouble from bandits lately. Nothing serious of course because we have taken stern measures in order to curtail their activities. There is only one answer for scum like that, we shoot them! Anyone working with these fellows, once they are caught are as good as dead. I do hope you will be sensible now that you are here, really you should have been sent to a prisoner-of-war camp, but it seems that you wouldn't tell our interrogators what you had been doing. That was very silly of you, you are wasting so much valuable time. This way, sit on the bench there.'

Sitting on a bench placed in the passage was Bill, the sergeant indicated that I should sit alongside him. 'Good morning, Sir.' Bill was not looking so good; he too must have passed an uncomfortable night. 'Hello, Charles, now remember, nothing unless you are hard pressed, and then nothing more than that story of the reconnaissance, remember?'

'I follow. There is one thing, Sir, that fellow they brought in the other evening. He may be called Peter Michael or Steven Peters, does that mean anything to you?'

'Yes, but forget it. We don't know them.' The sergeant returned, taking Bill into the room at the end of the passage. He was there for little more than an hour, and then was returned to his room which was on the same floor. The sergeant then escorted me to the interrogation room, where a senior sergeant-major of SD sat waiting. He pointed to a chair, the other side of the table, on which I sat. The sergeant interpreter sat at the end. The interrogation was set piece and was to be repeated, the same questions hour after hour at times spread over a month.

'What is your name, number and rank?' That I was always prepared to answer. 'Where are your identity documents?' This I always answered, 'You took them from me when I was first captured.'

'Curious, we haven't got them now.' I said, 'Then you must have lost them, that is not my fault.'

'It is unfortunate for you, because if you cannot prove your identity, we can only surmise that your activities were clandestine, in other words when you appear before the grand jury, they will believe that you are a spy. You were dropped by parachute into the Carnia. You are obliged to answer the questions. Very well, we'll continue. From now on you have no part in the war, what does it matter if you answer our questions, after all it is for your own good. You don't wish to be shot. That is the treatment we give to the bandits. Your number would indicate that you are a signals expert, where is the radio you were using, have you buried it?' I remained silent to all these questions but regardless, he wrote down various notes on the questionnaire. My silence did not disturb him in slightest for he continued with questions and suppositions which he verified himself.

'So, you are a wireless expert. Have you any cipher or did you bury that too? You must know what was contained in the text of any messages sent to your headquarters. I should like to know where your headquarters are, and how many messages you sent them. What type of aircraft brought you here to north Italy? What type of radio did you operate? Can you remember the frequencies used? At what time of day or night did you operate to your headquarters?' The sergeant hesitated at times, choosing the right word. Eventually, the SD man had written enough for what it was worth. Unless he were a thoughtful reader, I couldn't see what gains were made by the interrogation. He had pressed for a reply at times, but so far, so good, he hadn't used any strong-arm methods. Just the occasional reminder that I was at Gestapo Headquarters. He concluded by telling me that they were not a body to be trifled with, he then waved me away and the sergeant escorted me back to my cell. The questioning had lasted a little more than an hour.

Soon after the midday ration, a glass of water, I was sent for again; this time to another room with double doors. I looked carefully about the room after taking my seat and the doors closed behind me. The interrogator on this occasion was a surly faced captain, while the interpreter was the objectionable specimen we had met at Comeglians. They appeared to be a more business-like combination. I was told to sit down and be ready to answer the questions. I had wasted a lot of time the sergeant-major spat, it was now time for me to answer or else. It certainly sounded as if I were in for a rough time this afternoon. The captain perused the dossier that had been opened earlier during the morning's interrogation.

The captain opened the questioning. He said they had a long conversation with my Major today, and he had given them a lot of information which they wanted to verify with me. They wanted me to answer each question. 'When did you arrive in the Friuli? For what purpose did you come to north-east Italy, such a long way in front of your army? He waited for my reply, taking a cigarette from a packet and blowing the smoke in my direction. I said nothing.

The interpreter said, 'Well, you have heard the questions, answer the officer.' The captain studied me for a few moments and then decided he was wasting his time; he asked more questions.

'There were seven in the plane that brought you to the Carnia, I would like to know what happened to the remainder? Prisoners of war receive the same treatment as our own soldiers, but bandits and spies are not so fortunate. You will remain in this cell below until such time as you make up your mind to speak. Be sensible, after all you have nothing to lose by telling us the answers. You will not be able to write home or take exercise in the air or enjoy the privileges that a normal prisoner is given until you do, instead, you will continue to be locked up in that dark cell, you will rot there. It will be your own fault, the circumstances of your capture entitles us to treat you as we will, and if you make up your mind to be sensible, we will treat you well and send a telegram to your family through the Swiss Red Cross, informing them that you are safe, come, save your mother needless anxiety.'

He continued by saying that I landed in the Carnia and set to work, what was the purpose of my visit? What did I report to my base? What did the twenty messages contain. I did not reply, but nevertheless the captain paused to write something on the dossier. A point had occurred to him, seemingly a new angle previously unnoticed, he wrote quickly, reading over what he had written before continuing. 'We understand that you are a radio expert. What type of radio did you use, and when did you find it better to communicate? Some periods are better than others. You needn't mention all the frequencies, one will do.' Changing the subject, he questioned me on the places we had visited in the Friuli and the people we had met in our travels. The questioning lasted for 2 hours, he finally terminated the interrogation saying, 'I'll give you three days to think seriously and at the end of that period, you will be called for again, your answers will decide whether you are to live or die. I advise you to think seriously. He nodded to the sergeant-major who took me below.

Three days passed but I wasn't sent for. It was a week before they interrogated me again. Meanwhile from Neno I learned that Bill, who was extremely sick, had been taken to the Coroneo, another large prison, two or three streets to the north of the city; he had been placed in the sickbay. The other two Englishmen had been taken there too, Neno told me, 'I saw one, a small dark-faced man, do you know him?' I was interested, but not that interested if Neno wished to ask a lot of questions.

Chapter Seventeen

The First Month of Imprisonment

While there is life there is hope but constant speculation on how long you will continue to hope is a drain on the nervous system which, ultimately shows in your face, in your eyes and in every action you make. If you lack imagination, your nervous fibre weathers the storm for a longer period. If your make-up includes those remarkable properties which assist you to bear with pain, the thought of pain allows you to offer sustained resistance, commonly referred to as fearlessness, in some circles, courage. You are a source of comfort to those less fortunate than yourself, your example is a tonic. I had plenty of opportunity of studying my cell-mate's reactions to the wearisome taxation, applied by their skilled tormentors, and in turn, no doubt, they watched me. The inmates of the cells changed frequently, it was noticeable that there were always more Croats interned for cross-examination than any other group of nationals. In the evening they would sing their national songs, every one of them knew the words and those of us that didn't, listened to this harmonious message which pierced the gloomy walls and fortified us in our adversity. Somehow, although the words were foreign to my ears, they were nevertheless familiar, or perhaps it was that they were rendered with such feeling that I too was carried with them. Closing my eyes, it was easy to picture the quiet flow of life over gravel roads, the simple peasant pastures, and Sunday thanksgiving. These people had so little and yet they had everything and because of this, they were staunch in the face of oppression.

'Carlo, where do you live in England?' Neno asked. I thought it unlikely that he had heard of my hometown so I replied, 'In London.'

'Ah, London, a great city. I will go there one day. Would I be able to find work?' I told him that he would, but I added that he should be able to find work at home. He didn't answer immediately and then said that there would be much work, he had always wished to travel, and if possible after the war, he would go and, perhaps, he would visit me!

Neno had sounded doubtful. In the middle of his answer he had changed his mind as though various circumstances he had not considered intervened. He would like to go to London, yet conditions in the future may not allow it, or was he thinking of his imprisonment? He had yet to survive that. Normally he was cheerful, so much so that I was suspicious of his presence. The other prisoners were talkative at times, but they were cautious when they spoke with Neno. He was a tall youth for his age, well over 6ft with a pimply face, cavernous eyes and a shock of dark hair that he brushed straight back over his head. He was a friend to look at but an unknown quantity to listen to. He had a habit of asking sudden questions in the middle of conversations, which had no bearing on the topic you were at that moment discussing. With the walls between us, I pictured him listening, waiting for the answer to each question. When he failed to obtain the answer he was waiting for, he would hurry on with something bordering on the trivial. One couldn't help liking him and yet he was not to be trusted. No one was.

After each interrogation he would be waiting, anxious to know whether they had beaten me? What had they asked me? He was sympathetic too, for he would invariably say 'Povero Inglesi', Poor Englishman. I never really knew if he meant it. If the interrogation had been long and the questioning extra tiresome, I felt that it was mock sincerity, that perhaps he was a stooge waiting for me to relax to confide in him. Then I would let him talk, without answering until he tired. It was a great temptation for Neno was a good listener, he was never too tired for conversation. Each morning he would be taken upstairs by Kraut, he seemed to take a long time washing the dixies and the two cups. He was the only one who could take liberties with Kraut or Christian, sometimes they would kick him into his cell, sometimes he would be given a cigarette. Later, I did trust him, I gave him a message to carry. It never reached its destination, but I felt that it was instrumental in transferring me to the Coroneo where the Major and the other two Englishmen were imprisoned. I have often wondered what became of Neno.

Then there was a young man who was in the next cell but one who came from Zagreb. It was he who encouraged the remainder to sing and when they wouldn't, he would concentrate on me.

He told me to sing a song to which I replied that I couldn't sing, my voice was cracked. He then said, 'OK Englishman, you learn to sing our songs.' He would ask me to repeat after him. Phonetically, it went like this, but I never fully understood what it all meant.

'Moia Mati ma cuha café. Moia Mati ma cuha café. Sabotacoria, Saboticoria,

Moia Mati ma cuha café. Saboticoria, Saboti. Yeh!'

When I had sung the words right through, everyone sang the words over again. Each morning it was the practice for me to sing this little song, which never failed to draw laughter. Eventually, when I was sent to the Coroneo, I heard him singing in the yard below me, or if he didn't sing, he whistled the refrain. It wasn't possible for me to look below but I answered whistling the tune where he had left off. In this manner we kept in touch until he was taken away. 'Well done, Englishman, bravo! You sing well. Now, please sing an English song.'

Gaining confidence, I sang tunes that I knew, the words didn't matter, never remembered the correct words, but as I went along others served the purpose. I sang 'Wagon Wheels', 'Just a Song at Twilight, when the lights are low, and the flickering shadows, softly come and go.' Sometimes I had to sing this one twice. It was a sad song, the words and the tune. It was this song that they remembered and learned. The boy from Zagreb had a brother, he spoke of him sometimes and about himself.

'My brother is six years older, 26. He joined Tito and lives with a Partisan group just above my town. Sometimes, he goes to see my mother. Our house was destroyed but she is staying with my married sister. Who are you for, Mihailovitch or Tito?'

'If they are both fighting for freedom, I like them both equally well.'

He continued, 'I am for Draza, he is a good man, a good general. My brother says he is a traitor but then my brother is a Communist. I sometimes hate my brother, isn't it strange that we should be on opposite sides? I was studying to be an engineer, perhaps one day I shall be, who knows? There has been much fighting in Jugoslavia, Germans and Draza's boys, Tito and Draza's boys, Tito and the Germans.'

He went on to ask if I thought there would be another war. Will the English fight the Russians when this war was over? If they do, he will fight for the English, the Jugoslavs were the Englishman's oldest friends in war, 'Tell me Englishman, what will happen?'

'I'm sure, I don't know. We are all fighting Nazism, it is an evil, we shall always fight against tyranny, against any form of totalitarian power,' I said.

'Then the English will fight again after this war, you will fight Russia, they have dedicated themselves to world revolution. There will never be peace in the world until the people of Russia are free. You see Englishman, you wait and see.'

I had heard this theme so often, I almost believed that it was correct, although what foundations they had for this belief I could never discover. There were signs. The Russians were cautious, even of their allies, but then, in 1917 we hadn't accepted them, we had fought against them. One thing couldn't be overlooked, the fear that these people, working people, had of Russia.

Voices raised in argument were welcome and yet they were to be deplored. For one thing they were distracting but the theme was consistent, the same old repetition. The deep-voiced man was an ardent supporter of Tito. He would listen patiently to the young man from Zagreb then, persuasively, he would pursue his ideal.

'We are a poor country, yet we needn't be. It is strength of purpose through unity we require, and Tito is the man for us.' This would draw a moan of anguish from the youth, but the man continued to make his argument. A king was too costly, he deserted the people and ran away never to return. 'We have woods and minerals; we can feed ourselves. We need a large port, but most important, have faith in ourselves. Tito will bind us together; he is one of the people.'

The man was sure of his stance explaining that the army had disintegrated when the king fled, we were without leadership. But Broz stayed with them and gathered the people behind him.

So, it went on, argument and counter argument, a sure indication of the situation that exists in that part of the world. I was asked by both what my views were. I honestly did not know the answer, I was uncertain and weakly I remained impartial, as we had on past occasions with the Italian Partisans. In the evening, we were once more united in song, their folk songs, for tomorrow was another day, tomorrow was drawing near.

Christian offered me the end of his cigarette one morning after coffee had been distributed, he had allowed me to stand in the light of the passage near the cell door. He had been drinking heavily, his legs were unsteady and he supported himself with one hand placed on the wall. He was in a savage temper which worsened when I refused the cigarette end. He stamped on it and ground it into the floor of the passage, kicking it away from him, dazedly watching the tobacco scatter. Without warning, he lifted his whip and brought it down hard on my shoulder, I ran into the shelter of my cell, but he didn't follow, instead he crashed the door shut behind me shouting 'Schwein.' The other prisoners had remained quiet, nothing was said for several minutes, long after Christian had returned upstairs.

'Are you hurt Carlo?' Neno asked. 'No, it's alright, it was nothing. He was drunk.'

It was however a warning; an outburst of hate and it was humiliating. There was nothing one could do; it was futile complaining. I didn't look forward to the midday ration of water, not if there was to be a repetition of this treatment. If the guards were free to treat prisoners with contempt, unleashing the played-up bitterness of their feelings, what could one expect from their officers and seniors? One could only wait and see.

I received a surprise visit in the afternoon, Kraut came down in place of Christian, which was a relief, although there was little to choose between the two of them. Together with Neno, he issued the water ration, leaving my cell till last when he locked Neno up. While I drank the water, he stood, rather pensive, his right thumb stuck inside his belt. He looked a sad creature this afternoon, it may have been that he was tired or feeling the effects of his heavy drinking. I took my time and he didn't appear to mind; again unusual.

Pointing to the bucket when I had finished, he told me to follow him. We went to the entrance of the kitchen where I deposited the bucket. On the way back down the stairs, he took a packet of cigarettes and a booklet of matches from his pocket. 'Die Frau schickt diese Zigaretten,' he said.[1] He locked me in my cell, and taking the contents from the packet, I held the inner cardboard up to the light by the peephole in the door, discovering a few pencilled words, 'I have a son too; he is a prisoner of the British.' How odd, who could they be from? Who in this building would send me cigarettes? I ran the people over in my mind, finally deciding that the only one old enough to have a son, and any feeling for me, was perhaps the interpreter who had translated the general's questions on the night of our arrival, it must have been her kind heart.

The wealthiest prisoner of the cells I thought as I walked up and down, taking a cigarette from the packet. Unwisely, I took a deep draw of the freshly lit cigarette which set my head spinning, so that I was forced to sit on the bed for a moment. It was the first I had smoked for nearly a month, and it was strong, dark tobacco. Soon after I had finished it, I heard more steps on the stairs. It was Kraut again, making straight for my cell. When he had opened the door, I saw a ghost of a smile pass momentarily across his normally dour face, as he motioned thumb up and over his shoulder that I should accompany him. At the top of the stairs were two other guards who joined us. Kraut reported to the reception desk near the entrance, mentioning my name to the wooden faced sergeant who glanced up in my direction before he made an entry in the booking out log.

It was a grey day with a fresh wind blowing. There was little traffic on the roads. We crossed the road to the right of the roundabout in front of the building, taking a right turn and crossing to the left-hand pavement. People passed without looking in our direction. No curiosity here in Trieste, the sight of the uniforms was enough I thought. We turned left again after 200yd. The wide expanse of pavement was clear of people with the exception of an Italian soldier who paced idly toward us with a rifle slung over his shoulder. An occupied city with little in the shops and miserable-looking people scurrying about their business. The Triestini were a cheerful population normally, but I saw no indication of this as I walked quickly through the wide, thinly peopled streets. It was a pleasure to be out! The pavement on which we walked skirted a large four-storeyed building which we entered. So, this was the Coroneo, in normal times a civil prison; it suited its title for it was a grey, austere structure.

Kraut wasted no time, getting a signature for his charge, leaving me in the care of an Italian civilian who in turn took my particulars. Pushing a chair towards me he told me to sit down. The door opened again, and two men in battledress entered, one of whom I recognised as the prisoner we had met on the first evening at Gestapo Headquarters. They were equally surprised to see me. Ignoring the Italians, they introduced themselves, I had been right. It was Peter Michael and Steven Peters; these two were agents named Priestley and Turner. 'It's alright, we can talk in front of this chap, although he does speak English, he has lent me several English books, guess what, you'll never guess, Conan Doyle's book of Sherlock Holmes' activities,' said Steven.

He was a well-built, broad-shouldered, dark-haired, sun-tanned fellow of about 28 years. He was very cheerful and introduced me to Peter Michael, who said, 'It's a pity to meet another Englishman and a pleasure.' We shook hands.

The smaller man said that they had met my Major one morning. He was incarcerated here as well. He was in the sickbay but looked much better, though he couldn't walk without the aid of a stick.

I asked why we were congregating at this spot. One of them said he thought that everyone who entered the prison had to have his photograph taken, and that they also took fingerprints. He added that we might be waiting for the Major to join us. Indeed, in a few moments the Major appeared.

Outside a vehicle drew up, it was a saloon car, into which we scrambled, this was comfort. Bill had discarded his boots for felt slippers, a fair exchange with the Italian prison staff. He looked better than when I had last seen him sitting in the passage on the second morning, his face had more colour and he was cheerful.

Bill asked me if I knew the others and had I come to join them at the Coroneo, or was it just a visit? I replied that I hoped it was permanent as they had signed for me on the dotted line. The journey was a short one, a matter of 3 minutes before we pulled up in a narrow street about half a mile from the prison. We entered a photographer's shop (by special appointment to the Coroneo), where the owner was waiting for us. Using a plate camera, we were positioned full-face and profile frowning at the lens, then we dabbed our thumbs and first fingers into a black solution, pressing them onto a card, that was it! Finish. We were now fully-fledged criminals in the eyes of Fascist Italy and as such we were returned post-haste to the Coroneo. Peter was locked up in the ground-floor centre block. I was on the next floor and Steven on the third floor. Bill, assisted by the guards, was taken back to the sick ward. Just 2 minutes after I had been locked in the cell, it was visiting rounds and with great ceremony two guards entered, one placing a stool for the other to step onto under the barred window, tunefully, he ran a rod of iron along the bars, a security farce which was re-enacted every 3 hours. The cell was large and airy; and the bed was complete with mattress and a blanket. There was also a WC in one corner and a light high up in the centre of the ceiling. This was a palace after the basement cells of Gestapo Headquarters. In addition to this, I still had a pencil and four whitewashed walls, in this cell I could be artist, poet and *Everyman's Encyclopaedia*.

Chapter Eighteen

Trieste, December and January

'*Il Picollo, Picollo*, chi? Dove?' each evening the well-dressed news vendor hurried around the dimly lit corridors, accompanied by a guard who watched each transaction but rarely bothered to make any comment. With a regular customer, the vendor would stop for a few seconds, slipping a sentence of worthwhile gossip into his conversation that the buyer would never read, even between the lines of *Il Picollo*, such as 'The Eighth Army have captured Pescara' or 'The Fifth Army have reached Civitavecchia'. Twice-weekly, hawkers would make the rounds, offering fruit or cigarettes, they too brought news from the outside. On one occasion we learnt that the Partisans had blown up the SS canteen in Trieste itself. Within the hour, this item spread through the prison and while it did so, each whisper became more furtive for the Coroneo was a pool of hostages, and the SS believed in an eye for an eye, and a tooth for a tooth.

There were two brothers, they were the prison barbers and well known to most prisoners, both in their early 30s. For some time, they had expected to be released, eagerly, they had pressed for news of the day, 'When will we be free?' Ten or twelve prisoners, including the brothers, were warned to get their kits ready, they were going at long last, they were to leave at 4am next morning. It was known that they had assembled with their kits and had left the prison. Their kits were returned at 5am, but we never saw the brothers again. Each of these prisoners had expected to re-join his family after a long separation. The most horrifying aspect of this retaliation against helpless prisoners was the quiet efficiency with which the keyed-up hostages were coaxed to their sudden deaths. One by one, they had been shot.

Imprisonment in the Coroneo offered many compensations after the entombed existence at Gestapo Headquarters, and among these the most satisfying was equally the simplest pleasure, watching day change into night, and the pattern of shadows fade away with the weak winter sun. Through the broken windowpane flowed cold air, cleansing the cell. There was one meal a day, a watery bowl of macaroni and a portion of brown bread. It was a great temptation rationing the meal, for when it was served it was hot, but in its cold state, it was a tasteless mess. The guards were amusing, bad tempered, good hearted and corruptible. They had a sense of humour and because of this I was sure that their German over-seers would never make efficient watchdogs of them, not that anyone escaped, the prison was constructed too well. It was a maze of passages and intersecting iron gates through which one was forced to pass, exit by the window was impossible. They wore dirty, dark-blue overcoats and blue peaked caps. They might easily have been a company of broken-down opera singers who had finally been paid off with the ill-fitting uniform that hung from them in lieu of lira.

None of them sang, however, and neither would they permit the inmates to sing, but on occasions a well-known chorus would float from floor to floor, a corridor ahead of the aggravated jailers who implored the inmates to respect discipline. The tuneful words echoed throughout the whole prison; 'Si la guardia non voleva noi cantiamo, Si la guardia non voleva noi cantiamo' then to a crescendo; 'Canteremo Noi, Canteremo Noi, Canteremo Noi.'[1] Sung to the tune of any joyful aria.

One evening towards the end of the first week in the Coroneo, soon after the newsvendor had made his rounds, a gentleman whom I will always remember as 'Mr Providence', but commonly known as 'M. Mas-trovic', paid me a visit.[2] He was over 50 years old and his hair though thick, was fast growing grey which was, I thought, more in keeping with his dignity. He was portly rather than fat and his clothes, though coarse, were well tailored. There was nothing distinctive about his face, it was broad with high cheek bones, his dark eyes were active, searching and when he smiled, his face was kindly. He was the sort of person that looks genuine, stolid and reliable at first glance, and by his actions he proved this was in fact so. 'Hello, may I come in?' as he entered my cell. I had seen him once or twice in the end cell and had noticed the respect his fellow prisoners paid him, and for that matter the Italian guards. I welcomed the opportunity for a little conversation. 'Please do,' I said.

For some days following the hostage incident, discipline was more enforced; the guards accompanying the news-vendor hurried him along with his distribution, checking him when he attempted to make conversa-tion. All channels of gossip were effectively sealed and the inmates regard-ing their jailers with uneasiness, accentuating the atmosphere now filled with expectancy. But time is a great healer, and the paralysis which had enveloped the prison was a temporary affair, characteristic of the rapidly fluctuating passion pent up within its walls. Unobtrusively, hope over-came fear and the incident resolved into an unpleasant memory. The inmates were the first to react, sensing a change of temperament, their jailers no longer represented the jackals of oppression. They saw them for what they really were, the frightened employees of the Gestapo. The jailers too were relieved when the atmosphere relaxed, for they were loath to challenge the petty liberties that their captives took at the expense of discipline. Their prisoners lost their caged expression, and now found time to laugh. Human once more recognised human.

M. Mastrovic did not remain long for he realised the jailer, while granting permission, paced nervously outside the cell, curious as to the nature of the visit. Mastrovic was interested in Gestapo Headquarters, especially the prisoners in the basement. What were the prisoners like and what treatment were they being subjected to?[3] I described them to the best of my knowledge, giving him an outline of the procedure. He nodded his head as if to say he knew what I meant, 'I've heard it one hundred times before.' Finally, he asked if I was hungry, but smiled anticipating my reply, who wasn't hungry in the Coroneo? Grasping my hand firmly, he said 'Corragio,' and turning to the guard added 'Si, pronto' walking with him back to his cell. An hour later, I received the supper he had promised me, sheep brain on lettuce and a bottle of wine. All meals, purchased by the prisoners, came from the prosperous black-market hotel opposite the prison, the Black Cat.

Towards the end of November, I was transferred once more to Gestapo Headquarters. Steven and I went together one evening; on arrival we were taken to the fifth floor where we waited for interrogation. Steven was the first to be interrogated, he was in the room for about 30 minutes. He was smiling confidently when he returned to the passage, a heartening sign. I followed him.

'Sit down,' said the interpreter. The captain interrogator was reading my dossier and paid no attention to my entry. He read for several minutes prior to questioning me.

'Now, the time has come for you to clear up one or two points of interest.' He placed a watch on the table, then sat back folding his arms. 'You have exactly 15 minutes to think before you tell me all you know, 15 minutes, think seriously, Mister, for the time has come for you to identify yourself.' Bending over the watch, he checked the time, then waited. They lit cigarettes and I watched the smoke make crazy patterns as it rose towards the ceiling, listening at the same time to the double-beat of the watch. My chair creaked noisily when I moved. It was impossible to think clearly, and I found the slightest noise distracting. Their cigarettes had burned low before the veiled warning dawned on me. What had he said? You have exactly 15 minutes, think seriously, Mister, for the time has come. Why had he questioned Steven, what were they hatching now? They stubbed their cigarettes. 'Have you anything to say?'

I had to have a little more time. The 15 minutes had passed all too quickly, but what was there to say? There was nothing, nothing safe. 'Yes, I have. I would like to know why I am detained here without receiving the normal facilities granted to prisoners of war?'

The captain responded, 'You will be treated as a normal prisoner of war when you have convinced us that you are a soldier.'

'You have my identity documents, I am wearing a British uniform, I speak English, what more can I say?'

This was a new line of approach. I hadn't reckoned for this emergency, and emergency it was and they knew it was effective, hastening to seize their opportunity. 'We haven't received any documents and your uniform means nothing because we capture Partisans every day wearing uniforms identical to the one you are wearing, but Partisans are dealt with promptly when they are captured, they are shot. Shot because they are bandits. Come now, you are not a bandit, for your sake, we hope that you will be able to prove that you are a soldier.'

What was there to say if number, name and rank could not be substantiated with documents. They said that they hadn't seen the documents, suppose they were telling the truth. He continued, saving me the effort of making a reply.

'We believe that your comrade is a German Jew, he is, isn't he?' Again, something new, but where was the connection? Hellfire, let me think straight, let me think. A voice inside me snapped, 'Make him answer the questions, don't answer that, make him answer, go on, what are you waiting for? Ask him a question.'

'What on earth gave you that impression?' I asked.

'Never mind why, we believe that he is. He is dark, come now he is, isn't he?' He hadn't continued the description, but it gave me an idea.

'You can't go on looks. There are many Englishmen who are dark and swarthy, people who work in the Potteries for instance, the Black Country, many of them are dark.'

The more I said, the more ridiculous the explanation sounded, so I broke off as sharply as he had. Unbelievably, they were considering my answer. The interpreter found it difficult to translate my reply and demanded that I repeat myself. The captain was staring beyond me, pinching his lower lip while he concentrated.

Finally, he said, 'Curious, so you have made up your mind not to answer, well, we shall never learn who you are, a pity.'

There was no mistaking his implication but I felt now more than ever that he was bluffing, so obeying that little voice which had given me a lead, I replied, 'Whatever your decisions are, one thing you must remember, when the war is over, you will have to account for my disposal.' When he heard the translation, he was surprised for a moment, but he laughed, a humourless laugh. 'Keep thinking that way.'

That was the end of the interrogation. He curtly dismissed me and the sergeant-major escorted me to the basement to my old cell. I was never called for again. Two days before Christmas Day, Neno informed me that he was about to go to the Coroneo, this time it was definite. 'This afternoon, Carlo, at last, I shall go to the Coroneo. I will carry a message for you if you like?' I said that I had no paper or pencil. 'At noon, I will hand you one when I bring the water, you will have to be quick. I will leave one cup with you and then inform Kraut that it is to be collected, then put the message in the empty cup.'

I thought it improbable that Kraut would give him the opportunity, but I had made up my mind to accept his offer. It was much easier put into effect than I had imagined, too easy. But I had prepared the message for my captors rather than for Bill. At midday, Kraut opened all the cells and passed out of sight round the bend of the passage, enabling Neno to hand me the paper and pencil. I wasted no time writing the message.

It read, 'Dear Major, I cannot understand why I should be imprisoned here. If you can, please arrange for me to be returned to the Coroneo. Do not worry. If I do not see you again, if anything unforeseen should happen, please regard this as my will. I leave all to my mother. Good luck. Charles.'

Having served the remainder, Neno returned with Kraut, collecting the empty cup and the message. If this was an act, Kraut played his part admirably. Bill never received the message, I am sure that Neno was searched before he was transferred to the Coroneo, and the message was delivered to its intended addressee, my interrogators.

That same afternoon, I was returned to my cell in the Coroneo. Mastrovic met me in the passage on my return.

'We all wondered what had happened to you, we thought you had left us for good,' he said.

That was the turning point in our imprisonment. Conditions in the Coroneo improved steadily. The first sign that our captors had relaxed their attack on our morale and general vigilance was when we were allowed to take an hour's exercise in the prison yard, together. The hour always passed quickly, we had so much to discuss and for the first time in privacy. It was the first time we had really felt secure. We now planned further concessions, asking that we be allowed to pair up in our cells. Unexpectedly, the senior sergeant-major interrogator paid us a visit in person, notifying us that the request would be addressed to his superiors. He was polite and remained some minutes discussing the weather and other trivialities. We explained that we were already taking exercise together, a point he was obviously aware of, but he accepted the information as though it was news to him. 'I will see.' Then he departed.

Christmas Day brought yet another concession. We were permitted to attend the service in the prison chapel, and with the help of M. Mastrovic, we managed to spend the day in the infirmary, the happiest day of our imprisonment. Bill was still confined to his bed. Mastrovic joined us, bringing a bottle of the best wine to swell the provisions that the Partisans had obtained from the Black Cat. The prison bakery was close to the infirmary and the baker cooked some chicken and baked some rolls and bread, we probably fed much better than many of the guards and civilians in the city outside. The Slavs combined rendering several folk songs which together with the wine helped put everyone in the right mood. The English contingent were then asked to sing. Steven wisely suggested that we sing, 'I've got sixpence', we all knew the tune, but none of us knew the words. Without practice, we harmonised very well repeating the one sentence, 'I've got sixpence, jolly, jolly sixpence, I've got sixpence all [prolonged] to myself', which our fellow prisoners applauded heartily, calling out 'Encore'. But we had exhausted our repertoire and preferred to listen to them.

When we returned to our respective corridors, the other prisoners were fast asleep. Mastrovic pointed to one darkened corridor, explaining that the condemned prisoners were accommodated there. Some have been waiting many days for their execution he added. His explanation had a sobering effect, we passed by hoping that we hadn't disturbed them.

During exercise periods, we learned a little more about each other. Steven and Peter explained their capture which had occurred a week before we ourselves had been captured. They had been dropped on the wrong target area, right on top of the garrison town of Tolmezzo. Peter was taken straight away and Steven the following morning. We also learned smaller things, our ages, and every hour we expressed a special liking for a particular food. Food was a main topic for discussion, and we planned a reunion dinner with all the trimmings. On 6 January, the guard unlocked my cell just after the first inspection, throwing a paper parcel on my bed. Wondering what it could be, I hastened to undo it; two loaves of bread with birthday greetings from Steven. Two day's ration of bread and he had remembered my birthday.

The guards now came automatically to our cells each morning at 11 o'clock. Steven on the top floor was collected first, followed by Bill at the infirmary, then to the second and ground floors for Peter and myself.

This tour gave Steven, who made the complete circuit, the opportunity of assessing the internal maze and its various gate barriers through which one would have to pass to reach the one and only exit into the main street. Mastrovic took his exercise at the same time and on the way to the compound it was possible to engage in brief conversation when the guard was releasing other prisoners from their cells. He had a more intimate knowledge of the prison and, in addition, he was familiar with the city. Peter and Steven suggested that we made preparation for an escape, trusting that the opportunity would present itself. Much of our planning was formulated in the prison compound. We were all agreed that the Coroneo, by virtue of its construction and regular cell checks, was an impossible proposition unless we could bribe one of the guards. We consulted Mastrovic and at the same time asked for his assistance. He readily agreed to help us, but suggested we delay our attempt until such time as we were transferred. It now seemed likely that we should be taken to Germany or Austria. Mastrovic was of the opinion that our best chance would be in the course of the journey to Austria, the train would make frequent halts, he told us, and travel through the mountains very slowly. Many have been successful in the attempt, especially at night.

Towards the end of January after one such visit to the prison compound, we received permission to pair up in our cells. I had not long been locked in the cell when the guard returned, opening the cell door, in walked Steven. He had been to see the German overseer after the exercise period who was of the impression that we were already paired up in the cells. He had no idea when we were likely to be transferred. Together, we wondered what lay in store for us.

Mastrovic obtained civilian clothes for each of us which his wife brought in a succession of parcels daily to the prison. This was strictly prohibited and was only possible through bribing the German overseer. One morning he handed over 60,000 lira which Steven passed to Bill for safe custody in the infirmary.[4] Since the patients had bought their beds in the infirmary, where there was greater freedom of movement between wards, we thought it the safest hiding place.

It proved to be a wise choice for our cells were searched at odd intervals while we were in the compound taking exercise. The guards proved to be more amenable on the top floor allowing us to wash in the basin in the corridor first thing in the morning, after we had run ten or twelve times round the corridor. A necessary step preparing us for our premeditated eventual escape. Both inmates and guards eyed us with suspicion, who but the English would waste their energy in this ridiculous manner? And as for washing in January, stripped to the waste, totally unnecessary. We were now the proud possessors of a towel, also a gift from Mastrovic. Steven was widely travelled and proved to be an excellent companion. He had a varied selection of occupations prior to joining the army, and he had been keenly interested in European politics from the age of 18, shedding one ideal for successive 'isms' as he grew more mature. He filled the walls with general knowledge, the forty-eight states of the US, the counties of England, the eighteen regions of Italy, famous authors, cricketers, foot-ballers, athletes, rivers, mountains, until we could write no more.

We read in the local newspaper with some concern of the terrible damage caused in London by the revenge weapon, the 'V' bomb. Steven studied front-line reports carefully, trying to ascertain the Allies' progress on each front, but the maps were misleading and usually bore no relation to the current news. Place names in the paragraph were missing on the map, but each Line straightening movement meant an Allied gain. Several days after a manoeuvre of this nature, a fresh map would appear in *Il Picollo*, carrying a brief caption skilfully produced to veil the actual situation. Bill and Steven compared mental notes of the general situation, exchanging the conclusions they had drawn during the exercise period. One morning, Bill informed us that he had been approached by a Gestapo representa-tive with a view to recording anti-Communist propaganda for 'Adria', a department of the German news broadcasting service, which, with a shortage of successes to bolster its daily broadcasts, was now concentrating on causing dissension among the Allied ranks. Germany, they preached, was the bulwark among Bolshevist expansion. Communism threatened the World. Bill treated the request with the contempt that it deserved.

Our transfer came as a surprise. Steven and I had retired to our beds. We had been discussing the groups of Liberty Workers, who, from time to time, had congregated in the corridors of the prison overnight, prior to their departure for Germany. They were a pitiful collection, many of them lice ridden, having slept by the roadside for endless days during their forced march to the city. We learned of the steady withdrawal of the German forces from Greece through Jugoslavia, which was probably an excuse for the uplifting of village populations. Many were already refugees and homeless, but without exception none wished to be sent to Germany. On arrival at the Coroneo, they were crammed a hundred to a passage where they sank down on the cold stone floors, exhausted. Those who retained the power to move, the younger men, propped themselves against the walls, picking the lice from their shirts. Others, too tired to worry about the vermin eating into their flesh, fell fast asleep, chin on chest, lifeless. They carried small parcels of clothing, perhaps a little food, their worldly belongings, they had lost everything else. Early one morning, their hamlet or village had been surrounded, without warning or reason, they were forced to leave the warmth of their beds, with time only to dress and assemble a parcel of clothing and food. The men were separated from their womenfolk, father from son, mother from daughter. Only cripples and those close to death were left to tell the tale. The groups separated, marching days and nights, the guards, ill-tempered, merciless, anxious to be rid of their human spoils.

Everything that had meant anything to these people had been destroyed in one foul blow. Their family circle had been scattered, perhaps never to be reunited. In their physical and mental state of exhaustion, they cherished one earnest hope, the hope to live, but many knew that their days were numbered. The older men had nothing in reserve, the end of their life journey was in sight, the cold, waste ground of a foreign country. Their faces were drawn, their eyes open without seeing, their thoughts still numb with the picture of those last moments in the village. The frightened expression of their wife or child before they were forced to part and march their separate roads to Germany where they would work until they dropped. The men would find amenities. There would be the Auslanders Brothel for those who found the ration inadequate, but the money they received would buy them nothing more than the body of yet another Liberty Worker, in the Great State of the Master Race, or one of its satellites, wherever their destination lay. For the young women, the Auslanders Brothel lay at the end of the road, this was the purpose of their conscription, not the majority, the stronger ones could work. Those who were too weak or defiant were thrown into the brothels. That was where they died of disease or were left to the mercy of lust, tarnished, defiled, left without purpose or desire to live. These were the Liberty Workers. These were the people we saw through the small glass pane in the cell door. These were the people caught up in the German planned maelstrom of degradation.

It was about 8 o'clock, we heard several pairs of feet stamp down the passage, coming to a halt outside our cell door. There were two German soldiers with the Italian guard, one addressed us, 'Heraus, schnell.' We dressed quickly, taking up our rucksacks as ordered. So that was it, we were on the move. At the guard room we found Bill and Peter waiting. The sergeant-major explained that we were to be handcuffed. Outside the prison, a wild wind blew angrily through the deserted streets. We climbed aboard an army lorry which carried us to the main station.

Chapter Nineteen

The Journey to Kaisersteinbruck

Soon after we were settled in the compartment of the local train, it eased out of the main station along the line to Udine where we were to change for Austria. It made its way slowly, never exceeding 30mph, making shuddering halts at frequent intervals. Udine station, a main line junction, was a scene of devastation, noticeable even in the darkness. Recent heavy raids had taken toll of rolling stock and had severely shattered all buildings. Our escorts took us to the waiting room where we remained for an hour.

We hoped that the next train was heated, we were extremely cold, and the handcuffs were tight on our wrists, eating into our skin.

Steven asked us to follow him. He would speak to the officer who appeared to be in charge of the station; a fat, helmeted man who was then giving directions to one of his staff. Steven waited until he had finished before attracting his attention and pressing the question. For a second, the officer fought to control his temper, then spent his fury screaming his reply and waving us back to the bench, a very definite negative.

We sat down. Peter asked what the officer had said. Looking behind and to the right, Steven with humour replied, 'Are there any ladies present? Good, well, gentlemen you may have guessed. He said that I could kiss his seat, a man of excellent taste you'll agree.'

I suppose having been bombed by Allied aircraft was unlikely to improve the mood of the station staff.

Our escorts mingled with the Field Police who were sitting near the glowing stove in the corner of the room. The Field Police were responsible for the security of the marshalling yard; occasionally one would leave the warmth of the waiting room for a tour of inspection, after which they returned, taking their place in front of the stove. The cold wind outside blew with gale force, consequently, the reliefs changed every quarter-hour. Eventually, a train pulled into the station with a full complement of soldiers who were proceeding on leave, as were our escorts. The sergeant-major hustled us into an empty compartment, pairing us off either side; it was a corridor train, so the guards positioned themselves at each end near the doors. Looking at Bill who was handcuffed to Peter, I wondered if his thoughts were in keeping with my own. Handcuffed in pairs in a locked compartment, there was no chance of escape. As soon as the train got under way, the lights were extinguished as were our hopes of escape, at least for the present. The coach swayed gently from side to side and the wheels seemed to chatter as we were swept over the tracks, sleep if you can, sleep if you can, sleep if you can, the tracks seemed to talk to us. Sleep if you can, sleep if you can, your chance will come! It was wishful thinking but if you concentrate hard enough, you can make the wheels repeat almost anything, provide the sentences are short and fit the tempo. Maybe it was good advice at that, I was tired and inclined to accept it. I leant against Steven and dozed off.

During the night we crossed the frontier and met with a complete change of scenery, the Austrian countryside was covered by a white blanket of snow. I awoke simultaneously with the train's halt alongside a small station.

'Good morning, Charles, you gave us a hearty rendition during the night. I have never before heard tuneful snoring. I'm not criticising, I probably accompanied you for all I know, what's the name of this place, anybody see?' said Steven.

We looked outside but there was no sign to be seen. There were one or two dirty, brown coated figures wandering aimlessly beside the train. One was a Mongolian or a Caucasian, they were Russian prisoners of war.

They looked the worse for wear and were searching for something, later we knew what it was, they were in the throes of starvation, looking for anything that was edible, rotten potato peelings, scraps. We had stopped to change the engine. We thought we must have been shunted about in the night; we hadn't made much progress. We were still in the mountains and Steven thought we had only covered around 80 miles. Bill interrupted the train of thought, 'You've past this way before Peter, via Graz, how far are we from Vienna? What time should we get there?'

Peter thought that Vienna was roughly 300 miles away, bearing in mind the slow progress, it would be doubtful if we would arrive on time, the line might be blocked, or for safety's sake, they might have arranged a late arrival. The train might have been spotted by recce aircraft and, to confuse estimated progress, movement control might halt the train for an hour or so along the way. Steven added that it was only a guess.

With that, the train started moving again. The whistle blew and we moved off around a bend which enabled us to count the seven coaches and the guard's van at the rear of the train. The journey proved uninteresting as far as the eye could see, the whole countryside was a monotonous white, the snow hanging heavily on the trees which merged evenly with the landscape, giving a barren desert effect to the passing scene. When we had left the mountains far behind us and picked up a little speed along the more even gradient of the gently rolling plains, we saw some infantry soldiers running through the knee-deep snow. Every hundred yards they would simultaneously fall flat and level their rifles at imaginary targets and then, at a given signal, run forward to their next bound. They would have been vulnerable targets to the weakest opposition; the exercise was possibly to harden them. The sky was a dull grey, promising more snow. The people in these parts had probably had a white Christmas, as appropriate background for that festive occasion. It could only have served to remind them of happier times I thought. As Peter had visualised, we stopped frequently along the line for no apparent reason, and at each main station, leave parties disembarked, some remaining on the platform to wave their fellow travellers on. At Graz and Wiener Neustadt, once again we saw prisoner working parties unloading stationary goods waggons, carrying the packages to lorries or carts. The compartment was warm and conducive to sleep which we all accepted, waking with the stopping or erratic progress. The engine had difficulty getting underway, its wheels spinning round on the slippery lines, while it released a noisy rush of steam which quickly evaporated in the thin, cold air. We finally reached Vienna at 1am, halting in the South Bahnhof, a large squarely built station with track-level platforms, a relic of the busy past when Vienna was the envy of the Austrian Empire. The station was still busy, but the tourists all wore uniform and travelled at cheap rates on their way to the fronts, or inversely, back from the fronts. Many of them ruined; minus an arm or a leg which had been torn off by shrapnel, fired by an unseen enemy from guns which unbelievably seemed to multiply as the war lengthened, and the menacing enemy encroached on the frontiers of the Fatherland.

A red-capped, blue-uniformed woman walked hurriedly by the compartments, notifying sleep-lulled passengers that they had arrived at Wien. We clambered from the compartment. Directly the door opened, we felt the blast of icy wind which chased waves of snow along the platform leading to the exit through which we passed onto the street. Walls of snow were banked against the station and buildings on the opposite side of the wide thoroughfare over which we crossed, keeping up with our escorts who made for a lighted building.

The sergeant-major was familiar with the city, for when he was refused entry at the first building, he hurried on to a second and finally a third canteen where we found a vacant table. It was full of noisy soldiers, all without exception SS. Waitresses wound their way around the tables, carrying the one and only course, pea soup, a plate of which we were all glad to accept. Some soldiers were drinking pale-brown Pilsener beer, a white-topped gaseous brew which the waitress who served us said had long since been sold out. A feldwebel who had been sitting at a nearby table joined us, asking the sergeant-major who we were. He had been drinking and was rather talkative. Peter mentioned that he was an Austrian. He was curious to know what we thought of the war and when did we think it would end. He had no illusions with regard to its conclusion. As far as he was concerned, the war was as good as finished when the Battle of the Ardennes fizzled out, a fiasco, though he was careful to mention this fact when the sergeant-major was otherwise engaged. He might have been 30 years of age and had experienced fighting on many fronts chiefly in the East, where he stated the shortening of the Line was more due to lack of reserves than actual Russian pressure. We had neither the bullets nor the men to fire them quick enough to halt the hordes of rum-soaked Russian infantry. His knowledge of the Western Front was limited to information he had gleaned from men who had been posted to his unit which was in the process of reforming, prior to returning to the Eastern Front. He said, 'First, everyone wished to join the Afrika Corps and later, units of the Western Front, we do not mind being taken prisoner by the British or Americans; fighting on the Eastern Front has no future, you have the choice of four alternatives, to leave your frozen carcass rotting in the snow; to continue fighting against overwhelming odds; some shoot themselves; and lastly you can be taken prisoner. That is the worst of the four alternatives. There is nothing worse than living death, surrounded by animals. His conversation reached the height of morbidity, when he realised he had been talking too long; the sergeant-major was looking at him in disgust. He revived himself for a moment, cheering us up considerably with his parting words. 'This wonderful vengeance weapon we have heard a lot about, is not a war winner, the most we can expect is that it will obtain an honourable peace, but I think it will only cause a lot of damage and destroy all hope of that.' He left us.

Our escorts gathered their kits together, it was 4am, the connection was due to leave the Ostbahnhof at 5am. The high moon, which had magically changed the snow-bound streets into silver when we passed through them to the canteen, had evaded the break of day, leaving the ill-lit city dark and grim. We padded along, gathering cakes of snow on our boots. While we had been inside the canteen, a fresh fall of snow had laid a flaky covering over the previous falls which were now frozen hard. When our boots grew heavy, we kicked the cakes off, sending them slithering along the slippery road surface ahead of us. Crossing the main thoroughfare, we passed a three-coach tram, alongside which a long queue waited to board it. They were night-shift workers and one or two soldiers, homeward bound. The east station had been severely damaged, its room a mass of twisted metal. The train was already in the siding, so we made our way to a carriage which was partly filled, finding eight empty seats. Before we moved off all carriages were full, many people were standing. Our escorts were the only soldiers, the other passengers were women, clutching baskets on their laps, containing provisions which were scarce enough in the cities, but unobtainable in the towns and villages. The train trundled slowly south-eastwards, stopping at all the small villages, scattered along the southern borders of the Vienna plain which led to the Hungarian frontier, 35 miles away. Passengers stepped down from the coaches but no one joined us, travelling east. We watched each batch alight and make their way through the snow to small clusters of houses, laying remote and isolated. Peter remarked upon the barren land, he had been here before the war and even in summer the countryside was bare and lacking in colour. The earth, dark, was bisected into lots with ill-kept wooden fences. This was the poorest part of Austria.

We felt we were close to the Austro-Hungarian border, we thought that we would dismount on the Austrian side of the frontier. We asked the sergeant-major where we were. He replied in German that we were going to Kaisersteinbruck which was 3km from Wilfleinstadt.[1]

It was a bleak spot I thought as the train pulled into Wilfleinstadt halt. It revealed a small cluster of houses with a single road running through the middle and passing on towards the hill to the rear of the village. The aisle of trees bordering the road was stunted and lifeless but served to mark the route where the snow had covered all trace of its passage. As Bill stepped onto the platform, a small boy pointed at his felt slippers, laughing heartily, and dragging his mother's skirt, so that she too should witness Bill's discomfort. The mother glanced quickly before pulling the boy further along the platform.

'If that was my child, I should have warmed the seat of his pants,' Bill remarked irately adding that his footwear did look a bit odd, and that they were soaking wet already.

Peter offered to carry Bill's rucksack, he was limping, his leg was not improving. He refused any assistance saying there wasn't far to go now.

Reaching the top of the hill, we came in sight of the prison lager. By comparison, it was a town many times larger than Kaisersteinbruck, which nestled under the lee of a hill to its right. There were more than fifty huts surrounded by an oblong enclosure of double tear wire outside of which, at 200yd intervals, were sentry boxes raised on top of stilts, complete with searchlight and machine guns, an ever-present warning to the prisoners who might contemplate escape.

Peter broke the silence after viewing the long lines of huts, 'It may have been a cavalry barracks years ago. Look to the left of the camp, you can see what were once the stables. I wonder who they are reserved for now?' No one answered him, our interest was fixed on the prison ahead, a more miserable picture I never wished to see. The majority of the buildings were built of stone, while the portion to which Peter had referred to were wooden structures with a cobbled yard containing water troughs facing the main lager. Passing under the gate, we read 'Stalag XVII A', a place of unrest for more than 20,000 prisoners. Poles, Hungarians, French, British and Russians made up the living complement, but over the hill to the back of the camp were the breathless bodies of many hundreds of other Russians, rotting in large open pits, with a loose covering of earth and lime. Reaching the top of the camp, we entered the administration block, where we were duly registered and searched. They relieved us of the civilian clothing that Mastrovic had supplied but overlooked the lira. Steven placed a packet of cigarettes on top of his pack. For a moment, the soldier contemplatively fingered the packet. There were no words spoken, but the guard interpreted Steven's look, abruptly breaking off the search and allowing Steven to pass to the end of the counter. Bill had concealed the remaining lira on his person, but the soldier intent on turning his rucksack inside out, overlooked the clothing that he was wearing. Leaving the administration block, we passed a group of SA men who has assembled for guard duty.[2] One recognised our uniforms and spitting contemptuously on the ground, he said, 'English Gentlemen eh?' There was no mistaking the venom with which the words were spoken. He gripped his rifle firmly and watched us pass through the gate. Our fresh escort led us to the bathhouse, a small stone building at the eastern end of the camp. Extremely near the bath house, a wooden shed stood in the middle of a clear patch of ground. Two men carrying a stretcher deposited their contents inside the shed. Later we learnt that when the shed was full of bodies, a party of Russian prisoners would load them onto horse-drawn carts. The crude funeral party, of living and dead skeletons, would be escorted to the open burial pits, and to the guard's command, the dead were thrown among their comrades. There were no last rites performed, it was just a routine. In the shower room we joined a group of Russians. They were standing naked waiting for the water to flow from the showers. The barber had recently shaved their heads bare, and the hair was still floating on top of the filthy water to flow from the showers, left by a previous group of bathers. The guard suggested we have our hair cut but we adamantly refused. We waited for the Russians to finish, appalled at the state of their bodies, they too were walking skeletons, their skin clung to their bones, their heads were nothing more than a mask drawn tightly over a skull, each movement might have been their last, they were literally dying on their feet. Fortunately, the water was warm; the first bath we had been offered since our imprisonment and the first time in three months we had had the opportunity of examining the effects of our restricted diet. Our stomachs were flabby, full of the starch we had lived on while the rest of our bodies had wasted considerably. In comparison with the unfortunate Russians we were still in good condition, but then they had been in captivity longer. While we bathed, our clothing passed through the fumigator. We remained under the shower until they were returned, drying ourselves on the one and only towel. The preliminaries completed, we were escorted to the bunker, a block of cells reserved for special prisoners, invariably the mutinous, which stood in a compound of its own.

We were locked in one cell which contained a bunk, 5ft from the ground with a wooden ledge raised to form a head rest. Near the door we were thankful to find a stove and a supply of fuel sufficient to warm the cell before we retired for the night.

At 5pm the cell guard brought tins, a wooden spoon and the evening issue of food, an earthy beetroot swill unfit for pigs. Two of these meals were issued daily. If this was the same ration that the German Army was fighting on, they must have left many frozen dead on the Eastern Front, for this was nothing more than a dietician's menu of death. There seemed to be little to say. None of us could eat the swill and the light faded, leaving the cell in darkness. 'The bed will be hard gentlemen, but I'm settling down for the night,' said Bill. We laid in a line, Peter, Bill, Steven and myself with a blanket to cover each of us. A little later, we reorganised ourselves, moving closer together we nursed our mutual warmth, sharing the blankets, so that we had a double covering. No one spoke for fear of waking the others. The moon appeared without improving the outlook, its sickening light glistening on the snow banked against the window, the shadows of the cell bars extending across the walls, four black lines, one for each of us. I laid awake for more than 2 hours after we had settled down, listening to Steven's even breathing. Suddenly he screamed, a frightening soul-rending scream followed by unintelligible murmuring. It took my breath away and my heart raced madly within my breast. He lay perfectly still, as did the others, then suddenly flayed the air with his fists, giving another agonising scream after which he relaxed, moaning as he turned over onto his side. The cell, in fact the whole camp, was still, and I wondered if I had been dreaming, for Bill and Peter hadn't said a word. I was tempted to ask them if they had heard Steven just to reassure myself, I couldn't have dreamed that and yet I wasn't sure. The minutes stole by and I knew that I couldn't sleep until I had asked Peter or Bill. 'Is anyone awake?' I whispered. 'Who the hell could sleep through that?' Bill replied, but eventually we did.

Chapter Twenty

The Vertrauensmann and Dr Briefe

Steven suffered no ill-effects from his nightmare. He was the first to wake, a matter of minutes before I did. We woke the other two with our chatter. There seemed to be little point in leaving the warmth of the blanket, but we wondered what would happen first. Bill said that as official prisoners of war we would be entitled to Red Cross amenities, and that we must arrange an interview with the lager führer, or whatever he was called. Then, the British Camp Leader arrived.

'Good morning gentlemen, I heard that you had arrived last night, but I couldn't arrange to see you straight away. As a matter of fact, this visit is unofficial at the cost of two cigarettes. If you've got plenty of fags, you can move anywhere in this camp, it's good currency. I can't stay long, but if you like, I will put you in the picture later you see, when I come on an official visit, I will be able to remain longer.' Peter said, 'Good show.'

'Well gentlemen, I'm BSM Smith.'[1] 'I'm the British Camp Leader, the Vertrauensmann.[2] If the men have any complaints, I take them to the lager führer. We have a German representative as well, he's an Austrian actually, you will meet him later. He has been very helpful to us, in fact he's right on our side. There are about 500 British prisoners in this camp all told, but we have about the same number out on 'Arbeits Commandos', they are working parties mostly employed in farming. I make the rounds with Dr Briefe every now and again when we receive Red Cross parcels, making sure the working parties get their whack.'

He told us he would bring some Red Cross parcels later and that they typically got one a week, but for the past few months the quota had not been forthcoming because the trains had been bombed or too busy.

Most of the Red Cross parcels came from Sweden, but just lately a consignment from Switzerland had come through. The parcels varied, there were Canadian, which were the best, British and American. The Canadian parcels contained fifty cigarettes, used for bartering with the guards. 'At one time we paid twenty cigarettes for a loaf of bread, but we've come on the gold standard lately, a loaf only costs five now.'

Smith told us they had managed to build up a reserve supply of parcels and they had been issuing one between two a week. We were due two parcels later. As we were newcomers, we would receive a hospital parcel too. They contained milk, Horlicks, cocoa and benga's food, sometimes tea.[3] They also contained biscuits, a tin of Marmite and several other commodities.

Smith told us that when they first arrived, they were the only British prisoners and the Germans thought they could push them around like they did the Russians. That soon changed, the Brits stood up to them and as a result were treated much better. There was a special lager for the Russians who had fought for the Germans, and they were easy to spot, they had legs or arms missing, all lost a limb fighting for Jerry. This then is how they are treated, thrown back into prison with no future, looked down on by other prisoners. As well as ourselves, the French and Italians were the only others to get parcels. The Russians waited around the British compound all day, hoping for scraps of food to be given to them. Smith said he had seen the guards bayonet them without having any effect. Smith concluded by saying he was going to see Dr Briefe and he might return shortly.

I said after he had left, 'Well, things are looking up, a Red Cross parcel and a hospital parcel. Well done the Red Cross.'

We all liked the look of BSM Smith and with rising spirits tidied our cell in readiness for the arrival of Dr Briefe. Bill spoke of the 60,000 lira he was still carrying. He felt that it was only a matter of time before a search would reveal the money; they were consecutively numbered notes, all new and it would be awkward for Mastrovic if they were to find them. We could not foresee a use for them, and with a degree of reluctance, we decided the best course of action was to burn them. They disappeared in a flash, a few flames, ashes and they were gone. We wondered how Mastrovic was. Steven said that he had shown him a postcard of his family group one afternoon. He had two grown-up offspring, the boy was around 23 years and the daughter about 19. They were a handsome group.

Dr Briefe entered the cell.[4] He saluted. He wore the uniform of an honorary lieutenant. He bade us good morning and introduced himself. He was of average height, he looked a little pale, the result of a recent medical board he said. I was to hear his explanation in the course of a later conversation. He was Austrian and had no desire to fight for Germany. He felt Austria's interests were tied to Britain. He didn't theorise on this issue, but I gathered that his country's foreign policies marched in step with Britain's. He spoke of the great British politician of the past, Castlereagh, who was a good friend of the Austrian Metternich, both knew what was good for their countries.[5] He continued saying the war is a tragedy, he wanted no part in it. Every time they called him to a medical board, he dosed himself with aspirin and pleaded that his heart was weak. As a result, he had not been called to the front. He was glad the end was near and that Germany was doomed.

He then said, 'The purpose of my visit is to ask you to answer various questions. That is the official reason, but of course, I know that you are not disposed to answer them, so I don't waste time. It is forbidden for you to receive books here in the bunker, but I have brought you some, nevertheless. I hope they are suitable. Let me know later what you would prefer to read, and I will hunt through the library. I understand that Mr Smith has visited you already. He is a good man and has done much for the comfort of his fellow British prisoners. I have arranged that he will bring you parcels this morning. Perhaps you have some request to make?'

'Yes,' said Bill. 'Smith managed to look in for a moment. Dr Briefe, there are one or two requirements that you will no doubt be able to arrange which are of immediate concern to us as they affect our personal comfort. This cell is small, compact, but we shall make the best of it. It was extremely cold last night; we should like an extra blanket each. Secondly, since we are fortunate enough to have a stove, we should be grateful for some fuel, and lastly, but equally important for our health's sake, we should like to take an hour's exercise in the compound, morning and afternoon, dependent on the clemency of the weather. Naturally, if it was snowing hard, we would prefer to remain under cover.' Bill then spoke of the diet we had been on for the last three months and that it was insufficient to fortify us against the rigours of winter.

There was a faint suspicion of malicious humour underlining Bill's detailed requests. He had experience of German thoroughness, their set methodical direct application to any problem. He had agreed with Steven one day that their efficiency suffered for the simple reason that it was never elastic. Certainly on the field of battle, they had shown ability to exploit breakthroughs in the course of a successful operation, and their planning on the grand scale had enabled their armies to execute smooth manoeuvres, but, getting down to the individual, if something were to go wrong, invariably the whole machine was thrown out of gear; they were inclined to obey blindly, interpreting an order coldly and putting it into effect to the very letter. However, if one letter was missing, they were temporarily powerless to act independently. Dr Briefe was an Austrian, Bill realised that of course; I gathered that he wished to make quite clear that the guards were given to understand that we wished to please our-selves. We would indicate whether we were desirous of taking exercise or otherwise. If they weren't carefully briefed, we should find ourselves pushed outside in the middle of a snowstorm. Briefe was amused, perceiv-ing the unspoken thoughts which had prompted his detailed explanation, but he made no reference to it when he replied.

'Blankets are scarce; however, I will see what can be done. Mr Smith will be able to arrange a ration of fuel, the prisoners collect fuel in bulk and make their own compound distribution. He will make sure that your cell is included on the British compound delivery list. I will arrange with the cell guards that you take exercise twice daily according to your wishes. Now I must go.' Dr Briefe replied.

He walked towards the door, pausing when his hand held the handle. 'If you have anything you wish me to safeguard, I can promise you that it will be absolutely secure with me.' Steven looked at Bill, anticipating a negative reply, but Bill waited for Briefe to continue. Having ascertained that there was no one in the cell passage, he closed the door, adding, 'Mr Smith may have told you. There were ten or twelve British officers held in these very same cells several months ago. Perhaps you have heard of them. He mentioned their names. There was a British brigadier and an American colonel in this cell.[6] One or two had been badly wounded but they were not allowed to go to the hospital, although the British doctor demanded that they should be sent. They had been captured in Albania. The British brigadier gave me his diary before he left.[7] I have taken it to my family chalet and buried it in the grounds where it will be safe until the end of the war. I would be pleased to do the same for you. I leave you to think about my offer and I will return tomorrow.'

When Dr Briefe had left, Peter went to the window, watching him walk through the lager towards the administration block. 'What do you make of him, Sir? He seemed anxious to please; I would like to know his motive, there is more in this than meets the eye.'

Bill said he was hesitant to offer an opinion, but for the time being, we should be careful with Dr Briefe, allowing him to make the conversation. Although we were in an official prisoner-of-war camp, the SS knew where we could be found. We should be careful what we say, even inside our cell, we could always be recalled for further cross-examination by the SS.

If it were true that he had buried the brigadier's diary, then we could trust him. Bill thought the doctor's intention was clear, knowing which side his bread was buttered on. Bill didn't think he would be prepared to assist us to escape, it would be more than his life was worth, unless he was prepared to take the chance and accompany us.

Bill then spoke of the direction of any future escape. The shortest line would be to the east through the Russian lines. It would be extremely risky, and who knew what would happen once we were in Russian hands. Dr Briefe would not consider a plan involving a journey eastwards. Bill was not sure that it would be an easy matter convincing the Russians that we were British. Of course, Briefe would be taken prisoner and we would see him no more. No, the line of least resistance would be to make for the Jugoslav border, then again, the Partisans may be hostile, they would probably hold us captive and it has been known of them to dispose of British officers. If we got out at all, we should stick very close to Vienna, we could probably make ourselves more useful there. With a stroke of luck, pick up the threads of where we left off!

Bill then ventured, 'If Smith travels round the countryside with Briefe, visiting the arebeits commandos, he may have some useful information concerning the lie of the land and the feelings of the local peasantry.' It was decided to seek Smith's advice upon his next visit. We should at the same time, instruct him not to mention our conversation with the doctor.

We all felt that we could take Smith into our confidence if we were to attempt an escape. We then plotted the more intricate details of escape.

The first thing was to get out of the camp, the easiest way was to volunteer for work on one of the working parties, preferably on a farm. If we volunteered for work, we might have to give up our parole. If that is the case and we escaped from a farm, the warning would be circulated to shoot on sight, criminals at large, and we would have to confine ourselves to travelling at night. This led us into the next point. Would the locals be hostile or friendly? Smith may have the answer to that. We should then save enough food from the Red Cross parcels to see us through a week's travel, by which time, if we were forced to travel by night and were making for the Jugoslav border, we should take at least seven days and then be a day's journey away from our proposed destination. It was thought to be around 200 hundred miles distant. Peter thought it was less, around 150 miles but agreed that travel should take place during darkness. We had to consider assistance from the Austrian peasant, we would need a map and compass, and it was felt Smith may solve these problems.

Bill went on to discuss 'parole', it may be a thing of the past but if one gave up one's parole leaving the confinement of the camp, you are saying you will not escape. If you do, you give up your right to life, you can be shot. We then discussed if we were granted outside labour, could we choose to work on a farm to the north or the south of the Stalag. At that moment, BSM Smith returned carrying four hospital parcels and two Canadian boxes. 'When you open the box, you will find that all the tins have been opened, the Prison Commandant is bloody-minded on that score. They look for any compass or files hidden in the tins.'

We complimented Smith and Peter offered him a cigarette which he refused, saying Peter would need them himself. He then told us that they had a radio hidden in the lager. They were able to keep in touch with the outside world. A news bulletin was published and read out to the chaps each night just before 'Lights Out'. Last night, it was said that the Russians had almost encircled Budapest and had crossed the Vistula in Poland at several points. Greece was clear, but the Communist Partisans had been giving a bit of trouble. No change on the Western or Italian fronts. Smith felt it would all be over in a couple of months.

Bill then changed the conversation around to the subject of escape. He told Smith that none of the points to be discussed should be disclosed to Dr Briefe. He continued, we were new hands at prison life, and we trusted no one. Judging by Smith's conversation referring to Dr Briefe, we were prepared to believe him to be a well-meaning man, nevertheless, at this stage, our queries were not for his ears. Bill asked if Smith felt the local peasantry was friendly? How did he find them? They recognised him as a prisoner and British, were there any who were genuinely friendly, fully knowing what he was?

Smith replied that he hadn't met any himself who were hostile. Most of them got on with their work and paid little attention to the prisoners, but he had heard of some of them being hostile. He had recently heard a report about the crew of an American bomber that bailed out. Five of them landed, the local SA chased them into a churchyard and shot the lot of them. Smith had been trying to find their burial place. They don't like the airmen, and may have heard Hitler's order that all enemy airmen should be shot directly they are caught. Smith didn't know how many of the peasants pay attention to Hitler's orders anymore, but he felt sure that there are some who would. Conversely, there are some who would go out of their way to be friendly, like Dr Briefe's housekeeper at his flat in Vienna. Smith had been invited to stay there by Briefe on more than one occasion. She was very pro-British. He then related the story of the prisoner who was working on a farm not far away, it was run by the hausfrau and her daughter. The lad intended to make a getaway from the farm. He worked his plans very nicely, taking plenty of time. He used to work late, and the girl used to go and fetch him, he varied his hours so that she would be in the habit of expecting him anytime of the evening, well, within reason! The trouble started because he got too friendly with the girl and she fell in love with him. When he decided that he would make a go for it, he hadn't reckoned on the girl's feelings. He went out to work as usual in the fields, knowing that the girl had cycled into the village. Instead of going to work, he collected his food and map which he had hidden in a nearby field and set off south. When he was crossing a field, he saw a girl cycle by on the road a couple of hundred yards below him and he laid down until she had passed. The funny thing was that the girl had not indicated the village which she was going to visit that afternoon, and the chap hadn't recognised her as she cycled by. He continued on his way and was picked up an hour later. It was the daughter who had seen him and tipped off the police. He was sent back to the Stalag and put in the bunker on bread and water for twenty-one days.

Steven asked Smith if he thought the local peasantry would help if they were asked. 'What would be my chances if I knocked on the door of some out-of-the-way farmhouse at night. Do you think they would be prepared to feed me knowing I was an escapee?'

Smith replied, 'Without being long-winded, Sir, I think you would have to take your chance. You might be lucky, but I doubt it.'

That was not a favourable response, but Steven persisted with questioning Smith. He asked what the terms were for a man working on the arbeits commandos, could anyone work on them?

'Not anyone, Sir. All below the rank of corporal are accepted, although some prisoners may swap identity and go out with the intention of escaping. I have heard of senior ranks applying for work outside and being accepted, but they make sure that you work where you are under constant supervision and your chances of escape are limited.'

Smith was asked one last question, was there an escape committee in the camp and could maps and compasses be supplied? He replied that there was a sort of committee. Anyone escaping would place themselves in Smith's hands initially. Any unclaimed personal parcels that contained food were set aside for escape parties. Maps were a problem, but they had one of Austria and they made copies of it. Sometimes, they found small escape compasses inside the tobacco tins. Smith said that they always tried to get whatever the would-be escaper wanted and then cover up for him when he had gone.

Bill thanked BSM Smith and asked if we would be included on the fuel round today, and he assured us that we would. He made his farewell and disappeared back to the compound.

After he had gone, Bill summarised the situation:

If we were to make an attempt, it must be from the Stalag or from a working camp outside.

Which of the two start lines were the easier to cross? It would seem the working camp would be the better option. There was a danger of us being penned up in this bunker until the end of the war, or, on the other hand, we may be transferred to the main lager. It was more likely that Steven, Peter and Bill would be transferred to an officer's camp, while I took my chances here. If we wished to get to a working camp, we must exchange identities with a private soldier or a lance-corporal in order that we become eligible for a working party. That was point one. Once we were clear, it was essential that we should exist on our own resources to avoid the local peasantry. We should travel by night and rest up by day, which probably meant being forced to make detours and choose a hide-out by night. At present the weather was against an escape and we must wait for a break, probably until the spring, with luck the end of March or the beginning of April. To make himself clear, Bill reiterated that a quiet spot by night might be a busy one by day, we should be careful to avoid village localities for fear of stirring up noise, dogs chiefly who would cause some investigation. To sum up, point one, in order to get to a working camp, we must change our identities, and, secondly, if the attempt is to have any measure of success, it must be entirely on our own resources and therefore when the weather is more bearable.

I then said, 'May I add something, Sir, before you carry on?' 'Yes, Charles, what is it?'

'It is highly unlikely that we should all be sent to the same working camp, even if we succeed in swapping identities. That being the case, perhaps you would brief me for future reference. Do you suggest that the Jugoslav border is the safest asylum to strike for?'

Bill told me that my aim was to get back to Base as soon as possible. To pass through Russian lines might prove to be the shortest route. On the other hand, the safest route may be to strike for the Jugoslav border. It would depend on where you started from. It was really for me to decide once on the road.

The talk was over, it was time for food. Bill appointed me chief cook and asked me to rustle something up from the Red Cross parcels.

Chapter Twenty-One

The Parting of the Ways

On 3 March we had spent one month in the cell. The morning and afternoon exercise had helped to improve Bill's leg. He still walked with a limp but there was no doubt he was much stronger. Dr Briefe came to see us with some unexpected news, Bill, Steven and Peter were to be sent to Brunswick in northern Germany.[1] I was to be transferred to the main lager with the other British prisoners. The guard opened the door after our breakfast and proudly exercised the few words of English he had learned. 'Gentlemen, your air is served, this way please.' Putting on our jackets, we followed him into the small compound at the northern end of the block. Overnight, more prisoners had moved into the block opposite which was separated by a wire, one of the prisoners called to us, he was dressed in a Polish uniform, a man over 50 years of age, Steven and I went to the wire to speak with him. He understood English fairly well. We asked him where he had come from, he said a long way away, he had been on the road for a month, and he would be on the road again soon if the Russians got any closer. They were all Polish Partisans from Warsaw. He had fought with the British under Ironside at Archangel in the last war. He wore the Pour le Mérite, a Polish decoration, he said it was the equivalent of the Victoria Cross. We asked if he had been fighting in this war, he said he had, he was a regular Polish officer, fighting with an irregular army, the Partisans of Warsaw. 'We fought well, we were supplied with arms from the air by the RAF who flew low over the city, dropping guns right into our laps, and the Germans were powerless to do anything about it.' It had been a wonderful sight and raised hearts were then quickly trodden into the ground by the Russians. He portrayed a fascinating insight into the deprivations suffered under the rubble of bombed houses. They had lived like rats but hadn't given up hope. They had fought like thieves in the night, striking down the enemy in the dark, all the time growing stronger. The British sent in liaison officers and afterwards came the RAF, giving them the arms they sorely needed. One could see his passion as he continued his story. Then came the break-out. They struck in the enemy's rear and defeated him, chased him from Warsaw, clearing the banks of the

River Vistula so that the Russians could cross, but they never turned up, they didn't want to come. The Poles had fought their battle for them, their powerful army remained on the east bank of the Vistula. They waited for the German Army to lick its wounds and reorganise before they attacked the city yet again, while the Russians watched. They did not want a victorious Polish Army. The RAF could not save them this time, again the Polish fought in the buildings and cellars of Warsaw until forced to surrender and this is where they are now. Straightening up to his full height and looking at us as if he had seen us for the first time, saying, 'Long live Britain, long live Poland, the battle is not yet won boys by you, I or our countrymen; one day it will be won by all the Christian people who value freedom and the love of God.' He left us, joining his friends who were returning to their prison block.

I thought the war should nearly be won by now, perhaps in a couple of months it would all be over. Steven was philosophical; he didn't think the Pole meant the defeat of the Nazis and their satellites. The Poles live nearer to Russia that we did and have a greater understanding of Russians. He then delved into the Russian history, their recent history and the Red Revolution and the aims of Peter the Great and other czars, always wishing to control the Baltic and obtain effective control over land bordering on the Mediterranean. Steven didn't stop there, he continued to expand on a future world in which Communism would play a great part.

I was a little relieved when I saw Sergeant-Major Smith coming down the road, he was carrying another couple of parcels. He entered our cell, closing the door behind him. He knew that there was a move afoot as he addressed Bill. 'I hear you are on the move, Sir.' Bill replied that was the case and asked if Smith knew when. 'According to Dr Briefe, tomorrow, but I'm not sure, he'll be down in a minute. I thought I would see you alright for the journey, sometimes you are on the road for a long time these days. We were on the road for a month. We travelled on the train part of the way; we'd come from Stettin. You will need a couple of parcels to keep you going.' Bill thanked Smith profusely saying he hoped they would meet again in better circumstances, when he could be thanked properly. Bill asked if I would be joining Smith in the British compound to which Smith replied that I would be taken good care of.

Smith went on to say they had had a visit from the 'Free Corps' traitors who were on the lookout for volunteers. He had met him at the gate and warned him that if he set foot inside the camp, he would not be responsible for what happened to him.

Bill said that this was something new and who were the 'Free Corps', were they Englishmen?

Smith replied that some of them were, the rumour was that there were 445 so-called Englishmen in the 'Free Corps'. The Germans had asked for volunteers to fight the Russians, one of the earliest volunteers from the British element was a corporal, a New Zealander born of Russian parents.[2] The earliest volunteers were taken to Berlin and put on a course then sent around the camps to spread the anti-Communist gospel. They had a barracks at Graz. Dutchmen, Vichy-French, Spaniards, all sorts. Smith had heard them drilling, they had a reputation for smartness. A Russian general called Vlasov had several divisions of Russians who volunteered to fight against the Red Army, these were not classified as 'Free Corps' but were on their own.[3] They were easy to pick out, as they wore German Army uniform and the British had a small Union Jack sewn on their sleeve.

There followed comments on the future of the 'Free Corps', which was summed up quickly by Bill who said the ring leaders would be shot and the rest receive a prison sentence.

The Russian recruiter comes to the camp once a month, he always gets plenty of volunteers. He's smartly dressed, carries a briefcase, doesn't do much talking and then marches off volunteers in batches of a hundred at a time. When they come back, they are missing an arm or a leg, and they are thrown back into the swill pit. Nobody wants them.

Smith had seen Russian officers up to the rank of colonel, they are often in charge of a block. He dishes out the food, sometimes he has to kick the prisoners on past the swill tub, but they don't bother. They hover around until everyone has been served, and they make a dive for the bin, usually sending it flying and losing their own ration into the bargain. They lie on the ground licking up the swill. We watch them once, but once is enough, they are just like animals.

Smith then left followed quickly by the arrival of Dr Briefe. 'I have been informed that you will leave the camp at 10 hours tomorrow morning. The train leaves Wilfleinstadt at 10.30, and you will have to change at Vienna. From there you will probably travel to Munich and then north for Brunswick. It is a roundabout route and may take as long as three days, perhaps longer; these days no one can tell.' He hoped that the transferees would find improved conditions at their next camp, an officer's camp, not that amenities improve with status, sometimes they could be worse. After some deliberations of the demise of Austria at the war's end, Dr Briefe left the cell after wishing the group luck on their journey.

When Steven, Peter and Bill left, I went to the window and watched them pass out of sight. We had many strenuous arguments often without arriving at a conclusion. Sometimes, we were sick of listening one to the other, but we never lost sight of the fact that companionship was our main source of comfort. Bill had been our arbitrator, Steven provided many topics for discussion, continually probing into the future, and Peter was always cheerful, eager and trusting in providence for our well-being. Now the cell was empty, the ashes of the burnt-out fire were scattered round the foot of the stove while everywhere evidence of their occupation remained. The snow was thawing, and large pieces slid from the roof opposite into the compound where we used to take our exercise. It was a bright, hopeful day for the beginning of their journey to Brunswick, but the crude gloom of the cell matched my feelings.

Shortly after noon, a new guard escorted me to the British compound where I found BSM Smith and his brother, Jimmie, waiting at the entrance of their block. They had put my things in my room. It would be grub time soon and we would share it together in this room. I asked if they had both been taken prisoner at the same time, Jimmie said that they were, but they had been separated since, Jimmie had volunteered for a working party, he had worked on a bauer about 40 miles from the camp. It was OK during the summer, but pretty rough in the winter. There had been ten of them in the party all together in a hut. I asked him if he had ever tried to escape. He told me that once he did, but he didn't get very far, it's not easy and only a few are successful. He got twenty days in the bunker on bread and water.

Smith said, 'I've just had a look at the swill, it's deadly, I think we'll have toast and cheese, Jim, make some for our friend here as well. By the way, what is your Christian name?'

'Charles,' I replied.

'Well, Charles, my name is Francis, but I prefer to be called Frank; remember, you will always be welcome to join us in here. It's much quieter and even if we aren't here, come in if you want to read or sit on your own.'

Chapter Twenty-Two

A Hospital Bed Means Freedom

With the arrival of March, the weather rapidly improved for spring was premature and winter vanished overnight, leaving behind its mantle of snow. Fresh blades of virgin grass appeared, brightening the rolling slopes stretching across the Vienna plain to the north and spreading a carpet of green at the foot of the woods to the south. The trees were covered with sticky brown buds and new leafy shoots, thriving under a sun whose attentive rays aroused more than the countryside about us. Improved weather conditions enabled the air forces to renew their activity and take their proportionate part in the closing scenes, which were now being set on all fronts of the European Theatre. We in prison were thrown on the scent of things to come by a BBC news commentator who gave a brief review of the situation which explained the appearance of heavy bomber formations, attended by long-range fighter escorts in the skies about east Austria.

It was a small paragraph, but our news script-writer seized upon it to kindle the hopes of every prisoner in Stalag XVII A. 'American heavy bomber formations accompanied by strong fighter protection, have renewed their daylight sorties ahead of the Red Army on the Eastern Front, attacking strategic targets along the Red Army lines of advance. Red Air Force formations operate in close support of the front-line troops, concentrating their attacks on troop movements or formation headquarters.'

These daylight raids must have meant that the Red Army was close at hand; had not the commentator said that the sorties were attacking 'strategic targets along the Red Army lines of advance?' That surely meant the Red Army was close at hand. Wishfully, we believe this interpretation of the commentary, which was verbally retransmitted from compound to compound throughout the camp.

Jimmie alerted me to the latest news bulletin and told me I should go and read it.

Dr Briefe would be along at 8pm as he wished to speak to me, this is the message, it is from the King to General Eisenhower and Field-Marshal Montgomery:

His Majesty the King sent messages of congratulation to General Eisenhower and Field-Marshal Montgomery on behalf of the British Empire and Commonwealth expressing his gratitude to all those who participated in the crossing of the River Rhine. To the Field-Marshal he added, your triumphant passage of the Rhine into the heart of enemy territory has stirred us all deeply and I am prouder than I can say of the gallant part my sailors, soldiers and airmen have played in it.

Eastern Front: The Russians have encircled Budapest and the fall of that city is imminent. Russian Forces are pushing steadily on towards the Bratislava Gap leading to the Plain of Vienna. To the north Russian Forces have reached the estuary of the Oder at Stettin while Marshal Koniev's Forces have swung towards Upper Silesia. South-East of these Forces, the Red Army are threatening the Moravian Gap which is the gateway to the Czechoslovakian Arsenal. Ends [End note] More later if we can get it. The script writer bets ten cigarettes to one that we shall all be home in two months from now.

The end note had been added by an excited script-writer wishing to vent his feelings to all readers.

We felt that if the Russian Army was well on the way across the Hungarian plain heading towards Bratislava and the mouth of the Vienna plain, we should hear of a move at any moment. They were almost certain to evacuate the camp. Smith said he thought that was what Dr Briefe wanted to talk to me about.

Bedlam had been let loose in the dormitories, everyone talking two to the dozen comparing buoyant speculations, for the first time, conscious that the end was in sight. The British compound contained 1 block, housing 2 dormitories, each holding over 200 men. The dormitory over which the food syndicates warmed their meals or brewed tea. Mealtimes varied according to your place in the stove queue. The syndicates pooled their Red Cross boxes and, in this manner, managed to ration themselves for a month until the next issue, if it were delivered, thus avoiding the swill issued by the camp authorities which was given to the hungry Russians hovering near the compound wire.

Dr Briefe arrived. In view of the bulletin that we all had seen, Briefe told us that it had been decided that the camp should be evacuated should the Russians reach Stuhlweissenberg. Fit prisoners would be marched to Braunau, eighteen days on foot to the west.

After enquiry, Briefe said Stuhlweissenberg was 90km away, four days' march at the most. I asked if the sick prisoners would travel by train to

Munich. Briefe replied, 'I thought you might ask this question. No. They will be left here in the camp in charge of the British orderlies.'

I asked the doctor if he could arrange for me to enter the hospital block; this is the chance that I had been waiting for.

He thought it would be possible, his friend is the doctor in charge. Briefe foresaw no objections on his part, but he reminded me that I would have to be careful when the camp was being evacuated, because although there would be no prison guards, I would still have to pass through the retreating German Army and also the Russian Lines.

I told the good doctor that I had ample opportunity to consider the odds and make my plans. I felt that the Russian armoured units would make their way along the plain leading to Vienna, while their infantry units would move over the hills to the north and south. In that case, I didn't think the Wehrmacht would be long in following up the evacuating prisoners, for to remain entrenched in the hills, meant that they would be cut off from the rear with Russian infantry pressing down on top of them. If I could get out of the Stalag, I should walk over the hills to the south and head for the Neusiedler See and to the other side of the lake which is less than 10 miles from the Hungarian border.

The doctor replied, 'It is possible, you may be right. I would be inclined to remain hidden in the woods until the Wehrmacht has retired and then wait for the Russian infantry.'

I responded saying, 'In that case, I may just as well stay in the camp. No, doctor, I wish to travel fast and on my own. The Russians may force all prisoners to remain in the camps until they decide to evacuate them. That won't do for me, with any luck, I could be with my unit inside ten days from the time of departure from Kaisersteinbruck.' This was an unqualified estimate, but I hoped it would emphasis my anxiety and persuade Dr Briefe to help me obtain a place in the hospital.

'Very well, it is for you to decide, I will arrange for you to be transferred to the hospital tomorrow afternoon. You are sick with sciatica remember? Before the fit prisoners evacuate, I will bring you a route card of their intended journey to Braunau, it may be of use.'

So, on the morrow, I would be a very sick man, sick of sciatica and the prison camp!

The hospital differed little from any other block, an attempt had been made to distinguish it but the whitewash had long since been washed from the grey walls by the winter rains. There were fewer beds and the rooms were clean, small compensation for genuinely sick men. Among the British prisoners who shared the eastern dormitory, few fortunately required specialised attention, there were limited medicants available with which to treat the sick, but, the RAMC orderly, a kindly young man from Newcastle, using his best bedside manner, treated all minor ailments in addition to preparing morning and evening beverages made possible through the hospital parcels, thus supplementing the normal Red Cross box. The British ward served more as a rest centre for those who were run down and in need of peace and quiet, away from the noise and confinement of the compound, whereas in the adjacent dormitory housing the Russian patients, every bed was filled with men dying of TB, in their case it was a gesture, orderlies and patients alike were resigned to the fact that it was only a matter of time before a bed was available to release one more from the torment of the compound. The Red Cross couldn't help these men. No one could. Their bodies were past cure as they were laid in the bed, rotting, one stage from the large open pit over the hill.

The German medical orderly who was responsible for the hospital, an evil, cross-eyed man, had boasted in the past of the number of Russians he had helped on the way to the grave, little realising he was doing them a service when he injected poison into their wasted frames. He was known to the British prisoners as the 'Humane Killer'.

Mr Smith visited me telling me that they were going the following day. He wanted to wish me luck. He told me they had received a new prisoner, an American pilot, he thought he had been flying a Lightning fighter, he had been forced to bail out and broke his leg in doing so. He then gave me the route card as promised by Dr Briefe. It shows the route that they would take to Braunau. He wished he were staying with me and he would like to have seen Hungary, but he had been with the lads all the time and felt it right to stick with them to the end.

I thanked Frank for his kindness, I told him that I was glad of the chance to accelerate my freedom, even it was only by a day. I told him I would head for Budapest where the British and American Missions would aim for after being freed. We knew as a result of the news that they had been established for the time being in Debracen. I told him that Arthur the South African and Harry his friend were accompanying me.

Frank said the Red Army were very close. All camp lights were switched off last night, even the search lights. Dr Briefe had told him that he would walk with him to Braunau, Frank would be walking to freedom, he to prison.

It was time for Frank to go and pack in readiness for his long journey. He bade me farewell and told me to look after myself.

Under the cover of early morning darkness, long lines of prisoners left the camp. Mock roll calls were made in each compound, more in the nature of indicating that their authority was still alive instead of a dying order. Hasty searches revealed many absentees who had intended to remain behind, the truants made no sign of resistance for the gun was still in the enemy's hand. By first light, the fit men were on the road and the Stalag was left thinly guarded. The Camp Commandant issued final orders, that in the event of an attack by Russian units, the camp was to be defended to the last man, whereas if the Americans or British arrived first, fighting would be restricted to a minimum and the camp would be surrendered with all haste.

The night following the columns departure for Braunau, a Russian bomber dropped two bombs on the camp. They caused no damage, except to morale, our guards' morale! During the morning, we watched sorties of Stormovik light bombers escorted by Yak fighters sweep low over the plain in search of targets. Returning from their raids, they sprayed any sign of movement on or off the roads over which they flew. The Camp Commandant and his remaining staff waited no longer. This sign of the approaching Russian forces was more than enough for his peace of mind. Their departure was secretive and next morning we were free and did not realise the fact for some hours into the new day.

The front-line fighting which we had expected would give us warning of its approach, with the rumble of artillery fire and aerial bombardment, overtook us without advance notice; it suddenly sprang up round us when we were thinking it perhaps had bypassed the area.

A fellow prisoner with whom I had arranged to leave the camp and walk into Hungary suggested that we climb the hill which overlooked the camp. From there, we were able to see a great distance over the Vienna plain. It was a fine, clear day and the northern ridges concealing the Bratislava highway were plainly visible. Sitting within the shade of the trees which covered the hill, we were experiencing the wonderful sensation of being able to do what one wants and no one screaming orders to stop. We had wanted to climb the hill and look for signs of the approaching battle which we knew would eventually pass by; our late jailers by their very hasty withdrawal, had indicated this much. It was refreshing just to be able to walk that short distance up the hill behind the camp and breathe the air of a free man. Soon we saw the movement of some Russian units. Looking to the edge of the southern side of the plain near Wilfleinstadt, we saw a battery of Russian field guns drop into position. Almost immediately, they had sighted the guns and opened up on the northern horizon. We could plainly see the belch of flame from the guns, and the upheaval that the shells caused in the distance, though it was impossible to see the actual target.

'I expect they are firing by map reference on the Bratislava highway, you know that road behind those distant hills over to the north there. For all they know, some of their own troops may be moving along it right now, for they don't appear to have the means of finding out. I can't see a radio down there can you?' Arthur remarked. It's only harassing fire you notice, they were firing about one round per gun per minute. A group of infantrymen laid down to the rear of the guns; at first we had thought that they were refugees for they moved bunched together like a herd of sheep. Shells landed between the infantry and the battery of guns, but the gunners were the first to react to the attack, for as soon as they had located the fire which came from a factory at Bruckon Leiths, they turned their guns and fired over open sights into the factory not more than a mile away. The infantry moved along a flank, under cover of their own guns towards the factory.

At the close of the action, we decided to leave the Stalag before the battles round about us encircled the neighbourhood and prevented us from escaping. Returning to the camp, we looked for the third member of our party, Harry, and informed him of our intentions. He agreed with our plans and together we left early in the afternoon for the Hungarian frontier, taking the road leading over the hill which led to the Neusiedler See and, ultimately, to the Hungarian frontier.

Chapter Twenty-Three

Red Army Train

Komarno was a town of two-storeyed houses astride the main line from Budapest west, providing a home for 15,000 people, 90 per cent of whose interest lay in the soil, the people who worked it and the people who owned it. We had been travelling since early morning along the long, straight stretch of road from Otterveny without seeing much except the broad expanse of flatlands either side and to the front, for this was the northern fringe of the great Hungarian plain, the wheat country and granary of Europe. Arthur had corrected me when I had said that the land was lying fallow, explaining that there were a million, million seeds under that brown earth, but the early morning frosts were keeping their heads below the surface for the time being. The sun had been good company since we had left Kaisersteinbruck, for spring had arrived prematurely this year, a timely gesture of nature, for there were many thousands of refugees cluttering the roads and sleeping under the hedgerows. A heat haze lay as screen between us and the distant horizons, but we had no difficulty finding the way for there was only one road, and the horse seemed to know it. The squeaking wheels and the horse's hoof clops accompanied our conversation and sounded friendly to our ears. Everything was warm and kind and even if there had been rain falling, we would have welcomed it for such was our mood, we were free and could go where we pleased.

Harry, normally a quiet man but a good listener, had changed his disposition and today was talkative. He commented on the fact that each village we had passed through was devoid of young folk. Just old folk with one or two children. We wondered what had happened to them. Towards 3 o'clock, we arrived on the outskirts of Komarno. Simultaneously, we saw another British ex-prisoner of war walking slowly on the footpath; he appeared to be sightseeing and in no particular hurry. Pulling into the side of the road, Arthur reined the horse to a standstill so that we could have a word with the stranger.[1] Judging by his battledress, it was a safe guess that he had been a soldier, although there were no insignia on his clothing to confirm this. He spoke without haste and with a north-country accent. He asked us if we were looking for the staging camp where other prisoners were gathering? This was the first we had heard of a staging camp. Harry made further enquiries regarding a staging camp. He was told that Komarno was on the main railway line. When the Russians in the staging camp had enough escaping British/Allied soldiers, they would put them on board a train and take them to Odessa, the Black Sea port where a boat could be picked up bound for Britain. We were directed to the end of the road to the centre of town, at the main square, turn right and keep straight on, the camp could not be missed.

The soldier declined a lift saying he was out for exercise and a look round. That amused us for if he'd had the same experience as we had, he would have had sufficient exercise to last him weeks!

Continuing, we followed his instruction, we reached the main square, there might be a train for Budapest today, and if there were, I was going to have a shot at catching it. 'Hold on here,' I said to Arthur. 'This is where I leave you.' Harry, taken aback, exclaimed, 'This is a bit sudden.' 'Yes, it is rather, but I would like to carry on. We may have to wait in the staging camp for days before the Russians decide to move us to Odessa. There may be a train to the capital and if there is, I'm going to be on it, I'm in a hurry. It's been great knowing you chaps. You have my address; I hope you'll soon write when you get home. I'll be seeing you.'

They really had been great company. Friendly, kind and humorous, each with a turn for soldierly philosophy which had paved the way, making our companionship a living thing right from the beginning. I was sorry to leave them but equally anxious to keep on the move whereas they were in no great hurry and would be content to remain in the staging camp for days. We understood each other and they made no attempt to suggest an alternative. Instead, Arthur said, 'Well, if you've made up your mind, there's no point in arguing further. Goodbye, Charlie, and watch it!' Harry said a brief goodbye too and then Arthur drove the cart away. Pioneers I thought. In a way we had been for we had been among the first to cross the Russian lines into Hungary. When they had gone, I looked across the square in search of the route to the railway station.

Komarno was probably busier than it had ever been for months. There were obvious signs of the war which had passed through it not more than a week before. There hadn't been in any of the villages we had passed, but there was a note of sadness attached to them all which couldn't be associated with anything but the aftermath of war. The deserted appearance of a house full of wantonly destroyed furniture, but without the occupants. A derelict house is worse than a derelict ship. Ships come and go but houses are stationary, and the very life of the house and atmosphere is from the people who build them and live in them. They were colourful, yet lacked the beauty of life which only the missing villagers could have given them.

It was now flourishing with activity and the many noises of a township hard at work. Standing watching the scene, I could see little that was productive work, work that would give the people back the means of life. Passing along the main street were many Russian lorries, American made ones bearing the familiar white star on their bonnets, essential for recognition purposes. They bumped hurriedly by on the crumbling stretch of road, their drivers hooting at the many refugees and peasants who preferred the highway to the pavement. Some of the locals drove carts while others stood and simply watched, as I did, airing themselves in the warm sunshine and no doubt wondering what the immediate future contained. The harvest was a long way off and the granary was bare, all food was short and there seemed little prospect of adequate rationing. The war for them was just beginning, not with a blitzkrieg of bombs and ripping bullets, but the subjection of an occupation army, made up of people they had lived in fear of for years. It was no wonder that they looked dejected and helpless. It had been pleasant to stand in the warm and watch, until you found yourself looking at these peasants, old people, it wasn't that they looked sad and pathetic, there was more than that in their looks, which concealed a fear that had been dormant for some years. Searchingly, they looked at the ragged Russian soldiers who ambled about the town of which they were now the masters. A woman police officer directed the traffic with two discs which she wielded like at automaton. It was hard to believe that these soldiers, male and female, had been responsible for the destruction of the German Eastern Front armies. Or, had it been the 'decay of shortage' within the ranks of the German armies that had defeated them? When they had had plenty, they had beaten the Russians back, but when they had been without themselves, they had fallen back. Idle reminiscence would not get me a train. I crossed the square and asked my way to the railway station.

One train stood on the tracks, its engine building up energy. There were five Pullman coaches and twenty or more cattle trucks. It was a hospital train. The trucks were allotted to the wounded, some of whom I saw being deposited inside. The Pullman coaches were allotted to the doctors. Their nurses and whatever officers were moving East. Walking the length of the train, I searched for a vacant space, hoping that I would hear a voice of welcome and invitation to make the journey. Each truck was now full of wounded laid on the beds of straw, blood seeping through their hastily applied bandages. They laid quietly, patiently and apparently untroubled by the hanging palls of dust which the thick hot air carried in clouds through the open doors. I admired them for their fortitude, but couldn't help likening their powers of endurance to that of wounded animals I had seen from time to time. There was only one difference, animals lie with hurt in their eyes, they lay quiet but in their eyes there is a question and wonder, if there is something wrong, but they are unable to account for their condition. The wounded Russian soldiers lay without a sign of sorrow or pain, their eyes uninformative, a blank. Then I saw the doctor, he had stepped down from one of the Pullman coaches and was watching me approach him.

'Good afternoon,' I said, hoping that he would understand me. He had for he replied, 'Thank you very much.' It was not really a strange reply. It was the first time I had heard a Russian speak English or rather broken English. He spoke quietly and he looked at me not with suspicion but with studious interest. He had studied English many years ago at school, but he did remember some words that he spoke almost apologetically. 'You drive to Budapest with this train?' he asked. 'I would like to,' I answered hurriedly, hoping that I would not appear over-anxious. For some reason I felt that I must not arouse suspicion though why I should worry, I was at a loss to explain.

'Are you a soldier?' he asked a further question. 'Yes, an American soldier.' I replied untruthfully, hoping that this reply would carry more weight. After all, I had seen American made lorries and on one occasion, some Boston Light Bombers, fifteen of them flying in formation towards the front. They were marked with the Red Star but there was no mistaking their identity. I hoped that the doctor would regard me as a national of a friendly country and perhaps show his gratitude by offering me a seat in his compartment. It was an anxious moment, but he quickly dispelled it. I might have been truthful for in later conversation he would not agree that I had seen some American made machines. The planes and lorries were perhaps similar to those constructed by the Russians, but there it was, I had been mistaken. It was pointless arguing further for he was convinced he was right, and the important point at that moment however, had been the invitation to join him on the train.

'Good comrade, you ride with me,' he answered stepping back into the coach and leading the way to his compartment. Shortly after we had settled ourselves, the train moved off and we sat looking out of the compartment window at the passing landscape for nearly an hour, without a word spoken. The doctor lit himself a cigar, a black clumsily rolled weed which gave off a heavily scented aroma unlike any cigar I had yet smelt. The compartment was a picture of self-help and oddly equipped. It was obvious that the doctor had an eclectic taste for loot. There was an upright piano, a hospital type bed, some pictures, in themselves a variety of colour depicting hunting scenes, and a lone aspidistra. When the train had been on the move for little more than an hour, he took up a mandolin which he strummed monotonously; sometimes he accompanied his playing, humming sorrowful airs or so they sounded to my unaccustomed ear. They were melancholy and yet captivating. I listened attentively, hoping that I would thus be able to convey my gratitude for the lift which would save me several tiresome days on the road. I think he was studying me as well, for once or twice our eyes met, though I couldn't be sure whether it was me he saw or some distant place connected with his song and visible only to him, a village in the Ukraine, a small place on the banks of a large river. He was very fair, unique among the Russians I had seen, and he had blue eyes to match an almost boyish complexion. It was only his hair and the eyes which had suggested a Ukrainian village, the village of his melody, just that far east and no farther.

The sun dipped low in the west. A giant blood-red ball which balanced on the horizon for a moment colouring the whole western sky red. As the train swung slightly north or south, twisting beside the banks of the Danube, we were able to catch a glimpse of this magnificent setting. About this time, the nurse entered the compartment, a faint look of recognition passed between them as she took a seat on the bed beside the doctor. She was certainly the most feminine female wearing a Russian uniform that I had as yet seen. Her frame was sturdy, even angular, she would have had no difficulty lifting a man on her shoulder. There was power in her body if it lacked symmetry. She carried her head proudly as though she were acutely aware that it revealed her main attraction. Her hair was neatly plaited and was swept back from a broad temple in folds which met in a bun at the rear of her head. Her eyes in the weakening light appeared to be a dark blue. I think they really were her charm, for a light of understanding seemed to gleam in them, and besides, they were inquisitive and kindly, an odd combination. Perhaps it was her every closeness beside me in the compartment which gave birth to this appreciation. She asked me several questions but without success, for I couldn't

understand her, so she contented herself making solo conversation with
the doctor for he never made an effort to answer her. It was interesting to
sit and listen for a few minutes, though her words were a mystery.

When the last light of day receded giving place to a brilliant, starlit
evening, I accepted this change as a cue to leave the compartment, for I
had gathered that their acquaintanceship was a little more than doctor and
nurse. I was sure that they wished to retire, though they had not signified
that intention, nevertheless, I knew that they would shortly sleep together.
It was fresh in the corridor, and free from the unpleasant stuffiness and
scent that I had associated with the Russians. The journey was monotonous, for the train made frequent and apparently unnecessary halts; several
of the stops were made in small unlit stations but no additional passengers
joined the train. Wherever it was, the train idled, Russian soldiers were
'standing to', they crunched by on the stone-covered track beside the
coaches and although it was difficult to recognise them by dress, somehow it seemed natural for them to be Russian soldiers. When they raised
their voices, beckoning to each other or to the engine driver, I was sure.
Intermittently, I dozed off between stops, even in my subconscious mind
I encountered Russians. Long before I had ever met any, I had formed a
picture drawn from the books I had read about their country, its vastness
and the suffering that had overtaken it from time to time. My imagination
had served me accurately. Their uniforms were much the same, rough,
mass-produced but serviceable and their strange voices sounded remarkably similar. Hearing them speak made one look closer for the pitch of
their voices compelled a second look. Mongolians, Caucasian, Georgian,
light-skinned, dark-skinned, brown-skinned, they were all assembled in
my dream which was clearer than usual because those were the faces that
I had seen in reality. In the prisoner-of-war camp and on the road since.
They were quite different from the European peoples, the products of an
unshaped civilisation. Vaguely, their villages took shape and they wore
their customary costumes, some men with baggy trousers and fez hats,
peculiar to the East, walking in front of their women who trailed obedi-
ently behind. Then I saw the different breeds of Cossacks, wild men who
treated their women worse that their horses at times. They were numerous and one thing was common to all of them; they were undeveloped and
essentially Asiatic. Among the world of books, one could believe that these
people had struggled for the realisation of an ideal which had promised
them an un-dreamed of future. They had fanciful imaginations, all of
them. But they had not liked the shape of things to come, many of them,

but the war had come along to interrupt this discovery and they had been encouraged to defend themselves.

The world is a strange place, as strange as a dream; here was a race of young and vigorous people, accustomed to worse than austerity, whose leaders pointed the finger of scorn at the comfort of Europe, for even the poverty of Europe compared favourably with the average lot of these Asiatic peasants, who had come to assert themselves, and enforce their will, which had been steeped in years of misery, and the ignorant turmoil of a mismanaged ideal.

The engine disengaged itself, leaving the coaches in a marshalling yard. It was 5.30am and the grey light of dawn revealed a thickly populated suburb, surrounding the deserted marshalling yard, which was as still as the train and its sleep-drugged occupants.

The corridor was locked, but I found an open window through which I slipped to the ground making my way towards a single exit. I had no doubt that this was a suburb of Budapest, for buildings stretched as far as the eye could see. I was certain there was not another city of this dimension in Hungary. I passed out onto the street, a short way from a 'T' road junction. Turning the corner, I noticed a young woman walk from a house farther along the street, she saw me as well and stopped until I had joined her. She was pretty and trimly dressed, she carried a net bag and was evidently going shopping.

She had waited, half expecting that I wished to speak with her. There was no other person in sight, so I felt our meeting was fortunate and, possibly, time saving.

'Good morning! Do you speak English?' The question was simple and direct and though it was some seconds before she answered, I knew that she had understood. She was trying to find words with which to make a reply. Her lips curled round one or two silently before she finally gave them a voice saying, 'Thank you. Good morning. I speak not English very well, my friend speak very well. Come please.' After this explanation, she shook my hand, a delayed greeting but a sincere one I felt, for she found one or two more words. 'You are the first English soldier here, welcome, we 'ope others come.'

With that short but comprehensive wish, she led the way down the street. We walked a long way out of her way, but it seemed to be of no concern to her. Eventually, we entered a quiet street, there was a familiar ring about the name of it. It was connected with politics, past politics. The houses were stately, exhibiting a grandeur which the faded bricks enhanced rather than concealed. We passed under an arch into a small courtyard containing an ornate well, stopping outside a door to the right on the enclosed square. Her knock brought a young man to the door with whom she conducted a short conversation, departing with the first and the last word, but the young man was not put out, he smiled, his eyes following her fondly as she went. After the girl disappeared from view, he regarded me with a look I found difficult to fathom. Then he smiled once more, a change of expression I found more comforting.

Chapter Twenty-Four

Introduction to a Hungarian

The girl's voice matched her outward appearance. An attractive, pleasing tone which was infused with the pleasures of yet another fine day, carried on wings above the disorders of an unpleasant occupation. Her short musical conversation was, for the greater part, a mystery to me, but it was apparent that her words were spoken in my favour, and more important perhaps were being received with sympathetic concern, partially conveyed by the sincere warmth of feeling revealed in his face. Since I hadn't mentioned my name, neither did she. Her words trickled forth gaily and it was plain to see that she regarded her responsibility for my well-being more in the nature of a surprise joke than an imposition, and then, before the young man had had the opportunity of making a reply, she had hurriedly skipped away with a brief glance over her shoulder as she passed from the courtyard into the street.

My newly made acquaintance pushed the door wide open, holding it so until I had passed into the room, which was barely furnished, yet retained something of the man's character. The centre of attraction was a beautifully polished grand piano standing superior and looking decidedly out of place. When he had closed the door, it was as if he had sealed the room from the outside world, for the room was filled with the atmosphere of the man himself, although there was more evidence of the times through which we passed. It was unmistakably his room, his main pleasure still with him, for the time being safe and serving to remind him of past memories; the piano which, at his touch, would reveal whatever mood of the past he wished to recapture. Every other article in the room was makeshift, a temporary affair.

There was the air of the teacher about him, though at a glance, he looked young enough to be a student; his was the confidence of maturity. Here was a forthcoming character incapable of concealing what he believed to be the truth of the matter. He felt his way about cautiously once we were seated, but not without some concern, which the girl's presence had served to dispel. After a period, he relaxed, speaking with more confidence, dropping the screen of reserve. At first, his conversation was casual, but later he warmed to his subject. Forgetting to introduce himself, a normal method of breaking the initial awkwardness of a chance meeting, he asked, 'Do you play the piano?' his eyes following the direction in which I was looking. It really was a lovely instrument, a light mahogany coloured grand, aged but ageless.

'A long time ago, but it's such a time, I doubt if I could play a note now. During the war, there was little opportunity,' I answered.

He asked if this were my first time in Budapest and I answered that it was, I then introduced myself.

He said, 'I'm sorry, I had forgotten, my name is Stephen Kovacs, how do you do? I am pleased to meet you Mr Charles. You must forgive me; I've been thinking of other things and your sudden appearance on my doorstep confused me. I hope that I can be of service to you.'[1]

I explained that I was passing through and hoped to make my way to the British Embassy as soon as possible. Stephen told me that it was near the centre of the city in Liberty Square and that the British and Americans were sharing the same building, they had only arrived the day before. It was difficult to move about from one district to another, permission had to be sought from the Russian District Commissar. He has to sign a pass which must be carried, and you get it only if he is satisfied, but sometimes they are suspicious. He then volunteered to take me that afternoon.

Stephen Kovacs was born and bred in Budapest; in fact, he had spent the greater part of his thirty years there. He was rather a small man, except for his head which looked as though it might have been made for a larger pair of shoulders. Almost immediately, I was aware of the sincerity of purpose which had endeared him to all his friends. His face was pallid, the colour of a man recently recovered from a long illness, but for all that, he reflected strength, the firmness of a man blessed with the profound knowledge of what he wanted from life and how to set about getting it. He was gentle natured with but one fault; he was a forgivable dreamer.

He had never travelled far from the city, nor had he wished to do so, for him Budapest was the most beautiful place in Europe. His offices were in the new part of the city, in Pest, but all of his spare time was spent in the old city of Buda across the Danube. He had seen the builders create parts of the new city, the business portion, yet he had always felt more at home in Buda. It was here where he had everything that mattered to him, his mother, his music and his work.

At first, when he spoke of the recent past, I thought his motive was to excuse the part his country had played in the war, but he wasn't a man given to excuses, he was basically a pacifist but imbued with an honourable desire to serve his country to the best of his ability, as his country would have him serve her. Such a person was Stephen Kovacs.

'War is a tragedy I shall never understand. Its more secret purposes evade my notice. For some, the motives demanding a country's attendance at the battle are obvious, but in other countries, the reasons are complicated and beyond the understanding of the man in the street, who has not had the benefit of the information only available to the legislators. I foresaw that my country would become involved. Ask me to explain what those reasons were on which I based this conclusion, and I have to admit now that the evidence seems vague and meaningless; indeed, I do not profess to understand them.'

'Hungary was not a wealthy country before the war, but our economy was progressive, and, in the main, the people were well satisfied. Unfortunately, in the competitive market, our markets virtually meant an ever-strengthening link with Germany, for she was our chief buyer and to her, gradually, our economy became tied. Germany was the one reason why we went to war. We were forced to side with her but not at the expense of our friends. I would like to explain.'

Stephen said that people were easily led. When the public press and radio are united in purpose, the idea is as good as sold, especially when there was no voice raised in opposition. They were satisfied with life but complacent, alive to Germany's wickedness and afraid of Russia. Hungary had always feared her, and it was a case of choosing between the lesser of two evils. It was impossible to remain neutral, sides had to be taken, or else! The Hungarian economy was the deciding factor, it was perhaps a stock-exchange gamble inspired by fear of the ultimate consequences. With whom should they stand? That was the question. Hungary was in the passage of two giants.

Recent Hungarian history was complicated. They had had problems with Romania and Czechoslovakia. Germany skilfully resurrected those surface troubles stirring up strife among the Central European countries, sowing discord so that they were powerless to achieve an agreement, and so unite in opposition to Germany's territorial designs. Hungary was branded a guilty belligerent when, in fact, they were blackmailed. Hungarian war potential spent itself against Russia in a conflict that they hoped would preserve their independence, fighting for freedom from fear, and, like the British, cherishing those factors on which desirable peace depended.

Vaguely, I was aware of the trend of Stephen Kovac's conversation, I was only half interested, as far as I was concerned motives didn't much matter, the fact was his country had gone to war and she had backed the losing side. Now it would be a period of retribution for Hungary, as he had put it, and then, after a while when she had been guided back to the democratic fold, we would all work towards the permanence of peace through mutual prosperity.

Stephen continued saying that many Hungarians had emigrated to the US, none had crossed the frontier to go to Russia, a country nearer to the border. The American way of life was natural, a young, vigorous country of opportunity, that was the note that appealed to Hungarians. On the other hand, Russia was a closed book. He had been thankful for a posting to the Red Cross organisation, Stephen would never have made a soldier, he was thankful that the work exempted him from taking up arms. He didn't think he was a coward, but he would never have been able to shoot someone. Budapest had been in a state of siege for six weeks and was laid to the ground during the battle. It was a terrifying experience, but he had not been afraid. Then, the Russians requisitioned his home and, later, the Red Cross offices, and Stephen was forced to look for alternative accommodation in Ujpest. He had two rooms and he helped at the nearby hospital.

He then asked where I had been a prisoner and of my travels but in particular the circumstances of my escape from the prisoner-of-war camp.

The 6 April 1945 was a day of surprises, I explained to Stephen, for to commence with, we woke up to find our German captors had fled, and before leaving had even hurled down the red, white and black swastika-covered flag. The first person to realise our freedom in fact noticed the flag-less pole in front of the Staff Headquarters, and then, on closer inspection, noted the deserted sentry boxes and the open gates at the main entrance. There wasn't a German to be seen.

A lone bomber had passed over the area of the camp during the night, dropping one bomb which exploded so suddenly, that we did not at first associate it with the plane. There had been no warning whistle or swish. The Russian bomber was flying extremely high. It returned a little later, and again the sudden explosion as if to confirm the truth of the matter. There was no damage, but it served to keep many of us awake, listening for the next lone raider, but the morning arrived without further incident. I told Stephen about the condition of the Russian prisoners and the fact that we made them a hot meal of soup, scores of hungry men, rattling their cups in anticipation, waiting for the meal to be prepared.

I then continued with the events of 6 April. We had awaited the approaching Red Army with undisguised impatience and, yet, with some concern. When considering front-line fighting, we had pictured guns, explosions and the rattle of small-arms fire, but the battle arrived as suddenly as had our freedom, unannounced. Arthur and I had climbed the hill to the rear of the camp. It was a warm day and the shady, tree-bordered verge attracted us, from there we could see across the Vienna plain even as far as the Bratislava Gap. We searched the plain looking in the distance and nearly missing the recce party which rode by, almost under our noses.

Three Russian horsemen rode into the camp, riding straight through and away again across country, eastwards. Half an hour later, we were the spectators of a sharp action.

We watched the Russian artillery, as previously described, destroy German anti-tank gunners, leaving a soulless mass of battlefield human debris to rot in the sun, A few minutes before, they had the power to think and their last thoughts may have carried a picture of their wife, children, old mother or whatever a man thinks before a piece of metal wrenches the last breath from him. When Arthur and I had left that hill we were two very sober people, we had watched men being torn apart, close enough to see their twisted faces as they fell. We decided to waste no further time at Kaisersteinbruck, but to get on our way. We told Harry of our plan.

And so, my story continued, Stephen although tired, was still eager to listen to the escape unfold. It had been in the village of Magyarova where we found all the houses had been ransacked, I had killed a hen to eat and we set about cleaning one of the houses up a little so we could sleep. We had a visit from an old man, about the age of 70. He had been hiding in the basement. He spoke a little English and had been to the US as a young man. We learned that the owner of the house had fled with his wife and three daughters into the swampland area to the west of the village. The retreating Germans had carried tales of mass deportation and rape which the Red Army brought in its wake, a warning that most villagers had chosen to regard, judging by the empty houses. It was the old man who gave us the horse and cart that carried us to Komarno next day.

Stephen was about to make some comment when another young man entered the room. He was a tall, powerful looking man with a hearty, carefree manner. Seeing me he bade hello and said that he had heard his English friends had arrived. Magda, the young woman who had directed me to this house, had told him.

'Come, Stephen, are you ready? We must show our friend the hospital and I won't take no for an answer, because I have arranged a surprise for him.'

Bela was an unpredictable character in complete contrast with his friend Stephen, but he was equally sincere. His fiery conversation was a true reflection of his whole approach to life, for one minute he was amusing, and with the next breath, his mood would change, and his words would be full of bitterness and sorrow.

'Come, Charles, I want to show the two places in Hungary where you can breathe freely, and where there is real reconstruction taking place, sincere, honest, clean work. This is the first, it's the House of Forgiveness where men seek comfort and the purpose of life.' Bela led the way into a dimly lit church, standing at the corner of the street. We stood at the rear of the main aisle for a few moments. There were several people kneeling in prayer. We left them undisturbed.

As we entered the hospital, Bela spoke again saying, 'And this is the other place, where I work, helping patch up their bodies. I wonder how many will be really thankful, poor souls. What's the matter with me this morning, Stephen? Look, I have an idea, you show our friend here around the hospital for the time being and then come along to Ward C.' He looked at his wristlet watch adding, 'Yes. I'll expect you in a quarter of an hour at 11.30.'

It was a large hospital and every available bed was occupied. The floors were highly polished and the sheets on the beds were clean but there were many shortages, especially in respect of medicants. I was mildly surprised to find a spirit of cheerfulness everywhere in the building, as though the outside world was perfectly normal, damaged but on the way to repair. Entering Ward C, we found the patients sitting up in bed, smiling like children who just been told a secret. Belas's stentorian voice called for silence; we could see his back through the open door at the end of the ward, where he was seated at a piano. His wish complied with, he commenced to play the familiar strains of my own National Anthem. As a tear fell, it came home to me, I was indeed free.

Epilogue

Berlin, March 1950

The intention of Operation Arundel and the many other missions which were established in Europe had one purpose, and that was purely to assist in the destruction of the German war machine which held the Continent in a grip of terror, the memory of which will never be forgotten. British-trained liaison officers became the links with the free world and through them the spirit of resistance flourished.

The operation was successful primarily because it represented in person the will of the freedom-loving communities; and was responsible for strengthening morale in a mountainous neighbourhood where news was restricted, and rumour was the weed of frustrated hopes. The presence of the mission itself was a source of enlightenment, the forebear of liberty, and this fundamental of the peace to come was the earnest reason for launching this mission into the field of operations. The method outlined in this narrative may remain obscure, for though the mission was not continuously active with the business of sabotaging enemy material, it remained an inspiration to the people of the Provinces who supplied more recruits than there were guns to arm them, which is proof that the aims of the mission were successful.

As the weeks passed, it became increasingly evident that there were two Partisan movements, the politics of which contained no medium or genuine endeavour to collaborate, and to provide a united front against the common enemy. On the one hand were the Communists, suspicious of the motives which prompted the British to field missions in occupied Europe, though they suffered no embarrassment when accepting stores from the liaison officers. The other movement embraced principles of Western inspired ideals, while the bulk of the mountain population, acutely aware of this division, silently watched the veritable strongholds of 'thought' being prepared for the future.

The liaison officers, before venturing into the field, were carefully briefed that they should at all times remain impartial, which though desirous for the task of enrolling forces willing to destroy a common enemy, made it possible for the Communist-controlled Partisan movement to embrace and execute their two-fold aims, the war against Fascism and preparation for an East-West clash which their commissars promised would come to pass.

A world-famous German and man of letters once said, 'The word Liberty has so fine a sound, we could not do without it, even it was an error.' On another occasion, Goethe said, 'Our wishes are presentiments of the abilities lying within us, heralds of the things we shall be able to do.' Both Partisan elements seized upon the word 'Liberty' and used it to flavour their propaganda.

The peaceful desire of the world's population has been tossed about on a sea of propaganda which has confused the true value of such things as hard work, individual enterprise, family life and has thrust the faith, hope and charity of Christian outlook into the unusual place of secondary importance. While countries attempt to apply religion as a political instrument, and at the same time deny its free access to the hearts of the population, the moral integrity of those countries must suffer, and one of the corner stones of a realistic peace (which cannot be replaced) will have been discarded. When studying the passageway of time and these things which were once all important, experience enables one to evaluate, to appreciate the true value of that incident, period or particular desire. The passageway of time and the experience which I have referred to within the pages of this manuscript has provided a picture of suffering, endurance, hope and fear all bound up in a struggle, which, as yet, has failed to produce the desired effect, in fact the very word 'peace' serves only to describe something rather that we associate with from the past.

Near the heart of Budapest lies Liberty Square. Stephen Kovacs and I found the building which the British and American Military Missions were occupying positioned on one corner of the square. The military missions were the self-imposed lodgers who had arrived to prepare the way for a pact of peace. Already, the building was crowded with people anxious to leave the country or to establish contact with their friends or relatives abroad. Several hundred British nationals had survived the war in the capital, but they had had enough of military occupation and were putting their cases before the embassy staff in the hope that a speedy passage home would be arranged for them.

I had expressed my thanks to Stephen for his assistance and was about to step into the embassy when a young man approached me. 'Will you help me?' he said. Wondering what the nature of the request would be, I hesitatingly said, 'Yes, if I can, what is it you want?'

'Do you know the words to the song "Dipsy-Doodle"? You see my friends and I are putting on a show for the British and American soldiers, and we would particularly like to sing this song because we understand it is popular among them.'

The request, made in all sincerity, on the steps of a building, which, in the future was to become an island of Democratic representation, held me tongue-tied for a second or two. I was unable to answer his query, but he was not disappointed. Instead, he asked if I would care to visit a cinema with his sister and another young woman friend. With regret, I answered that I would not be able to accompany them.

This young man was a citizen of the new Hungary. He had been interested in the newly arrived Westerners' entertainment. His clothes were well tailored, and his general demeanour could be rightly assessed as bright and cheerful. It would be of interest to know how he is faring now, at a time when even the embassy staffs are being forced out of Budapest.

Since the war, the pace of world tempo has quickened; we are all kept jumping to political suggestion. Each crack of the Eastern or Western faction whip cuts across thoughts of a peaceful future, and the desire to plan ahead. One is continually thwarted with the prospect of yet another war. To speak with someone who genuinely believes the world is aiming for a stable peace is but a refreshing pastime, quickly quenched with a flood of warnings and impressions conveyed by press, radio and the European stage.

'For those that are not with us are against us.'

Charles Barker

Service Record of
Major Charles Barker, BEM

Other Rank Service

Enlisted as a Boy Soldier Apprentice Trainee and Posted to F Company.
Royal Corps of Signals on 30 April 1934.

Attained 18 years of age and reclassified as a Signalman on
6 January 1937.

Posted to A Corps Royal Corps of Signals on 16 March 1937.

Embarked for Egypt on 30 April 1938.

Appointed Acting Lance Corporal on 17 October 1939.

Reverts in rank at own request to Signalman on 28 February 1940.

Posted to Western Desert Force Royal Signals on 15 September 1940.

Disembarked in Greece on 3 April 1941.

Appointed Acting Lance Corporal on 31 May 1941.

Appointed Acting Corporal on 5 September 1941.

Granted War Substantive Corporal on 4 December 1941.

Posted to 17th Area Signals on 10 September 1942.

Posted to 4th Air Division Signals 1st Special Air Service Regiment on
1 January 1943.

Posted from Mediterranean Expeditionary Force to British North Africa
Forces, 4 Parachute Brigade on 1 August 1943.

Appointed War Substantive Sergeant on 21 April 1943.

Embarked for United Kingdom on 13 April 1944.

Posted to Depot Battalion and Embarked for Italy on 23 May 1944.

Disembarked North Africa and posted to 1st Special Forces on
25 May 1944.

Posted from British North Africa Forces to Middle East HQ Force 133
on 14 June 1944.

Posted from Mediterranean Expeditionary Force to Central
Mediterranean Force on 1 October 1944.

Reported Missing – Prisoner of War on 21 October 1944.

Repatriated on 5 May 1945.

Permanently attached to 161st Reconnaissance Regiment on
    22 June 1945.
Posted to 4 Holding Battalion on 12 July 1945.
Posted to 6th Division Royal Signals on 9 October 1945.
Permanently attached to 8th Battalion Sherwood Foresters for
    pre-Officer training on 31 October 1945.
Posted to 161st Officer Cadet Training Unit on 18 December 1945.

Soldier Service with the Colours
30 April 1940 to 2 May 1946.

Soldier Overseas Service
Egypt, North Africa, Middle East, Italy and Hungary.

Commissioned Service
Emergency Commissioned as a Lieutenant in the Bedfordshire and
    Hertfordshire Regiment on 3 May 1946.
Posted to 3 Battalion Infantry Training Centre on 31 May 1946.
Posted to Parachute Regiment Reserve Battalion on 6 November 1946.
Posted to Airborne Forces Depot on 16 June 1947.
Embarked for Middle East Land Force on 21 September 1947.
Posted to 8th Battalion Parachute Regiment on 8 October 1947.
Unit Amalgamated to form 8/9 Battalion Parachute Regiment on
    21 February 1948.
Disembarked for United Kingdom on 27 April 1948.
Posted to Airborne Forces Depot on 19 July 1948.
Posted to British Army, Rhine 16 Independent Parachute Brigade Group
    on 12 August 1948.
Posted to Public Relations on 15 August 1949.
Posted to Public Relations Photographic Pool on 4 September 1950.
Posted to Airborne Forces Depot on 9 April 1951.
Posted to Special Air Service Regiment Far East Land Forces on
    23 June 1951.
Promoted to Temporary Major and appointed Squadron Commander
    of 22nd Special Air Service Regiment on 16 July 1952.
Died of injuries sustained in a helicopter crash on 21 January 1953.

Commissioned Service with the Colours
3 May 1946 to 21 January 1953.

Total Service with the Colours
30 April 1934 to 21 January 1953.

Commissioned Overseas Service
Middle East, British Army of the Rhine and Far East.

Medals and Awards
British Empire Medal (Military) *London Gazette* entry 13 December 1945.
War Medal 1939/45.
1939/45 Star.
Africa Star.
Italy Star.
Defence Medal.
Palestine General Service Medal.
Malaya Clasp.

* * *

Major E.C.R. Barker's period of service lasted nearly twenty years serving in the British Army, almost half of which was spent in a theatre of war. His potential was recognised early and he was soon drafted into No. 1 Special Force, SOE. His participation in operations in northern Italy and his loyalty in staying with the injured Major Smallwood, knowing capture was inevitable, was commendable. His dogged resistance at the hand of his torturers is the stuff of heroes. His elevation to commissioned rank and his squadron command of 22nd Regiment SAS was meteoric and well deserved.

Who knows the heights he may have attained had he lived? The world fared well with his presence and, despite its dangers, he saw many things on land and in people that others did not. Above all else, Major Charles Barker, in the mould of like-minded special forces operatives everywhere exemplified his duty to the very end.

'We sleep soundly in our beds because rough men stand ready in the night to visit violence on those who do us harm.'

Attributed to George Orwell

Endnote

At 0900 on 21 January 1953, a Dragonfly helicopter took off from Kuala Lumpur. The destination was Legap via Ipoh. The pilot was Flying Officer Walters of the Casualty Evacuation Flight, RAF Changi. The passengers were Corporal Jarrett RAF and Major Barker, BEM, Officer Commanding 22nd Regiment SAS.

The first part of the journey was uneventful, the helicopter landing at Ipoh at 1030. It was refuelled and verbal permission was given for a police officer, D/CPO Toulson, to accompany Major Barker to Fort Legap. With no room left, Corporal Jarrett was left at Ipoh.

The pilot made usual R/T contact with the control tower on take-off at 1059. Shortly before 1109, the helicopter was seen by several witnesses who all heard unusual noises coming from it. Almost immediately, the rotor blades appeared to fold upwards and pieces were seen to break away as it crashed to the ground. All three occupants sustained fatal injuries.

A Court of Enquiry, held in March 1953, determined that the primary cause of the accident was the rotor hub arm, to which the yellow blade flapping link was attached, fracturing. This was sufficient to send the helicopter spiralling to the ground. It was decided to reduce the time between the crack-detection tests of the rotor hub arm and other adjacent parts from every 200 hours to 100 hours. Corporal Jarrett was an extremely fortunate man.[1]

Major Charles Barker rests in Cherras Road New Christian Cemetery, Kuala Lumpur.

Appendix

Extracts from the CLOWDER Mission In and Around Forni Avoltri, June–November 1944

Unpublished Paper by Alan Ogden and Martin Fielding, 2012 (rev. 2014, 2017, 2020)

Introduction

Following the fall of Monte Cassino in May 1944 the Allied armies were advancing towards the Gothic line. Partisan activity was seen as important to disrupt German communications and to divert enemy troops away from the main front where the objectives were to destroy the German armies in Italy in order to reach Vienna before the Russians and to occupy the Udine area which was being claimed by Yugoslavia.

General Raffale Cadorna was parachuted in to command the Voluntary Freedom Force (CVL) which was established to coordinate the Partisan groups. He reported the communist prominence in the resistance. This raised concern amongst the Allies who feared that Italy was sliding towards postwar instability, as were Greece and Yugoslavia. SOE therefore increased its missions in Italy in support largely of the Osoppo, i.e. non-communist groups.

[The Osoppo was raised from volunteers with lay, liberal, socialist and Catholic ideals whose groups were already active in Carnia and Friuli after the Badoglio Proclamation of 8 September 1943. The name 'Osoppo' was a symbolic reference to the history of the region during the Italian unification period when, in 1848, the nearby city of Osoppo resisted Austrian troops for seven months.]

From 13 June to 4 December 1944, two SOE sub-Missions – BALLOONET and BALLOONET VIOLET – of the CLOWDER Mission operated in and around the Forni Avoltri area. Their specific task was to infiltrate agents from North Italy into Austria where they were to start a resistance movement; similar SOE activities were also underway on the Austrian–Slovenian border. It was not the primary purpose of either sub-Mission to equip, train and advise Italian Partisan bands in fighting Germans and Italian fascists. These tasks had been allocated to other SOE Missions in the Western Veneto Mountains/Trentino Alto Adige/Friuli regions. Inevitably, however, both Missions formed close relationships with the Italian Partisans, particularly the Osoppo Brigade on whom they were dependent for security, local intelligence, food, and shelter. When attacked by the Germans and Italian fascists, both fought side by side. This is their story.

BALLOONET Mission

Arriving in Italy in November 1943, Squadron Leader Manfred Czernin [cover name Beckett] underwent the standard SOE courses to prepare him for operations behind enemy lines but it was not until June 1944 that he was selected to jump with his Italian signaller, Piero Bruzzone, into north-east Italy on a clandestine mission to penetrate into Austria. The first run was aborted when incorrect ground signals were seen. On the next night, 13 June, once more the signals were wrong but this time Czernin told the pilot to drop him and if the landing area proved secure, to make a second approach and drop Piero and the stores. It was a brave decision given the propensity of the Germans to attract Allied aircraft with bogus signals but fortunately proved to be the right one and the pair were escorted by their reception committee, members of the Osoppo resistance group, to the Partisan HQ at the nineteenth-century Castello Ceconi at Pielungo in the Friuli region.

The Mission was soon joined by Major Pat Martin-Smith and his W/T operator Sergeant Charles Barker who were dropped into its area on the night of 18 July. Martin-Smith's task was to act as assistant to Czernin until the first party of agents had been put over the border and then take over the management of the route while Czernin returned to Bari to report. Almost immediately they were attacked by a strong force of Germans and in their haste to escape both officers lost most of their personal kit and equipment; the castle was effectively demolished.

A week later, they moved to Tramonte di Sopra, at the foot of a large mountain called Monte Rest, an ideal area in terms of DZs and Landing Grounds but over 50 miles by road from the border. Shortly after, having attacked a German MG post at Casiago on 1 August, the Mission once again had to flee in the face of an overwhelming German response – '*I Tedeschi vengeno*', 'the Germans are coming' – and travelled non-stop for three days across country to Monte Rosso.

192 Behind Enemy Lines with SOE

Czernin's main task was to reconnoitre the Italian–Austrian border a 40km march away with a view to penetrating into Austria proper. The idea of using the Carnic Alps as a springboard for Austrian missions had been hatched by No. 1 Special Force during a meeting between Lieutenant Colonel Peter Wilkinson and Commander Gerry Holdsworth to supplement a similar plan which was being rolled out in Slovenia by Wilkinson. Czernin first established two lines across the frontier with the help of an Austrian guide, Georg Dereatti, alias 'VIENNA', and identified three other safe passages, which was a major step forward for senior SOE planners. He then asked the local Partisan commanders to send him any Austrian deserters or prisoners and after subjecting them to a screening process, he selected six to work with the mission.

On 12 August, a supplementary mission commanded by Major George Fielding [cover name Rudolf] was parachuted onto Czernin's DZ. It included an Austrian, SOE-trained 2nd Lieutenant Hubert Mayr, a.k.a. Georgeau, for Czernin to send across the border into Austria, and a party of a further three Austrians under Lieutenant Karminski. It was decided that Fielding, none of whose team had brought civilian clothes or documents with them except Mayr, should operate on the Austrian frontier with a group of twenty Partisans with his base in Forni Avoltri [Italy] while Karminski and his team should sabotage the railway system. Lieutenant Mayr was dispatched by Czernin on 18 August across the frontier with the help of Dereatti, returning ten days later with news that the Austrians he had met in Wetzman were all 'apathetic, lacking in patriotic spirit and very frightened of the Nazi machine'. However, he re-crossed into Austria ten days later, meeting up again with Czernin's chief guide Dereatti in early October to contact a group of Austrian officers at Villach who had said they wanted to defect. Later that October, Dereatti went back to join Mayr and set up safe houses in Zell-am-See and Salzburg. The two of them were spotted in the Upper Drau valley in January but never seen again.

Dereatti's Cross Border Journeys

Journey: 1
Objective: To recce route and obtain safe quarters.
Route: Timau – Pal Piccolo – Polenick – Mauthern – Wetzman – Oberdrauburg – Nikolsdorf and return.
Route: First contact was relative of A2 but name is unknown. This contact was in Nikolsdorf. Immediately after this contact was made Dereatti was arrested by Gendarmerie on suspicion of being an absconding worker and Partisan from Italy. Dereatti maintained the cover of being an Italian

having an Italian ID card. He claimed to have escaped from 'bandits' in Italy. Dereatti was immediately taken to Lienz where he was put to work. After 20 days he escaped, returned to Wetzman and thence to report.

Journey: 2
Objective: To contact A3 whom Dereatti had previously known.
Route: Same route as 1st journey to Wetzman, thence to Bannberg.
Comment: In Bannberg was chased by police and was therefore forced to return to Wetzman. Reported back in July.

Journey: 3
Objective: To insert Lt Mayr and to contact A3.
Route: Route taken as above journeys to Wetzman.
Comment: Mayr remained in Wetzman as A2's relative. Nikolsdorf had been compromised [see 1st journey]. Dereatti reached Villgraten and met A3 who stated he was ready to help provide men should arms be delivered. It was agreed that Mayr should come and help so that should A3 be away Mayr could contact C3. Dereatti returned to Wetzman in mid-August bringing Mayr back to report.

Journey: 4
Objective: To pass Mayr on to A3 and show new guide B4 the route.
Route: Route taken same as previous journeys to Wetzman.
Comment: B4 and Mayr successfully taken in. Mayr continued his journey to Villgraten alone while B4 returned to Wetzman with message from Mayr. Dereatti returned beginning September.

Journey: 5
Objective: To pass on message to Mayr and introduce route to new guide.
Route: Route taken was from Forni Avoltri over the Giramondo Pass to Birnbaum.
Comment: Dereatti took B2 and B3 in and accompanied the latter to Villgraten. B3 then remained with Mayr. B2 returned alone. Dereatti returned mid-September.

Journey: 6
Objective: To collect message from Mayr, show B2 route to Wetzman via Giramondo Pass and to contact an alleged group of Austrian officers at Villach, who, it was stated, wished to come over to the Allies.
Route: Journey took place beginning October. Route taken was via Giramondo Pass to Wetzman.

Comment: B2 went to Dellach im Drautal to visit family. Dereatti sent courier [B1] to Villach while he travelled to Villgraten to contact Mayr and A3. Mayr on being contacted on 6 October stated that no arms had been delivered and that if they did not arrive in ten days' time, he would have to move on as he would otherwise become discredited. Dereatti considered that Mayr had been premature with promises etc. and was trying to move on too rapidly.

Spokesman of group of Austrian officers was contacted at Villach, stated they were willing to come over to us providing they could be given assistance.

Dereatti then returned with Mayr's answer and the information about the group of officers in Villach. On arriving in Wetzman he found B4 with a gunshot wound in his arm. Dereatti and B4 returned to Forni Avoltri.

Journey: 7
Objective: To contact Mayr to discover safe houses up to Zell-am-See and Salzburg and to investigate the possibility of a British officer, in uniform, working in the Salzburg area [this he considers possible as he knows many people in this area, having been a local leader of the Social Democrat Party].
Route: Journey started end of October. It was also hoped, on this journey, to introduce B5 and B6 into Austria to use them as couriers.

Key:
A1   Josef, a 65-year-old gravedigger in Wetzman.
A2   Josef, a customs official in Unter Pirkach; brother-in-law of OTTO – possibly a farmer at Pirkach?
A3   Doctor Kirschbaumer in Ausser Villgraten.
B1   Finni, 25-year-old cook, granddaughter of A1.
B2   Brother of B4.
B3   Rudolf [HENRY], Ex-CSM German Army.
B4   OTTO, one-eyed Luftwaffe deserter – Stefan Hassler?
B5   Alois, 32-year-old labourer – Pucher?
B6   Albert, 38-year-old farmhand.
B7   Robert, former thief – Schollas?
B8   Karl, ex-Fallschirmjäger – Schmid?

In September, the disposition of SOE personnel was as follows:

- Major Fielding, Major Smallwood and Corporal Buttle at Forni Avoltri running lines into Austria.

- Captain Martin-Smith and Sergeant Barker either at Timau or Forni Avoltri running lines into Austria.
- Lieutenant Karminski training Garibaldini Partisans in sabotage techniques.
- Squadron Leader Czernin and Bruzzone at Tramonte di Sopra running School for Couriers.

A secondary task for BALLOONET was to establish contact with the local Partisans, predominantly communist-led Garibaldini units, and to assist them in sabotage and ambush activities. Two OSS missions in the area were also engaged in this. The first, under Major Lloyd Smith, arranged supply drops, the second, an all-Italian team of self-professed communists, provided liaison and leadership [one of them became the Garibaldi Chief of Staff]. Czernin collaborated with them in several attacks on the railway running through Carnia and as a result his mission was subjected to further anti-Partisan sweeps, on three occasions yet again losing nearly all his kit and equipment. The second mission under the command of Major Lloyd Smith was Captain Hall's blowing up of the Cortina railway line. He also blew up a bridge north of Tolmezzo which triggered German reprisals in Villa Santina. [See Dramatis Personae Captain Roderick 'Steve' Hall, OSS] On 10 October, the Germans launched a major sweep in Carnia and Friuli, capturing two of Fielding's men, Major Smallwood, and Sergeant Barker. Both Czernin and Captain Martin-Smith were engaged in bitter fighting in the Passo della Mauria; Tramonte fell on 17 October but the Germans withdrew soon after and left a small force of 150 Cossacks to guard it. The mission re-entered it on 20 October and found their Landing Ground miraculously intact. Throughout this period, despite repeated requests by both Czernin and Fielding, no stores were dropped to the missions or the Partisans. Among Czernin's many adventures were an uncomfortable 12 hours spent halfway up a ruined medieval watch tower while a German patrol camped out on the ground floor.

By now, it was essential to exfiltrate Czernin back to Bari so that he could report on the mission's three months in the field and most importantly explain how the lack of supplies was severely constricting their ability to produce results of any kind. The reality was that in three months the two Missions had only succeeded in getting one SOE-trained operative into Austria despite the comparative ease of passage and winter was fast approaching. On the evening of 25 October, Bari signalled that both Czernin and Martin-Smith were to come out. Given the position of various couriers over the border and that of those in the pipeline, this was unacceptable and it was Czernin alone who left by a Lysander aircraft on 29 October, in the company of two escaped POWs, Private Brown of the East Yorkshire Regiment and Private Clarke of the Sherwood Foresters. They arrived at SOE's new forward HQ in Sienna just in time to hear Field Marshal Alexander's order suspending the dropping of agents into enemy territory until the following spring.

Czernin's mission had been a qualified success. After proving the route into Austria, he had expected to support Fielding's mission; however, when only one man could go in, that support role fell on Fielding himself, so there was no scope for two Missions. However, there was a need to support the facilities at Tramonte and a need to continue to recruit Austrians. He had established six safe houses in Austria, formed a 'courier school' with Martin-Smith where they recruited and trained three internal and five external couriers, and nurtured five contacts within Austria. Dereatti, who he had employed as his chief guide, made no less than seven successful crossings.

However, due to no fault of Czernin, the almost complete failure to drop supplies to the Partisans undermined his credibility [and that of all the other British missions in the area] with the Partisan leadership and also severely compromised the Missions' ability to fend off German attacks. As he wrote in his November 1944 report, 'promises made by BLOs in all good faith which for one reason or another are not carried out, tend to damage Allied prestige and shake faith in the Allied promises. This inevitably encourages a dangerously cynical state of mind, particularly open revolutionary ideas and, consequently, susceptible to pro-Russian tendencies.' Furthermore he was not briefed to sort out the bitter political rivalry between The Osoppo and Garibaldi Partisans; his successor, Major Tom Roworth, managed to reach a temporary accommodation between the two but this 'unified command' soon fell apart in the face of a determined German *rastrellamenti*.

BALLOONET VIOLET Mission

Fielding's fluency in German made him an ideal candidate for SOE's plans to penetrate Austria and he was dropped, together with Major Bill Smallwood [also a fluent German speaker], 2nd Lieutenant Hubert Mayr, a.k.a. Georgeau [an Austrian] and their 20-year-old W/T operator Corporal Arthur Buttle on 12 August 1944 to Squadron Leader Czernin's reception committee at Tramonte. Their task was to penetrate the East Tirol and South West Carinthia and to establish a base and facilities for further penetration later. A second party of three Austrians jumped at the same time [cover names 2/Lt Cheney, 2/Lt McCabe, 2/Lt Simon]; they were earmarked for sabotage and demolition activity.

To the consternation of Czernin and his second-in-command, Captain Pat Martin-Smith who had joined SOE from 30 Commando in Italy, none of the new arrivals except Mayr had brought civilian clothes or ID papers with them, 'under the delusion that they could gaily march across the border in British uniform to be joined by a crowd of enthusiastic Austrian patriots'. The main body was delayed at Tramonte for fifteen days but Czernin managed to get Mayr, the only one with civilian clothes and ID papers, across the border on 18 August.

Eventually, Czernin arranged for twenty Osoppo Partisans under the command of a former Alpini padre, the priest Don 'Aurelio' [Ascanio de Luca – Aurelio], born Treppo Grande, 1912; died Udine 6 February 1990; ordained 1936] to escort Fielding's mission to Clavais to the north-east of Tramonte, where they arrived on 24 August.

However, it proved too far from the frontier to be practical and so they moved to Forni Avoltri [889m] where they were able to cover two excellent routes into Austria, the Giramondo and Val d'Inferno passes, both of which were unguarded. Mission HQ was installed in the Albergo Sotto Corona, where much to their surprise they discovered a North Country lass called Katie, formerly the Gräfin Donner and now styled Countess Sosic, wife of the harbour master of Naples.

Apart from the obvious dangers that housing the mission in the Albergo Sotto Corona involved to the Romanin family who owned it, four Cossacks were billeted in the hotel. The family stored arms behind the frieze of the dresser in which the plates etc. were kept. On one occasion the family were asked by a German if they had any arms and, naturally, they denied being in possession of any. The German in question was standing next to the dresser at the time!

Alpina Romanin later reminisced that the family was constantly short of food and were obliged to share what little food they had with the Cossacks. The Germans took all the livestock and, as is evidenced in the written order, the farmers were compelled to provide forage for the Cossacks' horses. Feeding the mission therefore imposed an additional burden on the family.

Alpina recalled that she stole food from wherever she could and used to walk to Udine to obtain flour. That was a two-day walk each way and she and her girlfriend slept in a barn en route. There was no certainty that they would find flour and if they were stopped on the way home, the

Don Aurelio and the Osoppo Brigade

Extract from Captain Pat Martin-Smith's Report on BALLOONET Mission

The Osoppo

This was started as a purely non-political movement to fight the Germans. The founders were Verdi, an artist born in Udine who became a Captain in the Bersaglieri, and Don Aurelio, parish priest born in Treppo Grande. Neither of these men is a politician. Verdi is probably the only man there who has anything approaching a sense of international politics. He is intelligent and, *rara avis*, a genuine patriot. Aurelio is a forceful personality and as a priest and founder of the movement was a great influence, though he has no official position.

Most of the troops are Alpini, the Giulia division, the local division of Friuli, which was punished by Mussolini for liquidating a Black shirt brigade in Albania. No political ideas and they imagine when the war is over then everything in the garden will be bright and beautiful.

Political Crisis in the Osoppo

The German attack on Pielungo on 19 July 1944 was used as a pretext to change the command in the Osoppo brigade. The politically minded were not satisfied with Verdi's attitude of political indifference and tried to oust him, using also as an argument his refusal to agree to the Unified Command with the Garibaldini. It was really a struggle between the Partito d'Azione and Partito Democrazia Christiana.

Osoppo's founders: Aurelio and Verdi.

A court of enquiry was held by members of the CLN (*Comitato di Liberazione Nazionale*) from Udine which nattered for a fortnight. The troops supported Verdi and Aurelio, but the members of the court were frightened by what the Garibaldini would do if Verdi remained. The Garibaldini realised too clearly that Verdi alone was the obstacle to their taking over the Osoppo, so he kept the business on a military plane by excluding politics; consequently, they tried to force the pace from outside. In the end a new commander was appointed, but he lasted for only 24 hours, as the troops revolted, put him under arrest and, facing him in a southerly direction, told him to march and never return. This was Aba [of Pola]; he is now living in Udine.

Ultimately the CLN of Milan exonerated Verdi and re-instated him in command, which he refused to accept, so Mario [Candido Grassi] was brought on from the 1 Brigade [from the Eastern side of the Tagliomento].

This suited everyone. It pleased the Partito d'Azione because it gave them, on paper, control over the Osoppo. It pleased Mario because it made him look important. It pleased Verdi and Aurelio, because it left them in a position of unimpaired influence, their reputation cleared and relieved of all responsibility while they still really ran the business. It also meant that all were now tacitly agreed that politics were the main issue, and the Germans were a secondary, though tiresome, consideration. Both sides were manoeuvring for position in the post-war.

* * *

Extract from Interrogation Report of Major T. Roworth of TABELLA Mission:

Don Aurelio

This man appears to have been a pupil of LINO [Don Moretti, Liaison officer, Udine CLN] at one time, although he is not very much younger. He is a priest and a native of Arba. He is outstandingly brave physically and has tremendous powers of physical endurance. [Awarded Croce di Guerra on Greek front in 1941 and Medaglia di Bronzo in Montenegro same year.] He was former commander of the Feldeta Battalion which was universally looked on as being by far the best battalion. According to subject, no other leader ever came near him for efficiency. Despite being intelligent, he is rather impudent and hasty and loses his temper easily. He is now administrator of the 1st Division. He has absolute control over his men whom he commands with iron discipline. He is the only Partisan commander who subject had heard give orders obviously meant to be obeyed instantly and without question. He is about 32 years old, very well-built, and strong. Has enormous will power. Height about 5 ft 8 inches; very straight, thin aquiline nose; wears glasses; large dark eyes; black hair, rather curly.

Germans would invariably confiscate it. When and if they got the flour home, they were obliged to feed some of it to the Cossacks.

Alpina said that the Cossacks lived very much in fear of the Partisans, whom they avoided. This is corroborated by Martin-Smith's view of them.

There was a Jewish family in the village that the Romanins knew. The parents did not look Jewish, but the children did, so they all went into hiding in one of the little barns below the Giramondo and Val d'Inferno Passes by the Refugio. Although the Romanin family had little if any food to spare, Alpina used to take food to them. It must have been an arduous journey in the winter and a bitterly cold time for everyone, especially the fugitives in the mountains.

Alpina Romanin had an uncle, Gino, who had fought in Russia where he was awarded the Iron Cross. Appalled by what he saw, as soon as he returned to Italy, he joined the Garibaldini. The Germans arrested him with a group of others from the village. On learning from the captors that he was destined to be shot, the family protested, pointing out that Uncle Gino had the Iron Cross. With Teutonic thoroughness the Germans demanded to see his medal which they took with them and as a result his life was spared at Mauthausen where sadly the others were shot.

Mayr returned on 26 August and brought with him a recruit, Rudolph Moser, alias 'Henry', a 24-year-old Wehrmacht NCO deserter. It was agreed that Henry should act as a courier for Fielding across the new route to Forni Avoltri until Mayr could find an Austrian with the necessary paperwork. Furthermore, if Mayr was to continue to operate across the frontier, he would need his own W/T operator and one was requested on 27 August. It was now clear from Mayr's reports that the Austrian people were apathetic, very frightened by the Nazis and appeared to have little patriotic spirit. From now until 10 October, the mission remained put, waiting for promised supplies to be dropped by the Balkan Air Force, the newly formed Bari-based organization responsible for supplying Partisans in Yugoslavia and North-East Italy by air.

The activities of the mission were now limited to reconnaissance through lack of any form of supply of arms and ammunition. Major Smallwood crossed over the frontier to the staging post at Birnbaum to persuade a farmer to hide an arms cache and to shelter mission members, the latter request being rejected out of hand. Plans were also made to launch a cross-border raid with the Osoppo Partisans to test the reaction of the local people; would they join the resistance or reject it? Once again, the lack of arms and supplies made the implementation of such a plan a non-starter. Fielding himself twice crossed the border to the small village of Liesing on the banks of the River Gail, both times to talk to the village priest who was fiercely opposed to the Nazi regime. The recruitment picture was not promising for the German call-up had left behind only males over 60, boys under 14 or those with disabilities; that said, the priest was of the opinion that if a safe area could be established, it should be possible to attract deserters, particularly from the training and holding regiment at Lienz. [Barker stated it was mooted that they should hang the mayor of Liesing to stimulate anti-German feeling.]

Life in plain clothes was never straightforward. Early in the morning on the day of his arrival Fielding went for a stroll in Tramonte di Sopra to get a feel for his new surroundings. An Italian, seeing him at such an hour, assumed he must have been to church and greeted him: 'Been to Mass?' to which he, thinking it could do no harm to appear a Catholic, replied: 'Yes'; only to get the answer, 'I don't go, I'm a Protestant from Piedmont'. On another occasion, Fielding and another member of his group were fishing in a river when some German Army vehicles appeared. One stopped and an officer approached them to enquire with typical Teutonic attention to detail if they had permits to fish that stream. They admitted that they did not, and the German officer merely told them that they must go to the town hall and obtain a permit before they fished again. He then got back in his vehicle and left.

From the perspective of security, the interests of the Mission conflicted sometimes with the Partisans and the OSS. For instance, the OSS [Captain Hall] blew up a bridge near Tolmezzo on 9 August which provoked German retaliation against Villa Santina and in early September OSS-trained Partisans ambushed a convoy, killing four Germans, wounding five and taking a number of prisoners including the commander of the garrison at Sappada.

Having crossed the frontier to Mauthen, Mayr had managed to reach Pirkach where he recruited another German as a courier, this time a one-eyed Luftwaffe deserter, codenamed 'Otto', but like Henry he was without suitable papers. He also contacted Dr Kirschbaumer at Ausser Villgraten, an important local figure, who agreed to provide a safe house for him. Based here, there was a real possibility that, provided the required drops of arms and supplies materialised, a resistance group could be nurtured in the valley and act as a springboard to a larger movement. The Italian Partisans were found to be inept at smuggling stores across the frontier, owing to their inadequate training in fieldcraft. It was therefore decided to recruit some British POWs and so Fielding dispatched Sergeant Barker,

Captain Martin-Smith's W/T operator, to Selva di Cadore near Cortina d'Ampezzo to contact six POWs known to be hiding near the house of a wealthy Jewish businessman. After a hazardous 200km round trip of eleven days, three of which were spent in persuading the POWs that he was not a German plant, Barker returned to Forni Avoltri with his charges, three of whom later left for Yugoslavia. While the Mission concentrated on running agents across the border into Austria, a dramatic twist to their fate was being played out in Ampezzo to their south. On 26 September, the CLN proclaimed the formation of the Government of Free Carnia Zone, an act of defiance verging on the foolhardy for Allied armies were still hundreds of miles away and winter imminent. Free Carnia lasted for a mere fifteen days until a German counter-offensive, Operation Waldlaufer, undertaken by Combat Group Schwerdfeger stormed into Carnia with the initial aim of clearing the road to Timau and recapturing the barracks at Paluzza. 20,000 troops [Cossacks, Germans and Italian fascists] moved on the region from all directions. Company strength fighting patrols penetrated the interior while an iron ring of roadblocks, OPs and ambushes closed the escape routes.

At the time of the offensive, Major Smallwood and Sergeant Barker were located at Forni Avoltri while Fielding and Corporal Buttle were at the Dropping Zone at Sauris, waiting for a promised drop by ten aircraft. Fielding quickly crossed the mountains back to Forni and agreed a plan of action with Smallwood; he, Fielding, would return to Sauris to wait for a single aircraft drop and Smallwood would withdraw with the couriers, Sergeant Barker and their six-strong Partisan bodyguard to join him if directly threatened by the Germans. At dawn on 11 October, Germans were spotted to the north of Forni, prompting Smallwood to leave with Barker for Sauris at about noon. After caching their radios and stores except for a B-set and their large packs, the two men reached the summit of Monte Tuglia about 1500 hours and, after burying their B-set, began their descent. They lost sight of one another in the thick mist and when Barker went in search of Smallwood, he found him with his ankle broken in two places and apparently suffering from internal injuries after a 30ft fall. Unable to carry him, Barker managed to drag Smallwood down to a cattle barn. As soon as it was light the next day, Barker descended further down the slope into the Val Pesarina and found some Garibaldini Partisans. Returning to Smallwood, they carried him to a group of barns 'above the valley bottom'. [The accident most likely happened either on the way up to Passo Geu or somewhere along the Vallone della Creta Forata. They were *not* on the summit of Monte Tuglia, as some reports have mistakenly recorded.]

At this point, Barker returned to Monte Tuglia where he had cached the B-set and after recovering it made his way back to the barn where he found the Partisans had managed to set Smallwood's leg in a splint. The following day, 13 October, enemy activity increased throughout the valley and after once more burying the B-set and all the plans, codes and diaries, Barker carried Smallwood down towards the village of Pesaris. Between 1700 and 1800 hours they were arrested by a Cossack patrol and taken to Comeglians where they were handed over to the Waffen SS. Barker could certainly have escaped but chose not to leave his severely injured commander alone in such dire circumstances.

Fielding signalled Bari on 21 October: 'Much regret Smallwood and Barker captured. Smallwood reported fell down mountain and injured leg and shoulder. Locals carrying him away surprised by Boche patrol. Barker gallantly refused to leave him. Both reported taken to San Stefano di Cadore or Cortina Ampezzo.'

By 15 October Smallwood and Barker found themselves at Gestapo HQ in Trieste. [Barker was interrogated fifteen times in twenty-three days before being sent to Coroneo prison; Smallwood joined him seventeen days later. Both had been tortured; Smallwood's broken leg was not attended to and he had been forced to stand in a telephone box on the roof of the prison for hours on end.] Fortunately, the cover story that they had been making a recce with a view to blowing up bridges and roads and assisting British POWs to escape held up well and merely served to confirm to the Germans facts they already knew.

With the loss of Smallwood and Barker and the cessation of all Partisan resistance in Carnia, Fielding's BMM [British Mission Officer] was now reduced to one officer and one NCO, with its attendant force of mostly unarmed and ragged Italian Partisans, found itself on its own and the target of intense German patrol activity. On 13 October, Axis troops at San Stefano launched a double pronged attack on *Commando Unico* Brigades Garibaldi Nord and Garibaldi Carnia towards Sappada and Sauris respectively. In the east, a thrust between Forni and Rigolato pushed up through to Cresto Carnico. The whole of the Mission's area was in uproar. To make matters worse, 255mm of rain fell in sixteen days [compared with a monthly average for October of 147.2mm], making movements across country even more treacherous than usual.

Despite the large numbers of Austrians in Allied captivity, SOE had great difficulty in finding suitable recruits who were prepared to return to Austria to kick-start the resistance. John Bruce Lockhart of SIS Bari was experiencing identical difficulties regarding a paucity of suitable agents and shortage of air support. However, one exceptional individual was identified by SOE, Wolfgang Treichl, alias Taggart. An ardent patriot who was determined to liberate his country from the scourge of fascism, Treichl had joined the Afrika Korps with the sole intention of being captured by the British to whom he would offer his services. Along with three other Austrians – Hauber who was to be infiltrated into Austria with him, Second Lieutenant Priestley who was to join Mayr as his W/T operator and Second Lieutenant Dale who was to join Karminski – Treichl emplaned on 12 October destined to be dropped to Czernin's mission. A mix-up by the pilot and navigator resulted in the team being dropped 12 miles from the DZ into the waiting arms of a German patrol by the Gendarmerie Barracks at Tolmezzo, Field Marshal Kesselring's HQ. [Hauber stated that the party had been dropped to four fires, 50yd apart, as opposed to the correct signal of five lights 100yd apart in a 'V' shape.] Treichl was shot and killed on landing; Hauber escaped in the darkness and reached Czernin a few days later with Lees and Grant of Karminski's party; the other two, Priestley and Dale, were captured but fortunately their story about being British officers was believed and they were treated as POWs rather than handed over to the Gestapo as Austrian spies.

Meanwhile Lieutenant Karminski [2/Lt Simon] and the other two Austrians had arrived from Cadore to add to the already fraught situation confronting Fielding; in addition to the general lack of arms and virtually no ammunition, no one had more than 24 hours of rations left at any one time for the Partisan caches, foolishly all stored in the towns, had been burnt by the Germans who had completely cleared the Tagliamento valley of resistance. In the middle of this critical period, a party of six Austrians arrived from Czernin to be put across the frontier. After a ten-day delay due to continuing German operations, Otto and Czernin's chief courier, Dereatti, safely dispatched them across the frontier. Lieutenant Hauber, the survivor of the Taggart mission, also arrived around this time and was sent with Karminski's party to Tramonte which they reached on 29 October.

On the night of 20 October, Fielding returned to Forni to see if the situation there had improved. While asleep in a hay barn, he was woken and warned that his location had been given away to the Germans, and moved to another building some way off. He watched at dawn as a German patrol surrounded the barn. After making a reconnaissance of the frontier the next day he established that both passes were still unguarded, but the Val Fleons was patrolled by alert Alpenjäger. Fielding bumped into one of their patrols which, although they gave chase, he managed to evade. Fielding returned to Forni to spend the night in another hay barn and the same chain of events happened. Once more, by moving promptly, he evaded capture. He returned to Sauris despondent and frustrated by the inability of the BMMs and Partisans to respond to enemy activity. Without arms, ammunition, boots and sturdy clothing, they were powerless. Frustrated and under relentless pressure from German patrols when the mission's survival depended on the Partisans for food, local intelligence and protection, he sent the Balkan Air Force a message asking that they display 'more of the spirit of the Battle of Britain and less of the Bottle of Bari'. Like many BMMs, he was fed up with making promises to the Partisans about air drops of arms and ammunition which inevitably failed to arrive and therefore undermined the credibility of the SOE mission. News reached Fielding, now back at Sauris, that Mayr's designated W/T operator, Priestley, had been captured by the Germans at Tolmezzo and therefore he returned to Forni to warn Mayr that his codes may have been compromised. Furthermore, he needed to discuss the status of the courier routes in the light of recent heavy snowfall and German troop movements. Setting out on 29 October, Fielding's first attempt to cross the mountains ended in failure after a 6-hour slog through thick snow. A second attempt the next day fared slightly better but a mule carrying a load of food fell over a precipice and the rest of the day was spent retrieving it. Yet another attempt had to be abandoned due to avalanches; this time both a man and a mule were lost. A fourth and final attempt got underway the next day, using the low cloud and mist as cover to move below the snow line. Five mules laden with food accompanied the party as it moved towards the Degano valley but to quote Fielding 'passing through the village of Mione in the early morning some enthusiast must have rung up the German garrison at Ovara as when we reached the next village [Cella] thorough which we were compelled to pass. Forty-five minutes away we found ourselves surrounded' by German troops from the Ovaro Garrison across the river. Abandoning the mules, the party managed to escape 'thanks to some very bad shooting on behalf of the mixed force of Germans and Russians', the only casualty being Fielding with a flesh wound to his arm. It was now that he discovered that the Germans had placed a reward of 800,000 Lire on his head for his capture. However, he always maintained that the betrayals were never motivated by the reward, rather by fear of the brutal reprisals meted out by the Cossacks.

During this period, Fielding had been observing 'an extremely bogus and suspicious' OSS Mission headquartered to the East of Comeglians. Consisting of 'Fred' [Fred is mentioned in Barker's manuscript], an Italian member of the PCI and his Italian-Egyptian W/T operator, the mission had the same brief as Fielding, namely to open courier lines into Austria. However, convinced that this was a cover for communist penetration of Austria, Fielding introduced a stooge, codenamed 'Fuli', through whom he fed suitably edited information to Fred, an arrangement that admirably worked until Fred broke his leg and his W/T operator went off the air due to severe syphilitic symptoms. However, the Garibaldini had their own programme based on two 'battalions', the 'Stalin' battalion formed from Ukrainian, Mongol and Cossack deserters, and the 'Karl Liebknecht' battalion composed of Austrian and German deserters, with the object of eventually sending them to Austria as communist agent provocateurs. Martin-Smith had information that the Austrian and German contingents were extremely unhappy with their lot, the more so since they had been told they would be shot if they crossed over to the Osoppo.

Thus, it came as no surprise when five Austrians and two Germans approached Martin-Smith, who immediately arranged for them to be received by Fielding under the formal protection of the BMM. The reaction of the Garibaldini was to send their Chief of Staff, Franco, who was also an American OSS officer [Joseph Gozzer, later captured and executed at Hersbruch in March 1945]. He explained that the 'Karl Liebknecht' battalion was an OSS creation and would be led in Austria by American officers who were expected any day soon. The seven deserters would have none of it and under the tutelage of Martin-Smith formed two three-man parties ready to be infiltrated into Austria, the first to Klagenfurt and the second to St Polten destined for Vienna. At the same time, he briefed Dereatti to prepare to move to the Salzkammergut to find a base from which the BMM could operate the following spring. The outcome was quite different. Otto Paulus, the leader of the Klagenfurt group [described by Martin-Smith as 'intelligent but domineering'], appeared to be on the verge of returning to the Wehrmacht and buying his immunity in exchange for betraying the BMM. Fielding took the hard decision to order the Partisans to take him away and shoot him in the village mortuary but to remove his uniform first. Unfortunately, Paulus escaped from his executioners and Fielding was faced with him rushing into the room clad only in his underwear and begging for his life. He was obliged to tell the Partisans to take him away and this time do the job properly which they did.

The next day, the group's Luftwaffe radio operator accidentally blew his brains out when his Sten gun went off in a truck. The remainder were handed over to Captain Prior, another SOE officer in Tramonte, for deployment as saboteurs.

Relations with the Garibaldini CLN had by now deteriorated to such a degree that Major Roworth, the BLO to the Udine CLN, was asked to arrest Fielding for anti-communist activities. He declined.

Captain Prior in his report on the Sauris–Tramonte route said the conditions were of 'very hard going owing to deep snow and later rain'. Fielding finally reached Tramonte on 6 November in time to find that the mission's first drop had arrived the night before; despite a guard and a lock, almost a third of it had been stolen. Ten days later and nearly three months after his original request had been submitted, he was notified that Mayr's W/T operator, Lieutenant Brenner, was due that night. Dropped at 3,000ft by the same Polish pilot, who had so carelessly deposited Hauber's party on top of the German HQ at Tolmezzo, Brenner landed half a mile from the nearest fire and after some difficulty in gaining admittance to the Drop Ground, was spirited off by Fielding to the Ampezzo area to get him across the frontier as soon as possible. The area turned out to be crawling with Germans and accordingly Fielding returned with Brenner to Tramonte where he started planning their evacuation. The idea was to exfiltrate by Lysander and after making final arrangements to get a message to Mayr, Martin-Smith stood vigil on the cold and wet 'Lizzie' field for the next week, only to watch one fly over and then disappear. It later transpired that soon after it was shot down by an American P-40 Lightning. With news of an impending German *rastrellamenti*, it became clear that the only way out was by foot and when the drive opened with a combined attack by 1,000 SS Alpenjäger, a brigade of Russian Cossacks and two crack Republican units, the 10th MAS and the San Marco Battalion, the mission set off for safe haven in Slovenia on 27 November on what was to become an epic 300-mile march.

Unknown to the Mission, on 27 November Phase Two of Operation Waldlaufer had been set in motion. This involved the complete encirclement of the Tramonte area and then tightening the outer cordon like a hangman's noose; the prize for the Germans was the Commando Unico Garibaldi-Osoppo, the nerve centre of the resistance located at Tramonte di Sopra. For the first five days, the mission was compelled to walk around the surrounding hillsides, unable to find a way through the enemy cordon. On the sixth night, after a 19+-hour walk, they managed to find a gap and the following night crossed the Tagliamento River south of Udine, 'fordable but cold' according to Martin-Smith. Three days later, after crossing the Pontebba railway line to the north of Udine, they reached the First Osoppo Brigade in the mountains to the north-east of the town. The following night they crossed the freezing Natisone River and from there reached the farthest West Slovenian Odred.

Their reception by the Slovene Partisans was discourteous and unco-operative; at one point, they were made to stand in a food queue with German deserters. After a difficult time crossing the River Isonzo, when the Slovene guide refused to accompany them to the bank, the mission arrived at IX Slovene Partisan Corps HQ at Strega [Plannina] where they were welcomed by the BMM and the 'A' Force representative. A further five-day march with virtually no food other than chestnuts took them to Slovene HQ at Črnomelj, one leg taking 23½ hours non-stop marching. On 27 December, they were finally evacuated by air to Bari. However, the airfield at Bari was unusable due to an accident on the runway, so they landed at Foggia, a US airbase. As a truck came to pick up the aircrew, the SOE group made to clamber aboard only to hear the stentorian bark of a sergeant: 'Only US personnel allowed on this truck.' Having walked to the canteen, where coffee, doughnuts and warmth awaited them, two British officers eyed their beards and general dishevelment, one remarking: 'Rather jungly'. The starving men were then made to wait for an hour and a half before the glass doors behind which the buffet was laid out were unlocked. They knew they were home and finally reached Bari in the back of a 3-ton truck late the same day.

Once back at No. 1 Special Force HQ, Fielding encountered a distinctly frosty reception. Major Charles Villiers gave him a dressing down for losing 20 gold sovereigns and threatened a board of inquiry; Fielding pro-tested that this was a disproportionate response, given that he had been on the run from almost the day he had been dropped. A further reprimand came from a senior airman who berated him for his 'Bottle of Bari' signal. This did not deter him from delivering a robust riposte and preparing a swingeing critique of his mission, including the following paragraph on 'Air Support':

Before the mission left base we were continually assured that during the summer and autumn we would be given air support in the form of drops of supplies and ammunition though the situation might be dif-ficult in the winter. In fact, the mission received no air support of any kind except during the last week when three parachute drops were received at Tramonte. Many promises were made including one of a drop by ten aircraft to the Italian Partisans, but nothing materialised. These promises were very nearly disastrous for the mission as the temper of constantly disappointed Partisans became very uncertain and perfectly naturally, I was held responsible. In fact, to outward appearances, we were playing the part of perfidious Albion to perfection. So much for the difficulties at our base in Italy.

Martin-Smith shared Fielding's view but was more diplomatic in the language he used in his own report: 'Close liaison with the RAF is essential, both before and during an operation, to ensure that it is possible to supply a mission in a given area; it is better to know this beforehand as it is extremely demoralising for all concerned to discover, after a great build-up of promises of supplies, that the RAF could not, in fact, and never imagined that they could drop into your particular area.' He followed this with a swipe at the Polish pilot who had dropped Treichl and Brenner: 'Pilots other than British [including British Empire] are extremely hazardous risks; no "body" should venture into a plane without assuring himself that the pilot is British, and secondly that he has experience of dropping "bodies" and knows the area to which he is going. This will apply *a fortiori* to Austria.' [To their consternation, the Big Bug mission under Captain Prior was dispatched from their aircraft by a Pole who spoke no English and furthermore had failed to hook any of them up.]

Fielding immediately succumbed to a bout of malaria and was confined to bed in a freezing cold room in a castle where an attractive ATS girl arrived to take down his report as he dictated it. Seeing that the girl's fingers were so cold she could hardly write, he told her to get into the other end of the bed assuring her that he would not molest her and in any event his malaria suppressed any such inclinations that he might have had. On being so discovered there was another almighty furor, but no further action was taken.

Sergeant Ernest Barker, BEM
Recommendation for MM
Sgt Barker was dropped by parachute as W/T operator to a Mission in North-West Italy which had the task of establishing a base for the penetration of East Tyrol and South West Carinthia. He made several journeys through enemy-occupied territory on one of which he took charge of a group of six POWs and brought them back to Forni Avoltri, a journey which involved Sgt Barker running the grave risk of wearing civilian clothes to pass through a village where the enemy were in force. Had he been discovered on this occasion he would without doubt have been shot.

On 11 October 1944 Sgt Barker accompanied his CO, Major Small-wood, when they were compelled to leave Forni Avoltri and take refuge in the hills on account of an enemy drive. Major Smallwood fell a consider-able distance over a cliff breaking a leg and injuring himself internally. Sgt Barker remained with him and managed to carry him to a place of safety. On 15 October, the enemy started to penetrate the hills where Sergeant Barker and Major Smallwood were in hiding and Major Small-wood ordered Sergeant Barker to leave him, but this Sergeant Barker refused to do. Later in the day both were taken prisoner and were imme-diately handed over to the SS. Sergeant Barker was imprisoned about six weeks in the Gestapo cell in Trieste. He was subjected to about twenty interrogations, housed in awfully bad conditions with totally inadequate food and was subject to solitary confinement and intense cold. He was severely beaten, and several times threatened with death to extract infor-mation from him. In spite of this terrible ordeal, he withstood all the tricks and resisted all the promises of the enemy of better treatment by 'invent-ing' a story to account for his activities which was plausible, wholly false, involved the identity of no other person and at the same time accorded with Major Smallwood's story. Sergeant Barker was finally transferred to Stalag XVIIa on 15 January 1945 with Major Smallwood. On 2 February Major Smallwood was transferred to an Oflag hut but by cleverly feigning sickness Sgt Barker got himself left behind and managed to effect his escape when the Red Army arrived. He immediately went to Budapest, reported to the British Mission, and was sent back to Italy by air.

As a result of Sergeant Barker's courage and devotion to duty the Mission's work in Northern Italy was greatly assisted. Major Smallwood's life was saved, and the enemy were prevented from obtaining information of great value about the Mission's activities and objectives. Furthermore, after his escape Sgt Barker gave much valuable information about the identity of other prisoners, enemy security personnel and counter-intelligence methods.

Awarded BEM

Smallwood's and Barker's Ordeal After Capture

Following Smallwood's fall, Barker managed to move him to shelter in a cattle barn. On the following day Barker moved to the valley where he met a group of communist Partisans who carried Smallwood to a group of three barns in the valley bottom where a group of patriots splinted his leg. Barker returned to recover the material (A set, two B sets and a plunger for blowing bridges) which he had buried.

On the following day enemy activity increased and the patriots fled. Smallwood's condition had deteriorated and neither he nor Barker had eaten for 48 hours. Smallwood told Barker to leave him, but Barker gallantly refused to do so. He buried the radio, plan, diaries, money, postcards with details of enemy locations and any other incriminating matter and then began to carry Smallwood towards Pessaris. On the way they ran into a group of Cossacks who arrested them indicating by gestures that they would be shot.

Taken to Comeglians, they were interrogated by members of the Waffen SS and one of the Gestapo. Fortunately, the interrogators were under the mistaken impression that Smallwood was the major [in fact it was Czernin] who saved two captured German officers from being shot by the Partisans during an attack at Pielungo. [Czernin had rescued the Germans and imprisoned them in the Castello Ceconi. They were left behind when the group abandoned the castle. Smallwood neither denied nor admitted it.]

After spending a night in the cells at Gestapo HQ in Tolmezzo they were transferred to Gestapo HQ at Trieste. Here during an air raid, they were taken to the cellar where they were both badly assaulted by two guards who beat them over the head with whips for 10 minutes and they were struck in the face.

Barker remained at Gestapo HQ for twenty-three days during which time he was interrogated around fifteen times for periods of between 2 and 4 hours. Priestley was brought into the room on one occasion but, as he had been captured on landing, Barker did not recognise him.

Conditions were squalid. Barker's cell was 3ft wide × 6ft 6in long × 6ft 3in high. The canvas bed had no blankets and there was no natural light. A latrine bucket was provided and this had to be emptied each morning into an upstairs lavatory in which Barker was also obliged to perform his ablutions. The rations were scant and sometimes stolen and in the event of a prisoner escaping or an air raid rations were stopped for 48 hours.

Smallwood received far worse treatment. His broken leg received no treatment and as a punishment he was forced to stand for 7 hours a day in a telephone booth at the top of the building. However, the treatment of political prisoners was far worse as they were regularly tortured. Their bones were broken, fingernails pulled out and they were treated with the electric chair. After forty-seven days Smallwood was finally transferred to the Coroneo prison hospital.

After a spell in Coroneo prison Barker was returned to Gestapo HQ where he subjected to further interrogation for seventeen days during which his already scant rations were reduced in an effort to make him talk. When the interrogations ceased Barker wrote his will in a letter to Smallwood with a request that, 'if however, an "unfortunate event" should occur would Smallwood see that the will was carried out'. This letter Barker gave to a prisoner whom he suspected was an agent provocateur as it was never delivered but probably served to convince the Gestapo that Barker was determined not to give any information.

Smallwood and Barker were transferred to Coroneo prison where they joined Priestley and a Major Turner and where they actually held a Christmas party together. However, during their incarceration at Corneo the Partisans blew up a canteen in Trieste and in response eleven prisoners including two women were shot.

Smallwood, Priestley, Turner and Barker were transferred from Trieste to Stalag XVIII A at Kaisersteinbruch, a journey which took three days and involved travelling via Vienna. Smallwood, Priestley and Turner were transferred to Oflag 17B (40km south-west of Brunswick) and it was there that Smallwood and Priestley were liberated by the American 9th Army.

At Kaiserbruch Barker was informed that the camp was to be evacuated and all but the sick were to embark on an eighteen-day journey to Branau-am-Inn. He feigned illness and when the camp was liberated by the Russians he escaped, passed through the lines into Hungary and after passing through Budapest to Debreczen was evacuated by air to Bari.

Notes from Sergeant Barker's SOE Report

Captain Martin-Smith and Sergeant Barker were dropped between Pielungo and Clausetta at 2340hr on 18 July 1944. They were met by patriots and made their way at once to Squadron Leader Beckett's [Manfred Czernin] castle. During the night, the Germans attacked the castle and the Mission was forced to flee. Beckett left behind two captured German officers whom he had saved from murder by the patriots and had treated correctly. The two officers were of course rescued by the enemy.

Italian patriots were found to be useless at smuggling stores across the frontier [to Austria] owing to inadequate training in fieldcraft. It was therefore decided to recruit British POWs. Sergeant Barker was sent on a mission to Selva di Cadore, near Cortina d'Ampezzo to contact six POWs hiding near the house of a wealthy Jewish refugee. At this time, Fielding's party moved to Forni Avoltri where a base would be formed at which Smallwood and Barker would remain, while Fielding, Banks and Buttle investigated routes into Austria. All of them therefore joined forces at Forni Avoltri, together with 2/Lieutenants Cheney, McCabe and Simon.

Sergeant Barker made the trip in eleven days. He was dressed in civilian clothing. Had he been captured he would have been shot. He returned with six POWs.

At about noon on 11 October, the arrival of the Germans at Forni Avoltri necessitated Smallwood and Barker's escape. They went into the mountains. They abandoned one spare B set, two A sets [radios] and a plunger for blowing up bridges, and Barker and Simon's packs, from which all incriminating material had been removed. They reached the summit of Monte Tuglia at about 3pm. Barker was carrying his B set and kit. Smallwood who was feeling unwell, was also heavily laden. They were so exhausted they buried the set on the summit of the mountain before beginning the descent. They became separated in the mist. Smallwood fell about 30ft and broke his leg near the ankle in two places, and apparently injured himself internally. Barker was able to move him into a cattle barn. The following day, they found a group of communist patriots who together, carried Smallwood to a group of three barns above the valley bottom. Barker returned to the summit of Monte Tuglia and collected the material he had buried. Another group of patriots arrived and set Small-wood's leg in splints.

On the following day, 13 October, the enemy became more active, and leaving the valley, began to penetrate into the hills. The patriots fled at once. Smallwood was unable to move and told Barker to leave him and make good his escape. Barker refused. Smallwood's condition was deteriorating and both had nothing to eat for 48 hours. They felt it necessary to give themselves up. Barker again buried the W/T set, plan, diaries, money, postcards with details of enemy locations and all other incriminating matter. Carrying Smallwood towards Pessaris, they encountered a group of Cossacks who immediately arrested them, indicating by gestures that they would be shot. This was between 5pm and 6pm on 13 October.

Taken to Comeglians, they were handed over to a major, the commander of the Waffen SS. Both men were interviewed by the major, one of his captains and an SS Staff Sergeant of the Gestapo called Mueller. Smallwood was asked by the major if he had rescued the two German officers at Pielungo. Smallwood neither admitted nor denied this.

Their journey to Trieste is outlined within Sergeant Barker's manuscript. On their arrival at Trieste they were interrogated after which two guards, Hans Kraut and Christian, took them into the cellars and beat them about the head for 10 minutes. An Italian civilian who was present also struck both men in the face.

During an interview, Sergeant Barker saw the name Turner on a piece of paper that was upside down in an office. An Austrian prisoner had been brought into the interview room and asked Barker if he recognised him. Barker made no sign of recognition; this man was Priestley.

Throughout, the Germans never suspected that there was a direct connection between Priestley, Smallwood and Barker.

Over the next thirteen days Barker was interrogated fifteen times at Gestapo HQ. His living conditions were abysmal. His stone cell in the basement was 3ft wide, 6ft 6in long and 6ft 3in high. The only light was admitted through a grille in the door from an ill-lit passage beyond. He had a canvas bed with holes in it and no blankets. Sanitation consisted of a bucket in the cell. It was emptied each morning into a WC upstairs in which Barker had to perform his ablutions. Barker's breakfast consisted of 50g of bread and ersatz coffee at 0800 hours. For supper at about 1800 hours, there was a bowl of hot soup. Food was sometimes stolen. When there was an air raid or when a prisoner escaped, rations were stopped for 48 hours.

All meals were served in the corridor so that prisoners actually met one another, though it was forbidden to talk, they did communicate when the guard was out of earshot. In this way, Barker made the acquaintance of Schuschnigg-Tugomair and the parish priest of San Antonio in Padua [Father Cortese]. He had helped British POWs but after being caught by the Germans he was horribly tortured and his condition was terrible. He was ultimately shot.

Barker hardly ever saw Smallwood, who received much worse treatment. His broken leg was not attended to and as a punishment he was compelled to stand for 7 hours a day in a telephone booth at the top of the building. After twenty-three days in Gestapo HQ Barker was sent to the Coroneo prison. Smallwood remained behind for a further fourteen days. He was then sent to the Coroneo hospital prison and Barker was returned to the Gestapo HQ. He remained there for seventeen days during which his rations were reduced in an attempt to induce him to talk. At this time Barker wrote a note to Smallwood telling him in the event of 'something happening to him' the note was his will and he wanted his mother to have all he owned. He deliberately gave the note to a prisoner, believing him to be an agent provocateur with a request for him to deliver it to Smallwood. The man had said he had regular access to the hospital for bathing. The letter was never delivered but was passed to the Gestapo. They must have thought that Barker was not going to be forthcoming with any information and, shortly afterwards, returned him to the Coroneo prison. The ruse had worked. It is a point of interest that the Germans never became aware that Major Smallwood could speak fluent German.

Major Smallwood, Barker, Priestley and Turner were all there at the same time but in different cells. During their time there, the Partisans blew up a canteen in Trieste. In response, the Germans shot eleven hostages among the prisoners, including two women [probably the same group that Barker mentions in his manuscript].

On 12 January 1945 Smallwood, Priestley, Turner and Sergeant Barker left Trieste bound for Kaisersteinbruch and Stalag XVII A. They were accompanied by RAF Warrant Officer I.E.H. Rapely, who had given an address of 31 Shelley Gardens, North Wembley, Middlesex. The conditions in this camp were poor but the European prisoners were well treated. The Russians were not. On 2 February, the officers were transferred to Oflag 79B, 40km south-west of Brunswick. They were rescued by the American 9th Army shortly before the 22 April.

About 1 April the whole camp was evacuated to Braunau-am-Inn. Barker feigned sickness and was left behind and when the camp was overrun by the Russians, he escaped, passing through the lines into Hungary and Budapest and Depbreczen where he was evacuated by air to Bari.

During his time in the Stalag, the four prisoners were looked after by BSM Francis White who came from Gloucester Street in Newcastle and an Austrian, Dr Bobleter. At the end of his report, Barker gave a detailed description of his interrogation. He felt that most of his interrogators were poorly tutored and only had a rudimentary knowledge of the skill.

The Cossacks

During the Stalinist repression, the Great Terror in the late 1930s, minority nationalities inside the Soviet Union, including the Cossacks, especially those who posed resistance, were among those brutally suppressed. Stalin therefore mistrusted the Cossacks and did not permit them to serve in the Red Army.

In 1936 Stalin reintroduced the Cossacks into the Red Army. Yet just sixty days after the German invasion Major Ivan Nikitich Kononov defected with his regiment of Cossacks, the 436th Infantry, to the Germans.

After Hitler launched the invasion of the Soviet Union several anti-communist Cossack leaders all publicly praised the German campaign. These included Kuban ataman Naumenko, Terek ataman Vdovenko, the

Cossack National Centre chairman Vasily Glazkov and former Don ataman Pyotr Krasnov, a former White Russian commander.

Nevertheless, Hitler and other top officials initially denied Cossack émigrés from having any military or political role in the war against the USSR. However, he later changed his mind and formed a Cossack Division under General von Pannwitz.

Despite his obvious affinity for them, Pannwitz ruled his men with typical German toughness, with penalties ranging from solitary confinement in darkened cells and flogging to execution for more serious offences. Nevertheless, he was granted honorary Cossack nationality on 21 March 1944.

In 1944 General Krasnov and other Cossack leaders had persuaded Hitler to allow Cossack troops, as well as civilians and non-combatant Cossacks, to settle permanently in sparsely populated Carnia. Presumably, Hitler was not prepared to allow those whom he regarded as 'Untermensch' to settle in his Aryan paradise. 30,000 Cossacks from the Caucasus including wives and families moved to Carnia where they established settlements, requisitioning houses and farms by evicting the inhabitants. They created several stanitsas [Cossack village communities], churches, schools and military units.

There, commanded by General Domanov, described by Martin-Smith as an autocrat whom the Cossacks would obey and do what he told them, they fought the Partisans and persecuted the local population clearing the inhabitants from their farms and homes committing numerous atrocities. They took reprisals [burning houses etc.] against the population for allowing Partisans from the hills to 'pass through the area alive' which did lead the Italians to the use of the epithet 'Barbarian Cossacks'. Not a single war crime arising from these measures was however attributed to the Cossacks.

By August 1944, the Cossack troops had been dispersed amongst the local population with whom they were billeted apparently to avoid them being concentrated in one place and becoming a target for a concentrated attack by the Partisans. They began negotiations with Squadron Leader Czernin before he was exfiltrated and later with Fielding whose mission wholly lacked any facilities needed to cope with such a horde as they sought a guarantee of immunity from the Allies, but these negotiations were forestalled by the first major German offensive.

Martin-Smith in his report described the Cossacks as 'savage nomads who lived on the country, pillaging and raping when drunk which was their normal condition'.

They were anxious to secure their future by coming to terms with the [Partisans] and consequently often turned a blind eye to [Partisan] activity. They were however 'white' so they were prepared to play with the 'green' Osoppo. The Garibaldini were a red rag to a bull in their eyes, they would have no dealings with them.

Normally they would not go out of their way to look for [Partisans] but when attacked by them would take revenge by burning whole villages and massacring the inhabitants. This happened in Carnia with the result that the population became so terrorised that they would betray any [Partisan] to the Germans. This finally made it impossible for Allied missions in Carnia. As fighting troops, the Cossacks were poor value. Their morale was low but when drunk they would make a furious charge: like Peter the Great at Narva they were as likely to run the other way. They were well armed individually with light automatic weapons but were the world's worst shots. They had few heavy weapons; these generally being supplied by the Germans for offensive operations.

The Germans were alleged to employ them, apart from the obvious motive of sparing their own troops as a subtle anti-Russian propaganda weapon. The population would be sickened [so ran the argument] by these barbarian Russians, they would never want the other Russians to come. This was not altogether without effect.

If there had been any prospect of an immediate Allied advance since last autumn it might have been possible to make an arrangement with them by which they would have attacked Tarvisio and Udine in return for some promise of immunity, dependent on their success. If they succeeded, they would have earned their pardon and it would have helped the Allied campaign; if they failed, they would have been wiped out, the problem would have been solved and the Allies would have lost nothing. It would not have been possible to maintain protracted negotiations over an indefinite period with no end in sight.

* * *

Martin-Smith's last paragraph is an incorrect summary of the position as there was never any possibility of any such pardon for the Cossacks but he was not to know that their fate had been sealed at Yalta under what was named Operation Keelhaul. Here Stalin obtained Allied agreement to the repatriation of every so-called 'Soviet' citizen held prisoner apparently because the Allied leaders feared that the Soviets either might delay or refuse repatriation of the Allied POWs whom the Red Army had liberated from Nazi POW camps.

Although the agreement for the deportation of all 'Soviet' citizens did not include White Russian émigrés who had fled during the Bolshevik Revolution before the establishment of the USSR, the Russians later demanded that all Cossack prisoners of war should be handed over.

The Cossacks were told to surrender to the British Army at Lienz to where they began their trek from Carnia. A giant wagon train consisting of an estimated 30,000 Cossacks wound its way to Timau, the last Italian village at the foot of the Plöcken Pass.

There they remained for three weeks while waiting for the thaw so they could start their journey over the mountains and down into the Drau valley to surrender to the British Army.

The Cossacks were eventually forcibly loaded onto railway wagons by troops of the Argyll & Sutherland Highlanders in scenes of some considerable violence and handed over to the Russian army. Many committed suicide as they were under no illusions as to the fate that Stalin had in store for them. Some escaped into woods and survived by being sheltered by local families.

The majority of the abandoned Cossack officers, after being found guilty of treason to a country they felt no longer was their country were executed. [On 12 August 1946, together with all his family, General Andreij Vasslov was executed.] The remainder of the survivors were sent off to the Gulags as slave labour. On 16 January 1947 Domanov was hanged along with Krassnoff, Shkuro, Klitsch and von Pannwitz, who, although a German national and under the provisions of the Yalta Conference not subject to repatriation to the Soviet Union, nobly surrendered along with his men to the Russians.

Notes

Introduction

1. P. Wilkinson (2002), *Foreign fields: the story of an SOE operative* (London; New York: I.B. Tauris Publishers), p. 109.
2. N.L.R. Franks (1976), *Double mission: RAF fighter ace and SOE agent, Manfred Czernin, DSO, MC, DFC* (London: Kimber), p. 109.
3. Extract from Sergeant Barker's personnel record. The National Archives WO 373/75/13.

Dramatis Personae

1. Czernin would later use 'Beckett' as his codename.
2. HS9/1375/3 PRO.
3. Information from The Battle of Britain London Monument (www.bbm.org/airmen/Czernin.htm).
4. The Clowder Mission was an SOE operation that included the infiltration of agents into Austria by using Slovene Partisans on the Carinthian borders to encourage resistance by persuading them to embark on a policy of open opposition, commencing in spring 1944. Within six months the whole operation had failed. There were a number of reasons for this: there was little interest from Austria in the liberation of Austria, but more regard for occupying the territory claimed by Yugoslavia. Secondly, the operation depended upon regular air drops of arms and supplies, not only for its credibility but, on occasions, for its very survival. The latter proved difficult because of the nature of the terrain. Dropping zones in mountainous regions had to be undertaken by aircrews of the Special Flight. With the establishment of the Balkan Airforce in the summer of 1944, these aircrews were no longer available, and consequently Clowder missions were accorded a lower priority. This was considered to be the most critical of all the factors that affected Operation Clowder. Wilkinson, *Foreign Fields*, pp. 207–11.
5. Franks, *Double mission*, p. 115.
6. *The Times*, Obit., 12 April 2005.
7. Ibid.
8. WO 373/59 Lieutenant (Temporary Captain) Martin-Smith, 1 May 1945.
9. CIA.gov/library/center-for-the-study-of-intelligence.
10. The diary was exhumed at the end of the war by Bobleter, who handed it to a Lieutenant Maynard, T Force in Saltzburg. See letter dated 22 July 1945 by Bobleter to Barker, plate 17.
11. Barker Affidavit lodged on 13 November 1945, at the Military Department, Office of the Judge Advocate General in London.
12. http://www.anpiudine.org/candido-grassi-verdi/.

Prologue

1. Sergeant Barker was attached to No. 1 Special Force.
2. Sergeant Barker's personnel record.

Chapter 1: Friends

1. There were many names given to hundreds of operations. Information on Operation Arundel cannot be found but we know a part of the operational brief was to open up a route into Austria.
2. Monopoli is a small port located between Bari and Brindisi. It had a parachute-training establishment, packing station and a paramilitary school. Malcolm Edward Tudor (2011), *SOE in Italy, 1940–1945: the real story* (Newtown: Emilia Publishing), p. 23. A Country Section house was a safe house where agents were accommodated before and after operations.
3. Pat was Captain Patrick Martin-Smith, known as 'Maggiore Pat' to the Italians. Franks, *Double Mission*, p. 117.
4. Squadron Leader Count Manfred Czernin, MC, DFC, RAF. Wilkinson, *Foreign fields*, p. 191.
5. 'Dickie' *may* have been Lieutenant Richard Mallaby. He was captured later and he met SS General Karl Wolff who allowed Mallaby to return to Switzerland bearing messages for the Allies. It is thought Mallaby was in Brindisi at this time, his nickname was Dickie.
6. The Bersaglieri were elite Italian soldiers.
7. 'Well done friend, well done friend, your comrade is down there.'

Chapter 2: Pielungo

1. 'Hey, best wishes.'
2. He is referring to Manfred Czernin.
3. Albergo is hotel in Italian.
4. Verdi's 'real' name was Candido Grassi; see Dramatis Personae. A small Bolognese man, Peppino's 'real' name was Piero; Franks, *Double mission*, p. 112. The Body-Ground was an area where the stores were hidden.
5. See plate 1, Castello Ceconi, destroyed by the SS during this raid, was rebuilt at the end of the war. Manfred's base HQ was in a farmhouse near Tramonti di Sopra at the foot of Monto Resto. Franks, *Double mission*, p. 117.
6. 'Where are we going now?'
7. 'Do you know the way?'
8. Mountain hut.

Chapter 3: Manfred Recalls the Recent Past

1. 'Waiter, can we have another bottle please?'
2. In September 1943, General Bagdoglio arranged an Armistice with the Allies.
3. Flight Sergeant Desmond did have a record in The National Archives (WO 3352/2464) but no papers have survived.
4. More information on 'Fred' is contained in the Appendix, 'Extracts from the CLOWDER Mission In and Around Forni Avoltri, June–November 1944'.

Chapter 4: A Sermon of Special Significance

1. Grappa is a brandy distilled from the pressed residue of the grape in the making of wine.
2. Colonel Harold Stevens (nicknamed Colonello Buonasera, 'Colonel Good Evening') was a British military officer who had lived in Rome, and, with his calm and reasonable commentary, was very different from the Fascist rhetoric commonly heard. He conveyed a sense of serenity and hope for the future.

Chapter 5: The Action was Unnecessary

1. It is not known if the group were successful in their escape.

Chapter 6: More Friends Arrive

1. 'We are lucky Verdi.'
2. We will be picking the white edelweiss flowers
Up on the mountain tops, close to the sky
When we are up there on the mountains
We will passionately sing our love song

The mountaineer with flowers in her hair
And the handsome soldier with fire (passion) in his heart
Those edelweiss flowers were to blame
Growing up there on the mountains close to the golden sun

A white flower and a black ink pen
Are about to unite them forever in eternal love
They took the oath up there on those mountains
Picking edelweiss flowers, the symbol of their love

Up there on the mountain, where lays that little church
The mountaineer is marrying her soldier
Her orange colour flowers mixed with the white edelweiss
Picked on a midday on the top of those mountains.

(Translation by Marios Papaconstantinou)
3. Major George Fielding, 3rd Hussars, code name Rudolf. Wilkinson, *Foreign fields*, p. 191.
4. Major S.F. (Bill) Smallwood. Intelligence Corps. Ibid. Charles Barker and Bill Smallwood were captured together later in 1944. Included in this party was Lieutenant Hubert Mayr, alias Lieutenant Banks, code name 'Georgeau' and the W/T operator Corporal Arthur Buttle. Georgeau disappeared in October 1944 looking for safe houses in Austria, probably the result of treachery by 'defecting' Austrian officers.
5. The inn was possibly the Hotel Antica Corte.
6. Arthur was Arthur Buttle.
7. There is no trace of Operation Royal and this must have been part of the Clowder Mission.

Chapter 7: Cleulis and Treppo Carnico

1. 'Here, the others are coming.'
2. 'How are you, Mr Captain?'
3. 'And best wishes.'
4. 'I fixed the appointment, we will meet them down at the mule-track.'

Chapter 8: A Radio and a Route Discovered

1. 'Good morning, are you hungry? I brought food.'
2. Formerly the Grafin Donner, now Countess Sosic, from Northern England and called Kate. Appendix, 'Extracts from the CLOWDER Mission In and Around Forni Avoltri, June–November 1944'.
3. 'Pash' means 'crush'.
4. Pierabec in Italian.
5. These men were Austrian SOE. They had the code names of 2/Lieutenants Simon, McCabe and Cheney. Appendix, 'Extracts from the CLOWDER Mission In and Around Forni Avoltri, June–November 1944'.

Chapter 9: To Points North and West

1. It is widely understood in the art of field craft that in combat situations troops should not silhouette on top of high ground, thus giving away positions and becoming easy targets.
2. The village of Leisinger, in the Gailtal area of Austria, a short distance from Forni Avoltri.
3. Edgar Wallace was a prolific writer of crime and detective mysteries.

Chapter 10: Auronzo and the Second Stage

1. 'There, the barracks.'
2. 'The Germans are ugly (nasty).'
3. SOE operatives wore uniform. Charles made the conscious decision to wear civilian clothing. Had he been captured he would have been shot.
4. The shipping line is believed to be the Lloyd Trieste Shipping Line.

Chapter 11: Selva di Cadore

1. 'Good evening, I am English, my friends want to eat.'
2. Captain Roderick Hall of OSS, parachuted with Major Lloyd G. Smith, 'Smitty', of State College, PA, into the Dolomites on 1 August 1944 to commit acts of sabotage. Smitty's brief was to organise and direct Partisans in Carnia, Hall the same in the Cadore. He made his way to San Stefano Cadore. (The Army Air Force would not drop them directly into the Cadore, the mountains were too high.) CIA.gov/library/center-for-the-study-of-intelligence. See Dramatis Personae, Captain Hall.
3. It is not known if Hall made contact with Tedeschini, if indeed that was his real name.

Chapter 12: Opportunity Seldom Knocks Twice

1. This was Hall's commanding officer, Major 'Smitty' Smith. See Dramatis Personae, Captain Hall.
2. Terza Grand, 2,595m.
3. The major was Major 'Smitty' Smith, Commander of the OSS Eagle Mission that landed on 2 August 1944 and based in Ovaro. Fielding SOE report.
4. The Cossacks, supported by the Nazis, intended to kill all Italians, and settle the area.
5. Manfred was with Piero, his radio operator, in a farmhouse at the northern end of the village of Tramonti di Sopra. His British liaison officer was Pat Martin-Smith. Franks, *Double mission*, p. 117.

Chapter 13: Austria Remains a Closed Book

1. The Angelus is a Catholic devotion recited at dawn, noon and dusk.

Chapter 14: We are Taken Prisoner

1. Bill was experiencing diarrhoea.
2. The major referred to here is possibly Manfred Czernin.
3. The reluctant natives of the recently visited hut may have alerted the enemy.
4. The cover story was: (1) They had dropped together on 14 August with five other officers and ORs. (2) They had not made contact with any other British personnel in NE Italy. (3) They had separated from the other five immediately and had never seen them again. (4) They had remained together the whole time and they had been accompanied by thirty Partisans who had left them shortly before their capture. (5) Their basic task was to make a recce with a view to blowing up roads and bridges and assisting British POWs to escape. SOE report by Sergeant Barker. Appendix, 'Extracts from the CLOWDER Mission In and Around Forni Avoltri, June–November 1944'.

Chapter 15: Enemies

1. SD (Sicherheitsdienst des Reichsführers-SS), the SS Intelligence Service.

Chapter 16: The Political Prisoners

1. The priest was Fr Placido Cortese, savagely tortured by the Gestapo and eventually murdered. He was seen by Barker while he was in Gestapo HQ in Trieste, and the former made an affidavit stating what he had witnessed. This was deposited on 13 November 1945 at the Military Department, Office of the Judge Advocate General in London.

Chapter 17: The First Month of Imprisonment

1. 'The woman sends these cigarettes.'

Chapter 18: Trieste, December and January

1. 'If the guard doesn't want to, we are singing, if the guard doesn't want to, we are singing.'
2. Barker's SOE report states Mr Providence, or M. Mastrovich, lived in Dalmatia. He had two sons, one of whom was a doctor, the other an engineer. Honorary head of the Croat Red Cross, he had been most helpful to Barker giving him 30,000 lira (Barker's manuscript says it was over 60,000 lira) and food and drink. Mastrovich did collect information regarding the mistreatment of prisoners and names of enemy officials.
3. Mastrovic's interest in the Gestapo HQ may well have been a way of enquiring into the welfare of Fr Placido Cortese who Sergeant Barker saw.
4. In 2019 this figure would be equivalent to £265.

Chapter 19: The Journey to Kaisersteinbruck

1. Stalag XVII A was a German prisoner-of-war camp run by the Wehrmacht and located south of the town of Wolfsberg in Carinthia, southern Austria.
2. Sturmabteilung or Storm Detachment, better known as 'Brown Shirts' or 'Storm Troopers'.

Chapter 20: The Vertrauensmann and Dr Briefe

1. Battery Sergeant-Major Smith is believed to have been Regimental Battery Sergeant Major 799731 Francis White, Newcastle upon Tyne. Leader of the British POW section. He had collected much information about atrocities and prisoners who had passed through the camp. Evacuated to Braunau-am-Inn. Barker's SOE report, Appendix, 'Extracts from the CLOWDER Mission In and Around Forni Avoltri, June–November 1944'. See plates 17.
2. Vertrauensmann means trusted representative.
3. Benga's food was possibly army jargon for Bengal food, a scant meal named after the 1943 food famine in Bengal, India.
4. Dr Briefe was in fact Dr Carl Bobleter. Bobleter was a highly educated doctor of economics. He claimed to know of an underground movement among members of the Opera Company of which the chief of the Gestapo in Vienna and two Gestapo officials from Linz were members. The three had all been shot. Multilingual, he had been in France in 1940 and was suspected by the French of Fifth Column activity. Barker's SOE report, Appendix, 'Extracts from the CLOWDER Mission In and Around Forni Avoltri, June–November 1944'. He wrote to Charles on 22 July 1945. He said that he had handed over Brigadier Davies's diary together with 'the other diary you saw' to the British Major Robinson at Braunau.
5. After Napoleon fell, there was a conference in Vienna the object being the restoration of peace and stability in Europe after the devastation of war. Central to this conference were the Foreign Secretary of the United Kingdom, Viscount Castlereagh and the Foreign Minister of Austria, Klemens Wenzel von Mettern Metternich. Together, they brokered a peace which lasted until 1914. H. Kissinger (2013), *A world restored Metternich, Castlereagh and the problems of peace 1812–22* (Brattleboro, Vermont: Echo Point Books & Media).
6. The Brigadier was Edmund Frank Davies, Royal Ulster Rifles.
7. See Dr Bobleter's letter, plate 17.

Chapter 21: The Parting of the Ways

1. Probably Oflag 79 at Waggum, Brunswick (officers' POW camp).
2. Roy Courlander, British by birth, joined the New Zealand Army. He was captured and recruited by the Germans and tried for treason in 1945 by the New Zealand authorities and sentenced to fifteen years' imprisonment. This was reduced on appeal in 1950 to nine years. He died in poverty in Lethbridge Park, Sydney, in 1979.
3. The Russian Liberation Army was a unit of mainly Russian soldiers that fought under German command during the Second World War. Their leader was General Andrey Vlasov, of the Red Army, who had defected.

Chapter 23: Red Army Train

1. The horse and cart had been given to them.

Chapter 24: Introduction to a Hungarian

1. I have been unable to locate Stephen Kovacs, although the name appears on Internet searches, and it has not been possible to link him and Barker.

Endnote

1. From the MOD Accident Report ADDA/WT 845 DRAGONFLY/21.1.53.

Bibliography and Sources

Anpimax (2011). 'Candido Grassi "Verdi"', online, ANPI. Available at: http://www.anpiudine.org/candido-grassi-verdi/ (accessed 28 November 2019).

Bailey, R. (2015). *Target: Italy: the secret war against Mussolini, 1940–1943: the official history of SOE operations in fascist Italy*. London: Faber & Faber.

Barker, C. (n.d.). SOE report 1 with supplement, second copy.

Cia.gov (2011). 'Roderick 'Steve' Hall – Central Intelligence Agency', online. Available at: https://www.cia.gov/library/center-for-the-study-of-intelligence/kent-csi/vol11no4/html/v11i4a05p_0001.htm (accessed 18 October 2019).

Contributors to Wikimedia projects (2010). 'British Army officer', online. Available at: https://en.m.wikipedia.org/wiki/George_Rudolf_Hanbury_Fielding (accessed 26 October 2019).

Fielding, G. (n.d.). SOE report Fielding/A, second copy (12 pp.).

Fielding, G. (n.d.). SOE report Fielding/B, second copy (5 pp.).

Franks, N.L.R. (1976). *Double mission: RAF fighter ace and SOE agent, Manfred Czernin, DSO, MC, DFC*. London: Kimber.

History Learning Site, 'British Free Corps', online. Available at: https://www.historylearningsite.co.uk/world-war-two/british-free-corps/ (accessed 31 October 2019).

Kissinger, H. (2013). *A world restored Metternich, Castlereagh and the problems of peace 1812–22*. Brattleboro, Vermont: Echo Point Books & Media.

Martin-Smith, P. (n.d.). SOE report PM-S/Austria P.1 (17 pp.) and PM-S/Italy P.2.

Ogden, Alan and Martin Fielding (2012; rev. 2014, 2017, 2020). 'The Clowder Mission in and around Forni Avoltri, June–November 1944', Unpublished.

Telegraph (2005). 'Major George Fielding', online. Available at: https://www.telegraph.co.uk/news/obituaries/1483676/Major-George-Fielding.html (accessed 26 October 2019).

The Times (2005). 'George Fielding', online. Available at: https://www.thetimes.co.uk/article/george-fielding-mz3z2z9wj96 (accessed 26 October 2019).

Tudor, Malcolm Edward (2011). *SOE in Italy, 1940–1945: the real story*. Newtown: Emilia Publishing.

Wilkinson, P. (2002). *Foreign fields: the story of an SOE operative*. London and New York: I.B. Tauris Publishers.

ww2inprague.com (2019). 'General Vlasov and Russian Liberation Army – true about the Prague Uprising – World War II in Prague', online. Available at: http://www.ww2inprague.com/general-vlasov-and-russian-liberation-army—hidden-true-about-the-prague-uprising (accessed 31 October 2019).

Index

References in **bold** refer to illustrations and plates.